TRADE AND COMMERCE IN COLONIAL BOMBAY

Trade and Commerce in Colonial Bombay

A History of the Emergence of its Business and Financial Establishments, c.1661–1935

MEENU KANOJIA

PRIMUS BOOKS

PRIMUS BOOKS
An imprint of Ratna Sagar P. Ltd.
Virat Bhavan
Mukherjee Nagar Commercial Complex
Delhi 110 009

Offices at CHENNAI LUCKNOW AGRA AHMEDABAD BENGALURU BHOPAL COIMBATORE DEHRADUN GUWAHATI HYDERABAD JAIPUR JALANDHAR KANPUR KOCHI KOLKATA MUMBAI PATNA RANCHI VARANASI

First published 2025

ISBN: 978-93-6627-219-1 (hardback)
ISBN: 978-93-6627-711-0 (POD)

Published by Primus Books

Laser typeset by Jojy Philip
jojyphilip@gmail.com

Contents

Tables

Acknowledgements

Undertaking this historical research on the bullion trade was both intellectually stimulating and challenging. While many valuable studies exist on different aspects of the history of Mumbai, there remained a need to delve into the financial and monetary foundations of Mumbai city. It is these foundations which enabled it to emerge as India's first leading commercial and industrial city—Mumbai, a 'City of Hope and Wealth' called Maya Nagri.

This research owes a great deal to many individuals and institutions. Firstly, I could undertake this research because of my professor, Dr Mariam Dossal who has been a great source of inspiration and encouragement at every step of the process. Her scholarship, academic competence, and analytical approach have enhanced the quality of my work enormously. An exceptional teacher and mentor, she gave me love and courage besides scholarly knowledge and wisdom. I will always be indebted to Dr Dossal for enriching me with her knowledge. I am also grateful to Dr Narendra Panjawani for his kindness, support, and encouragement.

It was a pleasure pursuing my doctoral research at the Department of History. University of Mumbai. I have benefitted greatly from Professor J.V. Naik's (Former Head of the Department), his erudite writings and lectures. I am thankful to Dr Manjari Kamat for her encouragement and support. Members of the office staff offered me administrative help from time to time, for which I am very thankful.

I wish to thank the librarians and staff of University of Mumbai at Kalina and Fort for their kind assistance throughout my study. I am extremely grateful to the Director and the staff of Maharashtra State Archives (MSA), Mumbai for providing me access to the vast repository of valuable diaries and manuscripts which helped me with my research on the monetary history of Bombay. My sincere thanks to the staff of the Asiatic Society of Mumbai.

I express my sincere gratitude to Dr Aubrey Macarenas S.J., former Director of the Heras Institute of Indian History and Culture, St. Xavier's College, Mumbai. His continuing encouragement and support have played an important role in completing this work.

I also wish to thank Dr Joan Dias, the present Director of Heras Institute for extending to me the facilities of the institute and her kindness. My sincere thanks also to the former librarians, Neeta Malik, P. Wilson D' Souza, and Shilpa Chedda.

I am truly grateful to Bazil Shaikh, Retd. Chief General Manager of the Reserve Bank of India, who has helped me with his invaluable insights.

I owe my sincere gratitude to Dr Medha Malik Kudaisya, (Associate Professor, Department of History, National University of Singapore), and Dr Ganesh Kudaisya, (Associate Professor in the South Asian Studies Programme, Faculty of Arts & Social Sciences at National University of Singapore); they have always supported and encouraged me in the journey of writing this book.

I am also very grateful to the Central Library of National University of Singapore and the National Public Library of Singapore for granting me permission to use their rich collections of books and materials for my research. I am also thankful to the librarians and staff of Central and Public Library of Singapore.

I am also extremely beholden to my parents and close members of my family for their continuing encouragement and unfailing support throughout these years of my research. My parents, Vishwanath Rajak and Titti Rajak, and my brother, Premnath Rajak, and sister-in-law, Kanchan Rajak, have supported me immensely. My special thanks to my sisters, Meena Prasad and Shobha Prasad, for always encouraging me.

Lastly, this book is dedicated to my dear husband and daughter, Ashish, and Parinistha Kanojia without whose love and encouragement it would not have been possible to persevere. Their love has been crucial to my intellectual journey.

I thank the Almighty for guiding me all these years and giving me strength and patience to complete this work.

I owe my sincere and deep gratitude to my publisher, Primus Books, for trusting my work and giving me all the possible support to see it through the journey of completion. My sincere thanks to Mr B. N. Varma, Dr Prasun Chatterjee, Amol Saghar, Lobsang Yeshi, and Vijay Kumar Sah for their immense support in making this book possible. I will always be indebted to team Primus.

Introduction

This book provides a detailed account of the Bombay Island, a small trading village which used to belong to the Kolis (fisherfolk), and other communities present there, and its transition from a small trading town to the commercial capital of India. Present-day India and its relationship with the financial centre, Mumbai (Bombay) holds a special place in the country's economic and financial history. This book traces the story from the colonial rule in western India in the seventeenth century until the establishment of the Reserve Bank of India. The monetary history of India is directly connected to the rule of the Mughals, the Portuguese and the English and their dominance in places like Delhi, Gujarat, Goa and Bombay. The uniform circulation of money throughout India today owes its due to numerous events in the past.

Bullion played an important role in trade in Bombay and other parts of western India, thereby, shaping the country's economy. The role of the Bombay governors, especially Gerald Aungier through his policies to improve Bombay Island, was instrumental in establishing the most important institutions, namely the Court of Judicature and the Bombay Mint, which in turn led to banking and setting up of other financial institutions. The East India Company played the most important role in maintaining a systematic practice of money circulation in the region and other port cities on the hinterland. The outfit controlled the debased coins in circulation through vigilance and law. The history of the bullion trade of Bombay town, thus, is linked with its trading connections with other countries to procure the supply of bullion for minting and monetary purposes.

The coming of the first European power, the Portuguese, in western India facilitated the establishment of Estado da India in Goa in 1510. Following this, they set up their first mint in Goa to carry out their financial needs. Minting their own currency ensured that they could establish their authority and influence over the inhabitants of Goa and other port towns on the hinterland of the western coast. Since many types of currencies were in circulation, especially during the Hindu Kadamba rule in the Goa kingdom and the rule of the Bahmani's the tenth to the fourteenth centuries, it was common to find currencies of other foreign nationalities in circulations too. These coins were minted in gold and silver both. Goa under the Bahmanis saw new currencies of the Bijapur rulers, and once Goa came under Portuguese power, their own currency was minted and their lingua franca imposed on the inhabitants. In fact, it was mandatory for locals to conduct business in the Portuguese language. After establishing their power in Goa, the Portuguese mints travelled to other port towns on the west coast of India, Hormuz in the Persian Gulf and the Straits of Malacca.

This book follows the banking institutions which came up after the inception of the Bombay Mint. The first governor of Bombay Island was Gerald Aungier, a man of great vision who laid the foundation of the Bombay Mint on 15 October 1676, to carry out their monetary concerns and to establish their authority over the Portuguese and other currencies which were in circulation then and to have their English currencies minted. The first bank of Bombay was established under the governorship of Charles Boone in 1720. Therefore, the journey from the Bombay Mint to the laying of foundations of the banking institutions in Bombay and other parts of India over the early eighteenth, nineteenth and twentieth centuries is truly a commendable work of both Indian merchants and the East India Company. Mumbai's ascension as the first financial capital of India owes full recognition to the East India Company.

During the years *c.*1661–1935, the town of Bombay developed as the most important commercial and financial centre, both under the English East India Company and even after the transfer of power to the British Raj. Chapter One entitled, 'The Portuguese Bullion Trade in Seventeenth Century Western India', provides an overview of the Portuguese bullion trade in western India between *c.*1534–1661. Bombay Island was under the control of the Portuguese Estado da India, with its headquarters in Goa (since 25 November 1510). During the Portuguese period, the island of Bombay was inhabited primarily by the Kolis, Bhandaris and Agris. There were also some Pathare Prabhus, Konkani Muslims and Portuguese Fazendars (land owners). The population of Bombay, however, did not exceed 10,000. The island possessed a deep natural harbour where trading vessels could anchor and find a safe haven even during the tempestuous monsoons.

The discovery made by the Portuguese of an all-water route in 1498 to the East Indies via the Cape of Good Hope was a major navigational achievement. The decades that followed are known as the 'Vasco da Gama Era', named after the Portuguese Admiral who led the convoy of four ships into the Indian Ocean at the close of the fifteenth century. This era marks the beginning of Asia's incorporation into the capitalist world economy centred around western Europe.

The success of long-distance Portuguese and Spanish sailings in the fifteenth and sixteenth centuries owed much to the astronomical, geographical and navigational knowledge acquired from earlier Arab, Greek and other Indian knowledge systems. Historian of Portuguese expansionism, A.J. Russell-Wood explains that Portugal was the only country in the sixteenth century to have ships sailing in the Atlantic, Pacific and Indian Oceans, as well as the Indonesian seas and the South China Sea.[1]

Improvements in transport technology brought with it structural changes in the older patterns of trade. These had a direct bearing on the transport of bullion which was vital to the establishment of the world economy. Trade between Europe and Asia had earlier relied on sailing ships and smaller boats which crossed the Mediterranean Sea, the Red Sea and the Persian Gulf to enter the Indian Ocean. Advancements in Portuguese ship design, notably of the *Caravel* in the 1440s, contributed greatly to multi-oceanic sailings[2]—galleons, caravels, fragatas and nao or carracks, which were sturdier and faster. These vessels carried bullion and commodities and helped the Portuguese establish their naval supremacy over the seas. The striking feature of the Portuguese empire was the control it exercised from its port-towns which were situated on the maritime rim of many countries. Portuguese power in the sixteenth century extended from the Atlantic Ocean, Salvador de Bahia in Brazil, to the Pacific Ocean, Nagasaki in Japan.

Chapter Two entitled, 'Monetary Concerns of the British and the Establishment of the Bombay Mint, *c.*1661–1710', reviews events which led to the transfer of the Bombay Island from the Portuguese to the English Crown in June 1661 to the East India Company on 27 March 1668. The seat of Portuguese administration on Bombay Island was located in the Manor House near the natural harbour. The Manor House was in the possession of Donna Ignez de Miranda, and in June 1661, the island of Bombay was given as dowry to King Charles II on marrying the Portuguese princess Catherine of Braganza.

There was considerable resistance from the Portuguese authorities based in Goa and Bassein against the transfer of Bombay Island to the English Crown. Bombay was finally acquired by the Crown representative Sir Humphrey Cooke on 18 February 1665. King Charles II's need for additional funding to improve the English Navy made him turn to the East India Company for a loan of £ 50,000. In return for the loan and the payment of an annual rent of £10, the island of Bombay was leased to the East India Company in 1668. The company administered Bombay town and Presidency until November 1858, when all British possessions in India came under direct rule of the Crown.

There were many currencies in circulation when the East India Company acquired Bombay Island. These included Portuguese currencies such as xerafins (silver coins), bazarucos (copper coins), pardaos, reis and other European currencies such as the Venetian florins and Spanish dollars. Mughal currencies such as the Surat rupees as well as the star pagodas from south India were also in use, as were larins and shahis from Persia and patacoes from Malacca. This made business transactions difficult. Numerous currencies reflected the lack of a strong administrative and political authority, and the continued usage of Portuguese business practices and the use of Portuguese language in the market too caused the Bombay government much concern. The monetary situation needed to be urgently reformed. Financial and monetary requirements led the East India Company to establish a mint in Bombay on 15 October 1676 during the governorship of Gerald Aungier.[3] The Bombay Mint was the first mint to be established by the British in India. The functioning of the Bombay Mint and the role of the assay masters as well as that of Sarrafs and Banias, who were vital to the indigenous banking system, are examined in Chapter Two.

Chapter Three entitled 'The Bombay Government and Merchants Engaged in the Bullion Trade, *c.*1710–40', reviews the efforts of Charles Boone in promoting trade and establishing financial stability. It was during Charles Boone's period of governorship that the Bank of Bombay was established on 22 December 1720.[4] The chapter deals with Bombay's bullion trade, the circulation of money in the island and the functioning of the Bank of Bombay.

An improvement in Bombay's defence was undertaken during this period. The building of the fort walls with ramparts, bastion, guns and cannons helped the East India Company to establish a more secure base. An improved defence system also enabled the Bombay government to develop its coastal and international trade.

Chapter Four entitled 'Theatre of Politics, Trade and Finance in Mid-Eighteenth Century Bombay, *c.*1740–80', highlights the period of intense political rivalry between the Bombay government and the local and foreign powers. These included the Maratha leader Kanhoji Angria of Kolaba, Khem Sawant of Malwan and the Siddis from the Janjira district, and the European powers—the Portuguese, Dutch and the French. These conflicts affected the Bombay trade as well as the trade in western India. This in turn disrupted the bullion supplies to the island; the piracy and confiscation of sailing vessels further disturbed the trade.

This chapter closely examines the activities of senior company servants engaged in private trade. These included

Bombay governors, Robert Cowan and William Wake. Leading private merchants such as Francis Pym, Lawrence Sullivan and David Scott who dominated Bombay's private trade were also important players in the bullion trade of western India.

The Anglo-French wars of 1742–4 disrupted the supply of gold, silver and copper metals on British ships to Bombay and seriously affected the bullion market. Scarcity in bullion supply led to the debasement of silver and gold coins. It also led to the introduction of small denomination coins such as pice.[5] The establishment of the Bombay Custom House in 1746 and the introduction of licenses and passes were measures by which the Bombay government sought to establish control over its monetary and commercial transactions. Passes and licenses, thus, became mandatory for all ships. These measures were often resisted by Indian rulers, merchants and brokers. Chapter Four also reviews changes in business practices brought about by the private agency houses such as Charles Forbes, Bruce Fawcett and Alexander Adamson. It examines the special features of 'bazaar'—hundis, shroffs, gumastas, purcchas and kaccharis—that enabled the circulation of money and promoted commercial activity in Bombay and the west coast of India.[6]

The late 1770s was thus a period of political instability due to the Maratha pressure on Mughals in Kathiawar and also the Anglo-Maratha War which created a chaotic situation affecting trade in western India. Therefore, Bombay became a thriving depot for commerce and a lucrative centre of finance, inviting merchants and traders belonging to the Parsi community, Gujarati-Jain Banias and brokers, Marwari bankers, Konkani Muslim traders, Baghdadi Jews and private European traders. These trading communities played an active role in dealing in bullion and financing trade, procuring bullion supply and exporting cotton and other goods, both in India and foreign countries.

Chapter Five entitled, 'Bombay's Bullion Trade with Europe, China and Japan, *c.*1780–1820', evaluates the sources of bullion supply from places such as Amsterdam, Antwerp, Seville and Tyrol in Europe and countries in South America such as Brazil, Bolivia, Mexico and Peru. In East Asia bullion was imported from Canton in China and Nagasaki in Japan.

During the 1780s Britain faced a serious trade deficit due to its increasing imports of tea and silk from China. Scarcity of silver metal forced the Bombay government to suspend the Bombay rupee between 1780–1800. This was due to the disruption of channels of supply from South America and Europe owing to the outbreak of the American Civil War (1861–5) and the French Revolution. As a result, the transportation of bullion supply to Bombay Island faced acute shortage. The British in Bombay were unable to acquire adequate sources of silver to mint coins. Wars waged in India such as the third Anglo-Maratha (1775–82) and Anglo-Mysore (1780–84) wars, required large amounts of bullion and this put additional pressure on the supply chain.[7] During this period when silver rupee was not in use, payments were made in gold. The problems were not restricted to Bombay Presidency alone; it affected all of East India Company's territorial possessions in India.

Exports of opium from the Malwa plateau through Bombay port offered a solution to Britain's balance of payments. By the early nineteenth century, the growing demand for opium in China resulted in large amounts of gold and silver being brought into western India. This increased the supply of bullion to Bombay and the silver rupee once again became the currency in circulation after 1800. Exchange of opium and cotton for silver, silk, porcelain and tea by the Chinese from the British brought in the white metals, but it was soon banned by the Chinese government during the war between 1839–42. The Treaty of Nanking put a stop on opium's entry into Chinese territory, and the existing opium in canton was destroyed and dumped into the river, taking a toll on marine life.

Chapter Six, the final chapter in this book entitled, 'The Emergence of Bombay City as the Financial Capital of India to Establishing of the Reserve Bank of India, c.1820–1935. This chapter presents in detail the development of Bombay from a mint to the establishment of the Reserve Bank of India. Thus, Bombay witnessed commercial growth as the capital city of finance in colonial India during the mid-twentieth century. Besides the local merchant communities, European agencies also came about for business transactions. This gave rise to banking institutions which created a money market for both merchants and traders.

Bombay's economy expanded in the mid-nineteenth century, making way for the new construction projects and the expansion of the railway lines. In 1836, Bombay Chambers of Commerce, one of the oldest in the country, was set up. The growth of commercial centres and the emergence of monetary policies in Bombay helped merchants and the development of many commercial buildings.

The rise in the price of silver affected the supply of silver bullion in the Indian territories, which became scarce. The Bombay town faced severe shortages of silver metal required for minting currency. This shortage and rise in prices forced people to hoard silver for personal profit. The situation led to the introduction of new monetary policies which brought in regulations among Bombay merchants and agency houses. The American Civil War, which had started on 12 April 1861, had created a huge loss for the merchants in Bombay, and therefore, the Bombay market underwent turmoil due to the fluctuation of prices and artificial boom. This concerned many traders and merchants who had invested huge amounts of capital in the cotton textile trade since an upsurge of demand for Indian cotton had lured Indian merchants into investing a huge sum in this trade. Later, they faced a severe crisis and saw their debts mounting, leading to a huge loss to property and capital. Many events across the globe in the mid-nineteenth century had brought in swift changes and new policies, all of which had an impact on the money market of Bombay.[8]

The steady decline in silver prices which started in the 1870s meant trouble for the Indian rupee since its content was silver. By 1893, silver prices were falling in world markets and the goal was to de-link the rupee from depreciating silver prices. A Currency Commission was set up to find the solution. The major cause for the fall in Indian prices lay in the government's attempts to hold a particular rate of exchange between the rupee and the sterling.

During the last quarter of the nineteenth century, World War I (1914–18) had already added serious constraints on the supply of silver metal to Bombay. The rising price of silver changed the old ratio, fixed in the early twentieth century, causing severe problems at the end of WWI in 1918. One of the many causes for the disruption of the Indian currency was the aggressive purchases of silver by the US Government from 1934 onwards, raising silver prices to the point that it was threatening to disrupt the Indian currency system because of the melting and exporting of silver rupees. The outbreak of World War II (1939–45) exacerbated the shortage of silver supply.[9] It hampered the global market leading to disruptions in global commerce as well as slowing down of the economy. Thus, Bombay saw a sharp decline in the banking institutions which had earlier flourished and soon found itself burdened with debt. The Bombay merchants and banking committees, to overcome this grave financial crisis and to protect the Presidency and Imperial Banks along with the merchants, founded the Reserve Bank of India on 1 April 1935. It was an effort to improve the financial and monetary system, for it to grow and strengthen; thus, making Bombay and the overall Indian economy strong and stable.[10] Bombay, thus, emerged as the gateway city and the financial capital of India in the twentieth century.

Notes

1. A.J.R. Russell-Wood, *The Portuguese Empire; A World on the Move, The Portuguese in Asia, Africa, and America: 1415–1808*, Baltimore: John Hopkins University Press, 1992, p. 126.
2. T. Bentley Duncan, *Navigation between Portugal and Asia in the Sixteenth and Seventeenth Centuries*, Variorum: Ashgate Publishing, 1997, p. 219.
3. S.M. Edwardes, *The Gazetteer of Bombay City and Island*, vol. II, Pune: Government Times Press, 1909, p. 271.
4. D.R. Almadi, *The Beginnings of Banking on Bombay Island*, Maharashtra Archives, Bulletin no. 12, Bombay: Government of Maharashtra, 1979, p. 5.
5. Bazil Shaik, 'Fortune, Probity, and Prudence (A Brief Narrative of Banking in Bombay)', *The Bombay Explorer*, vol. 47, 2006, p. 8.
6. K.K. Chaudhary, *Maharashtra State Gazetteer*, vol. II, Bombay: Gazetteer Department, Government of Maharashtra, 1987, pp. 495–6.
7. H.V. Bowen, 'Bullion for Trade, War, and Debt Relief; British Movements of Silver to around, and from Asia, 1700–1833', *Modern Asian Studies*, vol. 44, no. 3, 2010, pp. 341–2.

8. Radhe Shyam Rungta, *The Rise of Business Corporations in India; 1851–1900*, London: Cambridge University Press, 1970, pp. 72–6.
9. Bazil Shaikh, Ranjeeta Dubey and S.M. Khot, *Mint Road Milestones: RBI at 75*, Mumbai: Marg Publications, 2010, p. 60.
10. Rajat Kanta Ray, 'Indigenous Banking and Commission Agency in India's Colonial Economy', in *Money & Credit in Indian History; From Early Medieval Times*, ed. Amiya Kumar Bagchi, New Delhi: Tulika Books, 2002, pp. 118–30.

ONE

The Portuguese Bullion Trade in Seventeenth-Century Western India

Portuguese Conflicts with Indian Rulers

This chapter investigates Portuguese commercial activities with special reference to the bullion trade prevalent in seventeenth century western India. The important acquisitions of naval bases in the previous century are also reviewed here.

Four Portuguese vessels were sent out from Portugal in 1497 by King Dom Manuel I (1495–1521 AD). The *Sao Gabriel* was commanded by Admiral Vasco da Gama, who led the ships to India and reached Calicut on 21 May 1498. Other ships in the convoy were the *Sao Rafael* captained by Paulo da Gama, the brother of Vasco da Gama, and the *Berrios* commanded by Nicolao Coelho. The fourth ship which was a supply ship under the captainship of Goncalo Nunes did not reach the shores of India, as it was grounded in the Bay of Sao Bras. Its provisions were distributed among the other three vessels. These ships were guided from Kiliwa in Africa to Calicut on the Malabar Coast by an Arab navigator Ibn Majid.[1]

In the bustling markets of Calicut different local and foreign merchants traded. It included Armenians, Chinese, Gujaratis, Jews, Malays, Persians and Turks. These merchants traded under the permission of the Zamorin. The Arabs enjoyed special treatment from the Zamorin and dominated the trade of Calicut. The Arab quarters contained warehouses and shops and had their own judges and religious leaders.[2] The Arabs and Persians were central in controlling the trade in horses, having supplied horses to Indian rulers and merchants for centuries.[3]

The Portuguese carried goods as gifts and also for exchange. These included striped clothes, four scarlet hoods, six hats, four coral strings, a box of sugar and a jar of honey. Though initially trade was permissible by the Zamorin, the permission was soon denied to the Portuguese as was the right to anchor their ships off the coast.[4]

On 7 November 1502, Gama exchanged presents with the ruler of Cochin and also, the emissary from Cannanore, who had come to Cochin to negotiate terms for spice trade with the Portuguese. Between November 1502 and January 1503, Gama used Cochin as a central point to collect trade information from and conduct business with other towns of the Malabar coast.[5] Pepper was to be paid for in a ratio of three quarters of silver and one quarter of copper, at twelve gold ducats for a Cantera; cloves and benzoin were exchanged against textiles and cinnamon; incense and alum would be bartered for Brazilwood.[6]

Due to Vasco da Gama's atrocities on Ishmaelite (Muslims) sailors and the drowning of their trading vessels, he faced growing resistance from the Indian rulers and merchants which then forced him to look for a safer maritime base. The Moors, an Arabic nomadic tribes from north Africa had captured Portugal during the eighth century for around 400 years and had enslaved the Portuguese. Therefore, Vasco da Gama on his journey slaughtered hundreds of Muslims and had captured and drowned their vessels. Seeing the Arabs and Malabari Muslims in Calicut, Gama wanted to ban them from Calicut.[7] Thus Vasco da Gama was resented by these Arabs and Malabari Muslims. Vasco da Gama was denied the trading permission and entry into Calicut. To find safe base, Vasco da Gama moved towards Bandora (presently Bandra) and landed at Mahim (Bandar) in the same year. From 1505, the Portuguese made early incursions into the north Konkan coast. They sought to capture Mahim but were unable to do so until the 1530s. Mahim, a port town of consequence which traded with ports in Arabia, Persia, Red Sea and Africa, was also connected with towns in the hinterland.[8]

The custom bander from Mahim to the north-west, were used as anchorage for foreign and local sailing ships to load and unload goods through lighters (barges), and passengers on these ships could alight into the small barges. These landing anchorage points were not satisfactory or safe for both passengers and goods. They could only be used intermittently during the low tide, and both goods and passengers had to be carried out safely through the soft wet mud, as pointed out by Dr Himanshu Prabha Ray.[9]

The Portuguese, in search of trading sites as well as a protected coastal base, moved towards Chaul in 1507 and set up trade with the Bahmani ruler. In 1508 the Portuguese were defeated by the combined forces of the Sultan of Gujarat and Egyptian Mamluks. The Portuguese proceeded towards Dabhol and left it only on 5 January 1509, drifting towards the island of Bombay on 21 January 1509 AD. The population of Bombay comprised of Kolis (fisher folks), Bhandari's (toddy tappers), Kunbis (agriculturists) and Agris (salt pan workers). There were also small communities of Konkani Muslims and Pathare Prabhus. The Portuguese recognized the value of Bombay's safe harbour but could not establish their control over it until 1534. The name given by the Portuguese to the island '*Bombaim*' meant 'good bay' and applied to the seven small islets which were collectively known as 'Bombay Island'.[10]

The Portuguese soon set sail for Diu and upon arrival on 2 February 1509, faced attacks from Malik Ayaz, who with Amir Hussein, resisted the Portuguese. Malik and Hussein, however, lost to them and by 1513–14, the Portuguese were in a position to negotiate with Sultan Bahadur. Goa was conquered by the Portuguese Viceroy Afonso de Albuquerque after defeating Sultan Yusuf Adil Shah of Bijapur on 25 November 1510 AD, and the Estado da India officially came into existence in 1510. Before the arrival of the Portuguese, Goa was under the sultanate of Bijapur who had captured it from the Kadambas in 1350 AD. The Portuguese gained control of Mahim port and they plundered and burnt down Bandora in 1532. Bandora became the seat of the Portuguese administration in Salsette, where many churches came to be built for the Portuguese and the natives. It was situated at a strategic location, connected to both the islands, on the southern Salsette Island and towards the north of Bombay, and the sea.[11]

The Portuguese had first arrived in Chaul in 1507. It was an important port town on the west coast with an active sea trade. The Portuguese knew the importance of Chaul and attempted to capture it but got beaten by the combined forces of the Sultan of Gujarat and the Mamluks of Egypt.[12] Captain Vasco da Gama, recognizing the importance of Chaul and its strategic location, wanted Chaul to come under the Portuguese control in 1531 AD. They could not fortify Chaul, as the Portuguese had signed an agreement with King Bahadur Shah of Gujarat on 23 December 1534. The treaty stated that the Seven Islands of Bombay, Bassein (Vasai) and it's dependencies were ceded to the Portuguese Crown and which commenced after 1559–60. In November 1570, Chaul was attacked by Nizam Shah, Sultan of Ahmednagar, and in July 1571, a treaty was signed between the Sultan and the Portuguese. The Portuguese developed a shipyard in Chaul to build their own ships due to the availability of timber in abundance. The shipyard soon grew into a ship building centre to meet the demands of the Portuguese. Ships frequented Chaul, especially from the Red Sea and Hormuz in Persia. Items of trade included rice, sesame oil, fine cloth and cane sugar. Turbans were dyed and in demand in Arabia. The most important item of trade from Chaul, however, was grains, especially rice, exported to West Asia.[13] Russian traveller Athanasius Nikitin visited Chaul in 1470 AD and found it to be a flourishing trade centre.[14]

After many years of unresolved conflicts between the forces of the Sultan of Gujarat and the Portuguese, a peace treaty was signed on 25 October 1535. By the virtue of this important treaty, the Portuguese Estado da India acquired Bassein and Bombay Island. The terms of the treaty stated the terms on which Bahadur Shah:

> gave and bequeathed to the King of Portugal from that day forth and forever the city of Bassein, its territories, islands and seas, with all its revenues would be lost, in the same way as he, Sultan Bahadur, King of Gujarat, held them before, provided that all vessels from the Kingdom of Gujarat bound for the Red Sea should first stop at Bassein and collect passes, and on return voyage call there again, in order to pay duties under penalty and risk seizures.[15]

Finally, the control of these territories was transferred to the king of Portugal and his representatives at Estado da India.[16]

Under the governorship of Dom Joao de Castro (1547), important reforms were introduced in Bassein and its outlying regions. These included the plan to build a shipyard to construct and repair ships and churches and forts to protect themselves from enemies such as the Mughals, Marathas and the Siddis. It became the political capital of the Portuguese province of the north and soon developed into a commercial centre of grandeur and opulence. Bassein was often compared with Goa as it was among the largest and richest of Portuguese possessions in the east. French traveller Francois Pyrard de Laval, who visited Thane, commented on the beautiful churches and impressive fortifications. The Portuguese built a mint in Thane in the year 1611 AD, called the Casa de Moieda (House of Money), where Portuguese coins were minted.[17]

In the sixteenth century, Thane, an important trading centre, consisted of a population of Hindus, Muslims, Egyptians and Europeans. Other important port-towns located in north Kankan were Chaul and Sopara. The Portuguese ruled Bassein and Thane from 1535–1739 AD, after which Bassein was met with attacks from the Marathas. Under the leadership of Baji Rao I and his brother Chimmaji Rao, the Marathas were successful in taking over the political control of north Konkan by 1739.[18]

Thane was located in the north Konkan region and was ruled by the Portuguese for 200 years, from 1535 until 1739 AD. Foreign ships visited ports of Thane and established trade links. Items imported into Portuguese territories from the Red Sea, east Africa and Europe included horses, bullion and African slaves.[19] Thane traded with the adjoining ports in the interior and the items included cotton cloth, gold and silver embroidered fine muslin and fine gauze from Burhanpur. Other goods sent from the Deccan included gold and silver metal crafts, spices and cotton cloth. These items were later exported to Arabia, Persia, Africa and China.[20]

Among the most important items which were imported into Bassein or Thane were horses. Thane and Bassein were important centres for horse trading and merchants from all over the region were found there. These horses were imported from Basra, Ormuz, Muscat and Arabia since they were so valued in warfare.[21]

Goa became the political seat of the Portuguese power in western India in 1510 AD. It played an important role in supplying many essential commodities such as horses, timber, metals and spices to the neighbouring Indian state as well as to other Asian countries. It was also connected to other towns in the hinterland, products from which were exported to foreign countries. These included Balaghat textiles which were in high demand in Lisbon, Brazil, east Africa and other ports of Asia. Goa had also served as an important port for the Haj pilgrims undertaking their pilgrimage to Mecca, many of whom came from the Deccan. Trade in Goa and other Portuguese possessions on the west coast were made possible due to the establishment of the Goa Mint and other surrounding mints which provided currencies for circulation and enabled the growth of Portuguese trade.[22]

Portuguese Naval Supremacy in the Sixteenth and Seventeenth Centuries

The Portuguese set up high-technology shipyards for constructing ships of good quality and carrying ship repairs. Good quality large-sized ships were also built to carry valuable goods across the ocean. The trade items such as pepper, timber, ginger, cinnamon, cloves, nutmeg, camphor, sealing wax, indigo, sandalwood, ivory, ebony, benzoic, coir and several other items were exported from Cochin. Therefore, the Portuguese, the first European power, established a shipyard at Cochin.[23]

Cochin emerged as one of the most important political and commercial centres for the Portuguese. Even after the transfer of their political headquarters to Goa in 1510, Cochin continued to function as an important port for the Portuguese trade. Traders in Cochin used vessels that resembled the ones used by the Portuguese. The shipyard at Cochin, established in the year 1511–12, was the one in which *Santa-Catharina do Monte Sinai*, the most famous of the early Portuguese vessels, was built.

During the Portuguese rule in Cochin, the ship building yard was considered to be the finest. Strong vessels of different sizes and designs were built which promoted long distance trade. Sea-crafts were made accordingly for purposes of trade and war. Prominent among them was galleons for war and carracks for trade and commercial sea-faring activities.[24]

The ship building industry of Goa under the Portuguese in the sixteenth century, where the local craftsmen from Goa and the Portuguese craftsmen worked in the yards together, built large ton vessels, but these ships could only be used by the Portuguese. Therefore, the people of Goa resisted paying for these ships, which were to be primarily used for the advantage of the Portuguese and not for them. This refusal by the locals was due to the heavy taxes levied on the use of the ships, and the Portuguese continued using it for their own trade solely and denied the locals access. If they were to use it, they had to pay higher prices to load their own goods on the ship for trading.[25]

Chagas de Cristo, a great carrack of about 1,200 tons was built in Goa under the supervision of Viceroy Dom Constantino de Braganza. This officer, who built and designed this vessel himself, sailed to Lisbon in 1562. This vessel was in service for twenty-six years and later reduced to hulk in 1586. Another carrack used for trading named *Sao Pedro*, built in the Goa yard, set sail for Lisbon in 1538. The vessel remained operational for twenty years and was broken up similarly in 1557. From these vessels, the Portuguese earned substantial profits for Estado da India. The important trading vessels such as *Flor de La Mar* (1524–9) and *Nossa Senhora da Boa Viagem* (1576–85), brought in more revenues to the Portuguese Crown.[26]

Portuguese galleons developed in the early sixteenth century from the early designs of their ships, such as the caravel of 100–200 tons and galleons above 200 ton and under 500 tons, which were generally smaller than the Portuguese carracks but weighed heavier than the galleons. They weighed less than 1,000 tons. Galleons were war ships—stronger and heavily gun-armed. The designs usually were akin to the square-rigged caravel. Square-shaped designs were used for swift sailing at greater speeds when running offshore in order to protect the ship and cargoes from the enemies. Galleons were long, narrow and had a square-tuck stern instead of a round tuck. These vessels continued to be used until the early eighteenth century. *St. Teresa* of 1639 was the largest war ship ever to be built.[27]

Carracks were usually very large ships and over a thousand tons. For example, *Santa Maria* was a large carrack, its size and stability allowing cannon mounts. This extraordinary vessel gained fame with the Spanish and Portuguese voyages of discovery. The Portuguese used lateen sails. Joao de Liao represented the first Portuguese caravel. He was also the Portuguese architect who designed the ship *Caravel.* The carrack was the version taken from the caravel, which became the standard vessel for Atlantic trade and exploration in mid-sixteenth-century Europe. It was swift and strong, capable of transporting more men, military personnel and cargo.[28] The lateen rigged caravel was classified as a '*Caravel Latina*' and later modified as a square-rigged vessel called '*Caravel Redonda*'. It became a very popular model in the seventeenth century; the famous caravels among them being the *Nina* and the *Pinta*. These ships were built mainly to carry valuable goods and wealth safely across the ocean for trade.[29]

The Portuguese built huge vessels with guns and cannons, which were installed in these new vessels. These improvements could help the vessels to reach its destination on time and carry valuable cargoes safely to the destined place. The Indian Ocean was infested with both local and foreign pirates. They attacked ships and damaged valuable cargoes. Ships had special rooms to store valuable goods, especially precious metals. These precious commodities were stored in wooden chest boxes or metal boxes built in the special compartment. Therefore, to protect these goods, a safe vault was designed. Built of large tons, these ships could sail at high speeds without being disturbed or attacked. The Portuguese vessels carried cargoes from both local and foreign merchants.[30] The ship building industry thus, started by the Portuguese to promote trade through ships, brought in more revenues and helped the Crown earn profits from these vessels.

Table 1.1: Portuguese Vessels in the Seventeenth Century

Name of Vessels	*Tonnes*	*Years*
Ternate	200	1610
Hoope	150	1615
Diamant	300	1621
NA	600	1627

Name of Vessels	*Tonnes*	*Years*
Revengie	200	1633
Limburch	200	1634
Manhilhas	200	1635
Conjeher	200	1636
Negapatnam	200	1638
Nieuwe	200	1641

Source: M.M. Elbi, 'The Portuguese Caravel and European Ship Building: Phases of Development and Diversity', in *Revista da Universidade de Coimbra*, vol. 33, 1985, p. 553.

Establishment and Location of the Portuguese Mint in Goa

Portuguese Viceroy Afonso de Albuquerque ordered the establishment of the mint house in Goa. The mint house was known as the *Casa de Moeida* (House of Money) in 1510. In order to develop an effective monetary system, it was necessary to have adequate supply of coinage throughout the territories of Estado da India. Variety of coins varying in weight and values were minted in Goa. The Goa Mint issued currencies in gold, silver and copper. These included coins such as the manuels, esperas, half esperas, and leis or reis, and later other types of coins such as bazarucos, santhome, patacoes, tangas, pardaos, and cruzados came to be minted.[31]

The mint at Old Goa was situated on a road behind the bishop's house. The minting work was entrusted by Albuquerque to a brahmin merchant for 2,000 pardaos. Around 1552, under the administration of Dom Afonso de Noronha, the mint was shifted inside the city fort and then later shifted to Old Goa under Sam Pedro de Panelim on the orders of Dom Manoel. This mint in Goa was also shifted to Panjim. The French traveller Francois Pyrard de Laval who visited Goa between 1607 and 1610 recorded that the Portuguese coins were minted in the large *Praca* at '*Ribera Grande*' in Panjim.[32] The Portuguese Viceroy Afonso de Albuquerque introduced measures to improve the economy of Goa, increase the supply of bullion and struggle against the debasement of coin.

Afonso de Albuquerque invited leading *Cambistas* to assist the Goa mint in ensuring that no debased currencies circulated. These *Cambistas* were money changers with expertise in checking the purity of metals. They played an important role in ensuring that currencies maintained the specified quality of gold and silver when minted. They had served earlier under the Kadamba dynasty. Coins which were in circulation in Goa before the arrival of the Portuguese remained in circulation for decades after the Portuguese took control. The following chart illustrates the change from the pre-Portuguese currency to the new currency system in Goa introduced for the first time by Albuquerque.[33]

Table 1.2: Circulation of Coins before the Portuguese and the Introduction of Portuguese Coins under Alfonso Albuquerque.

Pre-Portuguese Coins in Goa	*Portuguese Coins Introduced under Alfonso Albuquerque*
fanam	cruzados
paream	meio-cruzados
partab	manoeis
partap	meio-manoeis.
tanke	espheras

Pre-Portuguese Coins in Goa	*Portuguese Coins Introduced under Alfonso Albuquerque*
hone	meias-espheras
sultani	–
pagodas	leais
barganis	dinheiros
zoitole	cepaiquas
jithals	roda
bazaruks (Persian)	–

Source: E. Lyon, 'The Nina, the Santa Cruz, and Other Caravels as Described in the Liro de Aarmadas and Other Spanish Records', *American Neptune*, 1993, pp. 239–41.

Table 1.3: Coins Minted in Goa under the Viceroyalty of Afonso de Albuquerque, Their Weight and Value

Names of the Coins	*Weight*	*Value*
Goan-cruzados or manoel (gold)	3.45 g.	680 reis
meio-manoel (gold)	1.70 g.	340 reis
espera (silver)	4.43 g.	40 reis
meia-esperas (silver)	2.21 g.	20 reis
capaiqua (copper)	1.15 g.	0.5 reis
lead	6–8.5 g.	2 reis
roda (tin-lead-zinc)	6–82 g.	7 reis

Source: E. Lyon, 'The Nina, the Santa Cruz, and Other Caravels as Described in the Liro de Aarmadas and Other Spanish Records', *American Neptune*, 1993, p. 550.

Portuguese cruzados in Goa were made of gold and similar in value and weight to those minted in Lisbon.[34]

Other coins included the gold manoeis struck in honour of King Dom Manoel I of Portugal. On the obverse side of the coins, an emblem with a Christian cross was embossed and on the reverse side, a sphere which was the mark of the majesty of King Dom Manuel I who ruled Portugal from 1495–1521 AD.[35]

Table 1.4: Establishment of Portuguese Mints in Sixteenth- and Seventeenth-Century Western India and the Neighbouring Countries

Location	*Date of Establishment*
Old Goa (Velha-Cidade)	1510 AD
Malacca	1511 AD
Cochin	1530 AD
Ceylon	1598 AD
Bassein	1611 AD
Daman	1611 AD
Chaul	1646 AD
Diu	1684 AD

Source: de Laval, *The Voyage of Francois Pyrard of Laval to the East Indies, The Maldives, The Moluccas and Brazil*, p. 79.

Albuquerque had opened two mints, one in Old Goa in 1510 and the other at Malacca in 1511. According to the numismatician Gerson da Cunha, Albuquerque's coins minted at Goa during his administration (1510–15) circulated along the entire western coast from the Persian Gulf to Ceylon. Copper coins began to be minted at Cochin around 1530 AD, and the copper was imported from Portugal but not permitted by the Zamorin of Calicut to be transported to the other towns in the Malabar region. This resulted in the shortage of copper coins in the Malabar coast of south India.

In 1525, Viceroy Dom Henrique de Menezes (1525–6) ordered that a few minters (*medeiros)* be sent to Cochin from Goa, to strike cruzados for promoting trade. Cochin gradually grew into a ship building and trading centre. In 1535, Manuel Botelho, the Portuguese governor of Cochin, who controlled the functioning of the mint, wrote to the king of Portugal about the need to import additional gold coins into Malabar if trade was to increase. The bullion imported into Goa from Portugal was to be utilized for making coins and later to be sent to Cochin. Copper coins were minted in Cochin especially during the second half of the sixteenth century. Cochin remained the Portuguese headquarter until 1662 AD in south India. The Portuguese power declined after 1662 AD due to the attacks of the Dutch East India Company.[36]

Portuguese control over Cochin declined due to naval attacks by the Dutch East India Company. Trade between Portuguese Goa and the east African towns of Monomotappa, Siena and Mogadishu consisted of imported goods such as rhino horns, elephant teeth, fish and sundry items and exported goods like fine cotton cloth, muslin, baftas and spices in exchange for gold, ivory, ebony, and cowries to other countries such as Manila, China, Japan and east Africa.[37]

Cowries were an important medium of monetary exchange and continued to be used for exchange where prices needed to be expressed in units lower than the copper coin. Thus, the metallic currency was supplemented by cowrie shells (*kauri* in Hindi; *khar muhra* in Persian) in Bengal, Bihar and Orissa, and bitter almonds (badam) in Gujarat. These shells were imported from Maldives and Iran respectively. Cowries and almonds were available abundantly at the coast but were in greater demand in the hinterland.[38]

Goa was dominated by prominent Indian merchants who collaborated with the Portuguese. Important among them were Saraswat brahmins from the Konkan and the Banias from southern Gujarat. These intermediaries facilitated the trade in Estado da India and Portuguese private trade during the sixteenth and seventeenth centuries. People who traded on their own account included resourceful Jesuits, mestizos and deserters from the army. This unofficial trade was largely financed by Indian merchants. Portuguese private trade was conducted in many ports, some of which were not even under direct Portuguese rule. Gujarat was especially important in the growth of official and private Portuguese trade; the value of this trade being estimated at about present-day 4 million rupees in 1600.[39]

German and Italian Merchants Engaged in Goa Trade

King John Afonso V of Portugal faced financial difficulties. To aid the Portuguese enterprise overseas, the king invited financiers to invest money in the Estado da India.[40] Merchants and financiers were to fit out vessels under the Portuguese banner. Private merchants were not allowed to trade in certain items such as spices which was deigned to remain under the royal monopoly. By 1504 the port of Antwerp was closely linked to Portugal's Asian trade. Portuguese consignments were received in great numbers and volume at Antwerp. In return, Antwerp supplied the Estado da India with bullion, armaments and medicine. European merchants played an important role in the development of Portuguese trade in western India. Prominent among them were German and Italians financiers.[41]

Bartholomew Marchione, a Florentine financier, commented, 'the merchants of Florence having fallen behind Venice, in the contest for the Oriental trade, were eager to invest in Portugal's exploration ventures'. Marchionni invested in the early Portuguese voyages to India. In 1507 and 1514, he provided King Manuel I with substantial amount of money to finance trade in the Indian Ocean. Other bankers Gualterotti and Frescobaldi participated in the trade of western India.[42] Florentine merchant Filipe Gualterotti acted as an agent for the Portuguese in Antwerp. He supplied large quantities of copper to the Portuguese factory in western India. King Dom Manuel I too granted the German merchants special commercial privileges. These included special concession in trading commodities such as spices and precious stones.[43]

Herwarts belonged to the trading families of Germany. They were specialist in the dealings of precious metals, precious stones and pearls, purchased large varieties of these commodities from Europe and Africa and exchanged them for commodities in India. The established trade connection between precious metals of central Europe and the spices of the East prompted the German merchants to set up shops in Lisbon and later in Antwerp. The new sea route to India around the Cape of Hope by the Portuguese helped in the growth of south German merchants and firms and gave them the necessary access to lucrative opportunities in the jewel trade of India. Precious stones available in Indian coastal towns arrived in Europe in large quantities. Jan Huygen van Linschoten, a Dutch traveller in sixteenth-century India, noted that amethyst, garnets, crystals, agates, fine amber and carnelians were sold in Cambay. Diamonds from India too were sold in Europe, especially by Venetian merchants.[44]

The Fuggers, an important German banking family, played a key role in the Portuguese Asian trade. The founder of the family was Johann Fugger. He belonged to the class of European bankers. Originally from Augsburg, these banking families were prominent since the sixteenth and seventeenth centuries.[45] Another family was the Welser family, who controlled much of the European economy in the sixteenth century and accumulated enormous wealth from their trade. This banking family replaced the de Medici family, who influenced all of Europe during the Renaissance period. The Fuggers seized many of the de Medici assets along with their political power and influence. Jacob Lucas Fugger and Anton Fugger along with the other rich and influential merchants of Germany began Hochstetler, meaning rich company, which was involved in Elizabethan copper mining venture and they remained the most hated monopolists of their time.[46]

The Fuggers played a significant role in the bullion trade conducted by the Portuguese in western India. They were not only financiers of the Holy Roman Empire but also supporters of the Papacy. Powerful bankers and capitalists with large investments in the fields of mining, banking, trading and the bill of exchange, they financed the Portuguese trade and earned special privileges for themselves.[47]

The Florentine merchants who supported the Portuguese trade in western India were Bartolommeo Marchionni, Filippo Glitterati and Frescobaldi, who financed the Portuguese trade in western India in the sixteenth century. Together they financed the bullion trade, helping the Portuguese in securing power and strength in building up the royal monopoly. They made profit in the trade in spices and precious stones. In order to acquire regular amount of goods for exports, special privileges were granted to the craftsmen, silversmiths, goldsmiths, coppersmiths, blacksmiths and men who worked in foundries. These special privileges included trade concessions, housing, trading licenses and protection to their families.[48]

Prominent among the local Indian merchants and also close to the Portuguese were the merchants based in Cochin, namely Mamale Marakkar, Cherina Marakkar, Pokkarachen of Cannanore, the Chetti merchants of Mangalore, and Khwaja Shamsuddin Giloni of Cannanore. The Portuguese collected large amounts of loans to carry out their trading activities. The Portuguese also traded with them and purchased their goods in order to export them to other regions.

In the sixteenth century, Khawaja Shamsuddin Giloni was a rich merchant who traded bullion with the Portuguese. Malik Gopi, Malik Ayaz and Khwaja Sofar of Gujarat and the Chettis of Coromandel Coast financed and participated with the Portuguese in conducting maritime trade in western India. These merchants were mediators for the Portuguese in securing permission from the rulers. The Nairs supported the Portuguese and fought for them.[49]

In the sixteenth and seventeenth centuries, Goa emerged as a great centre for trade in horses. Arab merchants flocked to Goa and sold a large number of horses in the city since horses were needed by rulers from different parts of India. An order issued by the Viceroy on 22 September 1515, stated that 'everywhere the order has gone out that the ships leaving the port of Ormuz with horses are to be given a guarantee of 100 Cruzados per horse and that they shall be taken to no other port but only to Goa'.[50]

Goa had developed under the Bijapuri rulers and it supplied both the kingdoms of Bijapur and Vijayanagar with Arabian and Persian horses which were imported from Arabia, Suvar, Ormuz and Turkey.[51] Indian rulers belonging to the families of Adil Shah of Bijapur and Nizam Shah of Ahmednagar signed treaties with the Portuguese in 1546 AD and became successful in making the Portuguese import twelve horses from Arabia every year without levying any taxes on them. Another agreement was signed on 22 August 1548 through which the number of horses was increased from twelve to twenty. Moreover, the Portuguese attempted to prevent independent horse dealers from entering the kingdom of Adil Shah. The Nizam Shahi rulers tried their best to ensure that the horses would not be sold to their rivals, Adil Shah.[52]

The Portuguese administration at Goa earned profits from the taxes levied on these horses—forty-two parados of gold to be paid per horses as excise duty. All merchants who brought horses to India were bound to come to Goa and obliged to pay the stipulated custom duties. When full payments were made on the duties of horses, only then were the horses allowed to be taken to places like Bhatkal, Chaul and Dhabol.[53] Obtaining of Cartazes and security arrangements were important components of the horse trade. Sometimes ten ships loaded with horses were found in Goa. In the years 1546–8, 1,000 horses were imported into Goa. The horse trade alone generated a revenue of 90,000 rupees which constituted half of the total revenue of the town.[54]

Tom Pires said, 'The best are the Arabian, next are the Persian and the third are those from Cambay. These are worth little'. The first two areas however produced very expensive horses. A good one could cost Rs.1,000 while the average one could cost between Rs.400 to Rs.600.[55]

By the beginning of the seventeenth century, Goa was the capital of the Portuguese empire whose trading connections extended from Hormuz in West Asia, Mozambique in east Africa to Nagasaki in Japan. The most important transport used in the Portuguese bullion trade were Naos or 'great ships'. These sailed annually between Goa, Macau and Nagasaki from the 1560s until 1618. The Portuguese later found it difficult to use these ships due to the competing Dutch forces. This new enemy of the Portuguese forced them to use smaller and faster galliots. These small-sized vessels enabled the Portuguese to conduct trade without disruptions from the enemies. In the seventeenth century, Manila became the first direct trade link between America and Asia across the Pacific Ocean. Spanish America became an important source for the supply of the precious metals, which estimated 150,000 tons of silver between 1500 and 1800, possessing 80 per cent of world's production. The second source for the supply of silver metal was Japan, almost a total of 3 cent of the world output; however, later, it declined to 16 per cent in the seventeenth century. Nagasaki was another source for the supply of silver, which was traded with China as it was one of the biggest buyers of white metal.[56]

Another source was the South American silver which traversed the Atlantic Ocean, passing through Europe for Asia, which came in large quantities of 150 tons of silver annually. This shipment also passed through Amsterdam. Another route for bullion supply was the Mediterranean-Levantine trade route which carried huge quantities of silver too, but the Cape route was the largest. Another important route was one through the Pacific Ocean where silver from South America-Acapulco passed through Manila and was later exported to China.[57]

The Portuguese conducted trade with the port of Macau in China and Nagasaki in Japan and the item of trade included Chinese silks, sugar, porcelain and Japanese silver. The Japanese silver mines profits increased, but gold and copper production soared in Japan only in the second half of the seventeenth century. Japan did not decline in the production of silver in the seventeenth century. Silver, like any commodity, lost its high value when supply exceeded the demand. This affected the structures of prices and the value of silver.[58]

China was among the biggest buyers of white metal, and

this demand was fulfilled by the Portuguese, as they found it profitable to exchange silver for tea and silk. Scholars have raised questions regarding the quantity of silver metal brought by the Portuguese into China. The writings of the English merchant named Ralph Fitch, who travelled in Asia between 1583 and 1591 recorded that the Portuguese carried 600,000 cruzados worth 15,336 kg. of silver from Japan to China.[59]

Table 1.5: The Portuguese Bullion Trade between China and Japan in Mid-Seventeenth Century

Destinations	*Year*	*Quantity of Silver*
Japan to China	1583–91	15,336 kg.
Nagasaki to China	1635	56,700 kg.
Nagasaki to China	1636	88,830 kg.
Nagasaki to China	1637	98,280 kg.
Nagasaki to China	1638	60,480 kg.

Source: Meenu Rajak (Meenu Kanojia), 'Trade in Horses by The Portuguese in Western India', (unpublished M.Phil. thesis), 2001, pp. 9-10.

From the table provided above, one can estimate that Nagasaki was an important port for the export of silver. The Portuguese were prominent in the silver trade and sought silver to meet the great demand from the Chinese. China was ready to pay any price for this precious metal.[60]

The year 1638 saw a sharp decline of almost 38,000 kg. of silver production. The drop in Japanese silver export was due to the declining power of the Portuguese in Japan as they were banned from trading in Japan. From the table, we can also calculate that the Portuguese imported around 1.65 million kg. Japanese silver into China.

Another 500,000 kg. silver was transported by the Portuguese from Goa to China or obtained through Manila. The Portuguese could get a total of 2 million kg. silver imported into China in the 1630s. They found the Chinese junks and Japanese red seal ships to be good carriers for their trade. Maritime historians Dennis O. Flynn and Arturo Giraldezs, highlight the importance of the trading route via Manila in the Pacific Ocean for transporting bullion. During the seventeenth century this route grew to be the most important and easiest route to bring South American silver into Manila. Manila became an important trading town and a centre of the Portuguese trade. The Portuguese found many Japanese residing in Manila from where they acquired silver for Japan.[61] Silver was shipped from Peru and Potosi in Bolivia, Peru and Lima. Rich silver mines in South America met the growing demand for this precious metal, especially in China. The Chinese took a special liking to silver and were ready to pay double its value.[62]

Goa's Bullion Trade and Trading Networks in the Seventeenth Century

Goa was the capital of the Portuguese empire which stretched from Mozambique in east Africa to Nagasaki in Japan and controlled the Indian Ocean trade in the early seventeenth century. From the 1560s onwards, Goa made profits between 25 to 40 per cent from the sale of silver Reals of Eight or pieces of eight. This silver metal was shipped from Portugal to India and was sold in Goa to money dealers there and in other parts of western India. The Portuguese trade in bullion increased in volume, approximately to 30,000 kg. silver per annum, as recorded in 1618. Imports of bullion to Goa in 1629 AD rose to a profit of 70 per cent.[63] Gold was imported

Table 1.6: Importation of Gold into Goa from the East African Region in the Sixteenth Century by the Portuguese

Destination	*Year*	*Quantity of gold (kg.)*
Goa	1585	573 kg.
Goa	1591	716 kg.
Goa	1610	850 kg.
Goa	1667	1,487 kg.

Source: Meenu Rajak (Meenu Kanojia), 'Trade in Horses by The Portuguese in Western India', (unpublished M.Phil. thesis), 2001, pp. 58-9.

by the Portuguese from places such as Sofala, Kilwa and Monomottappa, the gold-producing region in east Africa. A large amount of gold was sent to Goa. Annually, the Portuguese in east Africa exported 8,500 kg of silver a year, a large amount of which was sent to Goa.[64]

The supply of gold from Monomotappa in 1614 was approximately 400,000 parados, which was worth 1,000 kg. of gold. By the 1620s, a serious problem of adulteration and illegal smuggling of gold by the Swalilian and Portuguese traders arose. They were private traders involved in the piracy of gold from the mines. A letter from the authority of Goa to the king of Portugal in 1645 claimed that the householders of Mozambique falsified the gold with other base metals. The King of Mozambique responded that the gold from the mine was up to 35 per cent pure but adulterated by intermediaries resulting in great losses.[65]

The King of Mozambique wrote a letter to the Portuguese Viceroy in 1653 to control the adulteration of gold, but the governors of Portuguese India replied to the letter in 1658, saying that they could do nothing, as the gold was extremely pure when it was in the control of Kaffirs, but once the gold came into the hands of the Portuguese, it was falsified and adulterated to a large extent.[66]

Another letter in 1667 noted that in a rich area, 'the Kaffirs who possess these lands will not allow more gold to be extracted than is necessary, that the Portuguese may not covet and obtain possessions of their lands'.[67] The actual process of mining entailed hardships and danger. Rich gold mines of Monomottappa came under Portuguese control in the 1550s. Initially, the Portuguese thought that they could fill their sacks and carry off as much as they could, but when they saw the difficulties of spending a few days near the mine, the risk and perils the Kaffirs underwent and the reality of the gold mines, the Portuguese soon found their hopes frustrated and had to rely on the local population to mine the gold.[68]

The Levantine route was the oldest route in the transport of gold from Europe to India. The bullion which came to India had to pass through the Arabian and Persian territories and evade the monetary officials. It was more of an international trade in a regional economy. The European bullion was first minted into coins of their respective realm, either to finance the export trade or as a result of bullion measures. These coins were first used in circulation and then later exported to India in the form of Lari, Abbasi and Shahi Mohurs against the merchandise which was largely consumed within those regions. An important Armenian merchant active in bullion trade at the time recorded are as follows:

From the reign of Shah Abbas I to that of Shah Abbas II there had been plenty of silver in Persia than is to be seen now, and the Armenian merchants used to transport it from Europe into Persia and then got them converted in to local money (*le reduisoit en mannoye du pays*), but in these past years bring nothing but ducats and sequins since these are more portable. They have also invented new ways of hiding the money in their vests and shirts to safeguard against robberies which take place on caravans travelling from Turkey and also to avoid payments of customs and other dues at places which are not rigorous in searching for what the merchants are carrying.[69]

Historian Najaf Haider noted that according to Tavernier, those merchants travelling in caravans between Aleppo and Basra would be allowed to pass and had to pay the toll in the same currency. At other points, however, they were forced to convert these into local currencies at an official rate of exchange. The silk exports from Gilan and Georgia were financed by prototypal Iranian coins entirely struck out of European silver which the Armenian merchants brought to the frontiers of northern Iran. All of this was practised through a system of deposit banking and money-lending, which was quite widespread in Iran and controlled largely by the Indian Banias.[70]

Goa linked Surat and Golconda to the Mediterranean entrepots, and the remittance of commercial papers was matched by a reverse remittance of cash which was eventually transferred physically from Bandar Abbas to India. As a result of regular trade between the Portuguese and West Asian merchants, the lari had already become an established medium of payment on the coasts of Gujarat and western Deccan. In another testimony, Gomes Solis, who was a big merchant in Indo-Portuguese trade at the turn of the seventeenth century, described how the reales were converted into Turkish and Iranian coins and then taken to India in large quantities. By 1602, the annual export of bullion to Hormuz by the Ottoman merchants was as high as 2 million cruzados (41.74 metric tons of silver). These also included payments in the form of shahi, lari, and reale, which were brought not only to the western coasts of India but also to the other hinterland port towns of the Mughal Empire as well.[71]

The export of bullion out of Persia was never popular among the authorities; the merchants could always found ways and means to circumvent official prohibition. However, due to large amount of bullion being exported which led to the depletion of wealth from the country and an ensuing monetary crisis, the bullion export came under the strictest scrutiny. This was later reported to Shah Suleiman. Looking at the serious condition, he took strict measures to regulate the supplies of silver to the mints. Armenians were now no longer bringing foreign bullion into the country of Persia and were exporting it to India. This movement of the Armenians was causing silver crisis in the empire and all of this led to serious drainage in Persia. Silver coins were found debased in value. In 1684, foreign coins were undervalued at the official rate of exchange and it became practically impossible for the merchants to get correct values for their bullion in Persia. All of these developments put together forced the merchants to export directly to India.

Thus, evidence suggests that Gujarati shipping in the western Indian Ocean for trade with Iran was increasing in this period. The English reported in 1660 AD that the number of non-European ships at Surat had increased considerably from 15–20 in number to 80. The customs revenue at Hormuz in 1610 was 3.6 metric tons of silver and that of Bandar Abbas in 1643 was 5.5 metric tons. This trade later rose to 6 metric tons in 1654 and 7 metric tons in 1657. In 1656–7, the average of the total which was exported from Surat to Bandar Abbas was 22 metric tons of their silver value.[72]

Important sources for the bullion supply to western India by the maritime route was the Red Sea. Indian ships called at the ports of the Red Sea in the course of the seventeenth century. Mocha brought 200,000 reals of eight and 100,000 Venetian and Hungarian ducats and Ottoman sultani. Mocha was believed to be one of the busiest markets for exchange of Europeans bullion against the spices from Malabar and Achin, textiles and indigo from Gujarat and coffee from Yemen. These items of trade were brought to the market of Mocha, and traders came to buy these commodities. Therefore, 'a great deal of money passes on to India that way'. Thus, these goods brought to Mocha were sold to the Arab and Turkish merchants, mainly for silver and gold.

The above information gives an important account of the Mocha region, which adds to the economy of western India and the magnitude of overall trade with India. The Portuguese sources speaks of 12–15 ships going to the Red Sea from Gujarat each year, and a modern estimate has put the total value of this trade at 20 million rupees (approximately 226.6 metric tons of silver) on the basis of the duties paid to the Portuguese by these ships.[73]

Table 1.7: Bullion Imported into Gujarat through the Red Sea Route

Year	*Amount*	*Fine Silver (in metric tons)*	*Number of Trading Ships.*
1582	1,200,000 rupees	13.63	On one imperial ship
1622	2,500,000 rupees	32.10	On two Gujarati ships
1624	-	24.00	Bullion and goods on a Diu ship
1628	1,200,000 florins	11.30	On one imperial ship
1641	1,700,000 reales of eight.	43.50	On Gujarati ships
1642	1,000,000 reales	25.59	On one English ship
1643	600 to 700,000 rupees	6.8–7.9	On a Gujarati ship

1645	485,000 reales and 10,000 ducats	12.85	On Gujarati ships and one on Dutch ship
1648	1,167,853 reales	29.88	On Gujarati ship
1653	961,000 reales	24.59	On eight Gujarati ships
1654	1,000,000 reales	25,76	On five Gujarati ships
1679	4,000 ducats	56.67	On Gujarati ships
1685	5,000,000 rupees	56.67	On Gujarati ships
*c.*1700	6,000,000 rupees	68.00	

Source: Najaf Haider, 'Precious Metal flows and currency circulation in the Mughal Empire', in *The Journal of the Economic and Social-History of the Orient*, vol. 39, no. 3, 1996, p. 312.

From the above table, one can say that in the last quarter of the seventeenth century, there was an increase in the imports of Red Sea bullion to Gujarat.

Table 1.8: Bullion Imports of the Mughal Empire in the Seventeenth Century

Source	*1588–1602*	*Percentage of the total*	*1630–45*	*Percentage of the total*	*1679–85*	*Percentage of the total*
Persian	27.8	22.4	25.0	29.5	30.0	22.9
Isfahan	10.0	8.1	5.0	5.0	10.0	7.6
Red Sea	75.0	60.5	40.0	47.2	56.0	42.8
Portuguese	11.2	9.0	3.0	3.5	–	–
English	–	–	5.2	6.1	25.1	19.2
Dutch	–	–	6.6	7.8	9.7	7.4
Total	124	100.0	84.8	100.0	130.8	100.0.

Source: Najaf Haider, 'Precious Metal flows and currency circulation in the Mughal Empire', in *The Journal of the Economic and Social-History of the Orient*, vol. 39, no. 3, 1996, p. 323.

Gold: An Exclusive Metal for Trading

Mughal scholar Abul Fazl's famous book *Ain-i-Akbari* describes the foreign coins which were in circulation in the Mughal Empire. The book does not list any gold coins which were minted in the Mughal mint, while the account of gold minting gives an impression that the gold had to be drawn by the Sarrafs (money-changers) from the private hoardings. In the seventeenth century, gold was exported both by the European and Asian merchants. The imports which came from Persia until 1600 were mainly in silver, but after 1666, gold began to replace silver in great quantities. However, from 1684, it can be seen that the silver which was exported to the Mughal Empire was revived once again.[74]

A Note on the Sarrafs and their Role in the Bullion Trade

Sarraf is derived an Arabic word *Sayrafi*, referring to money testing as well as to fix their value in the markets. The Sarrafs also organized commercial credit, and their position as deposit bankers and discounters of Bills of Exchange (Hundi) enabled them to not only supply the bullion seller with cash but also provided the facilities to transfer funds from one place to another. These Sarrafs made their profits out of wholesale buying of all kinds of bullion such as gold, silver, copper and tin, foreign and regional coins. They acted as mediators and also chose auspicious days to finalize a good bargain. Sometimes, these Sararafs were faced with competitors who also fixed the bullion price and exchanged the rate of foreign coins carefully, evaluating the cost of precious metals and adding extra cost of minting to price they offered to the sellers.[75] As for the Red Sea shipments of gold, it can be seen that from the first half of the seventeenth century, gold ducats were carried on the ships and also by the merchants caravans on land between the Levant and Gujarat in varying proportions, approximately between 4 to 27 per cent. The evidence from the second half of the seventeenth century suggests that gold came to Gujarat in increasing quantities from Levant between 1665–82. Another source states that the Dutch, who also imported gold to Gujarat, depended very largely on the availability of Chinese gold as well as supplies from the Netherlands.[76]

However, a major portion of bullion was not meant to be imported to Surat but to Coromandel, where gold was used as a currency. Therefore, the periods of high prices of gold in the Mughal Empire might have provided an inducement to increase the share of gold exported from the Mughal Empire. Another source, from where we get an insight, is from the Spanish records, which recently revealed how the drop in the American silver which arrived in Spain in the 1670s and the 'annual Plata fleet was importing gold in surprisingly large amount'. The total quantity, however, needs to be examined.[77]

It was examined that bullion and foreign spices were obtained through trade and brought to the Surat mints of the Mughal empire to be struck into rupees (Mughal silver coins of 179 grains) and mohurs (gold coins of 169 grains), which were of a very superior quality. The importance of precious metals lay in sustaining currency circulation, commodity trade and taxation and the fiscal and mercantile considerations. The custom duty imposed on the imported silver and gold was 1 to 2.5 per cent, lower than those on merchandise.[78] The mint had an open coinage system in which freedom rested with the bullion supplier and they were granted the permission to obtain Mughal coins on the payment of minting cost and seigniorage. The Mughal currency itself was usually of a very high degree of fineness and accepted at a premium over and above its weight in fine metal. This policy was thus applied to allow the merchant access to a free market and to keep away from currency manipulations and administrative interventions.[79]

Bullion sales usually took place when the returning fleet of Indian ships brought huge quantities of silver and gold from the Red Sea and the Persian Gulf. The abundance of precious metals lowered the price of bullion relative to specie as a result of the Mughal coins for country investments or the settlements of debts. The Sarrafs fixed the bullion price and exchanged the rates of the foreign coins, skilfully evaluating the cost of precious metals and adding the cost of minting.[80]

Estimates of the Portuguese Bullion Import into the Mughal Territory

According to the Portuguese historians, James Boya Jian gives us an insight into the Portuguese imports—derived from the Casa da India (Lisbon), how the Portuguese traded during the Mughal Empire, how the entire export to Lisbon was paid in precious metals, mainly silver, and how the merchandise which the Portuguese brought added to their supplement of bullion. The assumption estimated over the values on imports in silver represents the volume of Portuguese exports of bullion into the Mughal Empire.

Later this trade saw a decline, which was seen in the Portuguese exports of silver which came to India from about 26.71 metric tons in 1585 to 6.55 metric tons in 1615 and 1618. There was a sharp fall in the exports of silver when compared to the last quarter of the seventeenth century. The lowest level was seen in the year 1608, when another power, the English East India Company, entered the Mughal territory and later a regular shipment began to arrive in Gujarat till the middle of the eighteenth century. The English exports of bullion fluctuated between 1.5 and 6.4 metric tons from 1614 to 1672 with an average of 3.3 metric tons per year.[81] The exports were virtually suspended during the second Anglo-Dutch war.

Table 1.9: Estimated Output of the Mughal Silver Mints

Years	*A: Number of Coins*	*Annual Output in Metric Tons of Silver*	*B: Number of Coins*	*Annual Output in Metric Tons of Silver*
1556–65	20.5	4.28	32.0	5.79
1566–75	122.0	25.49	226.5	40.99
1576–85	231.0	48.28	424.5	76.83
1586–95	440.0	91.96	854.5	154.66
1596–1605	584.0	122.05	1147.0	207.60
1606–15	368.0	76.91	516.5	93.48
1616–25	308.0	64.37	432.5	78.28
1626–35	574.0	196.96	758.0	137.19
1636–45	384.0	80.25	499.4	90.41
1646–55	306.5	64.05	398.0	72.03
1656–65	299.8	62.65	365.0	66.06
1666–75	223.5	46.71	256.0	46.33
1676–85	258.3	53.98	294.5	53.21
1686–95	395.6	82.68	453.0	81.99
1696–1705	585.1	122.28	670.0	121.27

Source: Najaf Haider, 'Precious Metal flows and currency circulation in the Mughal Empire', in *The Journal of the Economic and Social-History of the Orient*, vol. 39, no. 3, 1996, p. 340.

The Role of the Portuguese Merchants in the Bullion Trade of Gujarat in the Seventeenth Century

The Portuguese merchants bringing reale from Lisbon in September had to exchange them for the lari in order to obtain spices such as clove, cinnamon, cardamom, pepper and other spices, which earned them a profit of 12 per cent easily. These gold coins were used to settle the purchase of spices. The demand for laris had outgrown the demand for the rising silver influx and the currency which had been acquired on the western coast to settle regional trade balances.[82]

One of the important merchants named Gomes Solis from Goa, who was a big merchant in the Indo-Portuguese trade at the turn of the seventeenth century, described how the reales of Lisbon when coming through the Mediterranean Sea into Turkey and Iran, were converted to Turkish and Iranian coins and later shipped in large quantities to India. By 1602, the annual export of bullion to Hormuz by the Ottoman merchants was as high as 2 million cruzados, which equalled 41.74 metric tons of silver. This silver was in the form of shahi, lari and reale, which was brought not only to the western coast of India but also to the Mughal Empire. Lari was first brought by the Persian merchants to the Konkan region and was accepted by the people and also the Sultans of Bijapur. Therefore, we find different types of laris bearing the names of places where it was struck, e.g. Dabhol, Chaul, Basra, Hurmuz and so on.[83]

The term 'lari' meant a unique silver coin of high fineness minted at Lar (the capital of Laristan in southern Iran). On numerous occasions, laris were described by foreign travellers and observers who took care to note their size and shape, which testified their high degree of fineness. These bullions which came to western India by the Red Sea, linked the Levant with the Arabia and Iranian ports and exchanged merchandise with bullion. An Ottoman imperial ship sailed every year to Mocha laden with huge quantities of gold and silver coins. In 1616, exports to Mocha by one such ship consisted of 350,000 reales of eight and 50,000 Venetian coins. The Red Sea ports of Jeddah, Mocha and Aden were visited by merchants belonging to Cairo and Aleppo, where European bullion came through the ports of Alexandria, Smyrna, and Iskenderun.[84]

The first quarter of the seventeenth century was an important period for Portuguese trade, especially bullion; Indian ships sailing through the Red Sea halted at these trading ports such as Jeddah, Mocha and Aden. These ports were of immense importance as they exchanged spices for European bullion. Spices, textiles, indigo and fine muslin cloth from Gujarat and coffee, ivory and bullion from Yemen were exchanged. These commodities brought to Mocha were sold to the Arab and Turkish merchants mainly for silver and gold.[85]

M.N. Pearson records from the Portuguese sources that twelve to fifteen ships from Gujarat sailed to the Red Sea annually. In 1622, two ships, the *Sala-Mati* and *Tawakkul I Ali*, sailed from Mocha to Gujarat bringing silver worth 32 metric tons. Ships from Jeddah and Hodeida richly laden with bullion came to the Gujarat port. The Portuguese helped the Mughals to go on pilgrimages and undertake trading activities, by protecting their ships and goods. They also forced the Mughals to take Cartazes from them for smooth sailing. A royal imperial ship of the Mughals travelling to the Red Sea was an important advantage, as pilgrims visited safely and in return carried bullion.[86]

Table 1.10: Estimates of Portuguese Exports of Precious Metals to the Mughal Empire, 1586–1631

Year	*Gujarat and Sind*	*Bengal*	*Annual Total*
1586–90	50.45	5.65	11.22
1591–5	22.54	2.74	5.04
1596–1600	42.81	3.93	9.34
1602	3.38	0.43	3.81
1605	0.00	0.00	0.00
1608	1.02	0.13	1.15
1610	2.28	0.19	2.47
1615	2.14	0.27	2.41
1616	4.98	0.61	5.59
1618	4.12	0.47	4.59
1630	5.76	0.54	6.30
1631	1.99	0.34	2.33

Source: Najaf Haider, 'Precious Metal flows and currency circulation in the Mughal Empire', in *The Journal of the Economic and Social-History of the Orient*, vol. 39, no. 3, 1996, p. 315.

Import of Bullion by the Portuguese in Seventeenth-Century Goa

Precious metals like gold, silver and copper were imported in Goa in the early seventeenth century. These metals in the form of bullion were used to carry out official trade, known as *Cabedal de Pimenta* (pepper money). Goa became an important trading town for both Portuguese as well as Indian merchants, since ships loaded with metals, horses, ivory, rose-wood, glass-ware and other luxury items were imported to Goa. Through these imported commodities, the Portuguese made huge profits from the sale made to both

Indian as well foreign governments and rulers in India in the early seventeenth century.

These metals were shipped from Lisbon (Portugal), it came in the form of gold, silver and copper. Metals also came from South America via the Cape of Good Hope to Goa and from China and Japan. This bullion trade became the most important maritime trade of the Portuguese in the sixteenth and early seventeenth centuries. The Portuguese continued to accumulate large quantities of copper, gold and silver, which came from European places like Antwerp, Tyrol, Sweden, Denmark, Flanders, Servile, Valencia, Bremen, Hamburg, Danzig, Augsburg, Nurnberg and Urn.[87]

Introduction of Custom Duties in Goa

In the year 1638, other Europeans are said to have paid duties amounting to 3.5 per cent on imports and exports, especially on gold and silver coined in bars, which when imported to Goa, one had to pay only 2 per cent. Precious metals in different forms of gold dust, coins, gold bar and Spanish dollars were given concessions on custom duties. This can be explained by Fernao Mendes Pinto's travel account in 1638 AD, which recorded that there was a special custom duty imposed on religion. That is, 2.5 per cent on Muslims and 5 per cent on the Hindus. The 2 per cent levied on the Muslims was paid for *Zakat*, or charity, which was considered mandatory for Muslims who set out for pilgrimage and was a holy custom for Muslims to donate selflessly.[88]

The Cartaz System: Ways of Controlling Sea-borne Trade

The Portuguese Viceroy Alfonso de Albuquerque introduced the Cartaz system in 1502 which led to the establishment of trading stations at Calicut, Cochin and Cannanore. Cochin was the early capital of the Portuguese. To control trade and shipping in the Malabar Coast and obtain revenues for their Estado da India, the Cartaz system was introduced. The revenue collected from this system was spent on the manning of the Portuguese garrison and navy. The system thus enabled the Portuguese to exercise some control over trading networks which they were not able to dominate otherwise. Later, in the sea-faring world, it came to be called a passport or CDC (cargoes' discharging certificate).[89]

The Cartaz system was a trading license to authorize ships to carry cargoes and conduct trade. This certificate would thus protect those ships that had this certificate, duly signed by the Portuguese custom officials in charge of the port. The Cartaz required all merchants to purchase this trading license. Without it the trade was deemed illegal and goods could be confiscated. The trading license, being in possession of the Cartaz, provided merchants protection offered by the Portuguese authorities. Purchasing the Cartaz helped the merchants from being attacked or looted by the pirates. Thus, taking in to account the many advantages it served, it forced the merchants to buy the Cartaz from the Portuguese custom houses, which were erected at the Portuguese port.

The Cartaz listed the ports a ship could visit and the cost of the Cartaz depended on the quantity of goods and its value. The Portuguese Cartaz system was later used by the Dutch and the English to control the Indian Ocean trade. The Cartaz had impressions of Virgin Mary, Jesus and the Portuguese kings stamped on it.[90] The Portuguese intended the Cartaz to be bought by both Indian rulers and merchants. This was, however, resisted by Indian rulers such as the Zamorin of Calicut.

In 1518, the Portuguese governor Lopo Soares issued

orders that there be a book in which all the Cartazes issued from time to time could be registered. The Cartaz list was to be duly signed by the authorities in charge of the factory or fortress. The cost of one Cartaz was five pardaos. The record or registry was to be maintained and shown to him whenever he desired to consult it. The number of merchants purchasing this sailing permit or license increased as the Portuguese power grew. Indian and foreign traders purchased these Cartazes from Portuguese control ports such as Cochin, Cannanore, Goa, Chaul, Bassein, Daman and Diu. The practice of the Cartaz system continued until the mid-eighteenth century.[91]

Among the Indian rulers who purchased these Cartazes were Khwaja Sofar, the merchant governor of Surat and Khwaja Sham-din-Giloni, the administrator and governor of Belgaum in the kingdom of Bijapur. Malik Gopi—the merchant governor of Surat—and his son Amir Gopi too collected 20 Cartazes for his ships in 1533 AD. Armenian merchants too collected these Cartazes for ship-trading in India as well as the Red Sea. Nizam Shah of Ahmed Nagar purchased these Cartazes to import horses from Arabia. Adil Shah of Bijapur too collected six Cartazes for their ships sailing to Mecca, Hormuz and other ports on the Red Sea in 1613. Changes were evident in the system of the Cartaz, when the Portuguese faced increasing competition for control over the seas by the seventeenth century. Many merchants and rulers disregarded the system of Cartaz completely and could avail the Cartaz from other European powers as well. The Indian Ocean now was controlled not only by the Portuguese, but by the Dutch, French, and the English who too had entered the sea politics and were gradually weakening the power of the Portuguese. The Portuguese, therefore, could not force the merchants to buy these Cartazes, as they refused to take it from the Portuguese. The reason being that other European power such as the Dutch too issued Cartazes to the merchants and in return granted protection to both, ships and goods.[92]

The Declining Phase of the Portuguese Bullion Trade in the Seventeenth Century

The European wars of the 1620s had disrupted the normal channels of trade between Mediterranean countries and north Europe, and all this led to an acute crisis in the supply of silver rials and bullion. Silver was exported in the form of Spanish coins known as rials of eight. These coins were supplied for the English Company, mainly from the Middleburg, Amsterdam, Netherlands and France, considered to be the chief sources for the supply of bullion.

The early seventeenth century saw the decline of the Portuguese maritime power in Asia due to the new competitor Dutch, who took control over the Portuguese centres in India and Asia. The early years of the seventeenth century were a period of instability and crisis, for both the Portuguese and the English East India Company, as the Dutch had become powerful with their fast-moving vessels. The Dutch attacked and captured the Portuguese trading stations in India as well as Malacca in Malaysia and Hormuz in Persia. Since the Dutch had become bitter enemies of the Portuguese, the English too wanted to control and capture Portuguese trading stations. The Portuguese power started weakening, as both Dutch and English were competing to take over the Portuguese centre. On the other hand, England was involved in wars with Spain and France, which interfered with the supply of bullion.

The seventeenth century thus witnessed a major setback for the Portuguese Estado da India. However, the decline of the Portuguese empire in Asia in the seventeenth century was mainly due to the rivalry of other European powers in the Indian Ocean. During the early seventeenth century, many trading activities underwent a change, which was due to the military maintenance on local and foreign land, Portuguese private trade and accumulating wealth individually instead of filling wealth in the royal treasury. The 1630s and 1640s brought a major downfall for the Portuguese as they lost their hold over important trading centres such as Hormuz, Canton and Nagasaki.

The elimination of the Portuguese from Nagasaki in 1639 saw a sharp downfall in the volume of Japanese silver entering China, as they had lost their trading permission and because their trading prowess moved to the hands of the Dutch. The decline of the Portuguese trade proved beneficial for both the Dutch and the Chinese. In 1640 AD, the Dutch became one of the acute enemies of the Portuguese and were importing Chinese and Persian silks via the Cape route and later re-exporting it to Manila. From 1637–41, 150,000 to 200,000 kg. of Japanese silver was carried to China each year, but also, silver came from Acapulco via Manila. Much of this white metal continued to flow through the Mediterranean during the seventeenth century.[93]

At first this was very profitable commerce open to all traders, but the Estado da India moved to extract the maximum return for the crown—a single ship to make the Goa-Macau-Nagasaki for each round trip. Spanish merchants at Manila were also drawn to the trading networks, as they purchased Chinese silk with American silver and sent it back to Europe via Mexico. In 1641, the Dutch captured Malacca and closed the straits to the Portuguese vessels, lowering its revenue and trade.[94]

The Portuguese maritime trading started weakening from

the early seventeenth century due to the arrival of the new power, the Dutch, and its naval supremacy. The Portuguese witnessed the decline in the trade of almost all commodities, especially precious metals, copper, ivory, horses and precious stones. The reason for this decline was that the Portuguese faced challenges both from the Dutch and the English East India Company, as they attacked the Portuguese factories and forts, and took over their control. All this led to the gradual downfall of the Portuguese trade. The new European power in the Indian Ocean forced the Portuguese to give in, as the new enemies had more sophisticated sailing vessels and technology.

Another reason for the decline of the Portuguese power was the temporary union of Spain and Portugal in 1580–1640, which meant that the Estado da India came under assault from the enemies of Spain as well, most notably the Dutch. Once the Vereenigde Oost-Indische Compagnie or the United East Indian Company persuaded the merchants in Amsterdam of the value of cooperation, concerted efforts were made to monopolize the import of spices to Europe and transport it to inland markets which required it the most. The advent of the English and the French converted commercial rivalry into warfare, especially in India, where the decline of the Mughal powers provided ample scope for the acquisition of territory.

The Portuguese saw its decline in western India due to the aggression of the French, the Dutch, the Maratha, the Mughals and the Siddhis. The marriage alliance weakened the Portuguese power further when Bombay was transferred to the English King. Bombay was one of the most prominent islands among the seven islands. The loss of Bombay made way for the loss of Portuguese power gradually. The expellation from Nagasaki in 1640s, loss of Hurmuz and other factories brought in the decline of Portuguese power and their trading activities. The British and the Dutch became the next supreme powers in the Indian Ocean.[95]

Notes

1. Sanjay Subrahmanyam, *The Career and Legend of Vasco da Gama*, New Delhi: Cambridge University Press, 1977, p. 77.
2. Glenn Joseph Ames, *Vasco da Gama: Renaissance Crusader*, New York: Pearson Longman, 2005, p. 55.
3. C.R. Boxer, *Race Relations in the Portuguese Colonial Empire (1415–1825)*, Oxford: Oxford University Press, 1963, p. 69.
4. Subrahmanyam, *The Career and Legend of Vasco da Gama*, p. 217.
5. Ames, *Vasco da Gama: Renaissance Crusader*, p. 56.
6. Subrahmanyam, *The Career and legend of Vasco da Gama*, p. 217.
7. K.S. Mathews, *Trade with India during the Sixteenth Century*, New Delhi: Manohar Publications, 1983, p. 161.
8. B. Arunachalam, *Mumbai by the Sea*, Mumbai: Maritime History Society, 2004, pp. 64–5.
9. Himanshu Prabha Ray, 'Ethnographies of Sailing – From the Red Sea to the Bay of Bengal in Antiquity', in *The Indian Ocean Trade in Antiquity, Political, Cultural and Economic Impacts*, ed. Matthew Adam Cobb, New York: Routledge, 2019, p. 12.
10. Mariam Dossal, *Theater of Conflict, City of Hope: Mumbai, 1660 to Present Times*, Mumbai: Oxford University Press, 2020, pp. 4–5.
11. K.S. Mathews, 'The Economy of Bassein in the Sixteenth Century', *Indica*, ed. John Correia Afonso, vol. 24, Bombay: Anand Press, 1978, pp. 42–3
12. De Barros, 'Portuguese Coinage and Currency in Goa', p. 8.
13. Om Prakash, *Portuguese in India*, vol. I, New Delhi: Anmol Publications, 2002, p. 274.

14. Ibid., vol. II, p. 318.
15. Boxer, *The Portuguese Seaborne Empire*, p. 73.
16. Ashin Das Gupta, *The World of the Indian Ocean Merchant, 1500–1800*, New Delhi: Oxford University Press, 2001, p. 79.
17. Om Prakash, *European Commercial Enterprise in Pre-Colonial India*, Cambridge: Cambridge University Press, 1998, p. 73.
18. Boxer, *The Portuguese Seaborne Empire*, p. 69.
19. Peter Gay and R.K. Webb, *Modern Europe*, New York: Harper and Row Publishers, 1973, p. 210.
20. K.S. Mathews, *Portuguese Trade with India during the Sixteenth Century*, New Delhi: Manohar Publications, 1983, p. 69.
21. Christian John Le Roy, 'Portuguese India and its Historical Records', in *Hispanic American Historical Review*, vol. 25, 1945, p. 232.
22. Mathew, *Portuguese Trade with India during the Sixteenth Century*, p. 71.
23. T.R. de Souza and G.V. Scammell, 'The New Worlds and Europe in the Sixteenth Century', *The Historical Journal*, vol. 12, no. 3, Pembroke: Cambridge University Press, 1969, pp. 389–412.
24. K.S. Mathew, *Indo-Portuguese Trade, and the Fugger's of Germany: Sixteenth Century*, New Delhi: Manoharlal Munshi Publications, 1997, pp. 73–4.
25. Gay and Webb, *Modern Europe*, p. 204.
26. Ibid., p. 75.
27. Le Roy, 'Portuguese India and its Historical Records', pp. 235–6.
28. Celsa Pinto, *Trade and Finance in Portuguese India*, New Delhi: Concept Publishing Company, 1994, pp. 79–80.
29. K.S. Mathew, 'The Portuguese Chronicles of the Sixteenth Century and the Socio-economic History of India', in *12th Conference of the International Association of Historian of Asia*, Hongkong, 24–8 June 1991, p. 16.

30. C.R. de Silva, 'Empire, Horses and Trade', in *International Conference in Indian Ocean Studies*, Perth, 1979, p. 215.
31. T. Bentley Duncan, 'Navigation between Portugal and Asia in the Sixteenth and Seventeenth Centuries', in *European Commercial Expansion in Early Modern Asia*, ed. Om Prakash, Vermont: Ashgate Publishing, 1997, p. xix.
32. Rajak, 'Trade in Horses by the Portuguese in Western India', pp. 8–9.
33. Ibid., pp. 9–10.
34. Ibid., p. 9
35. Ibid., pp. 48–9.
36. Ibid., p. 272.
37. Ibid., p. 273.
38. Ibid., p. 58.
39. Ibid., pp. 58–9.
40. Brian Moloughney and Xia Wei Zhong, 'Silver and the Fall of the Ming', in *Metals and Monies in an Emerging Global Economy*, ed. Thomas Bracewell and Heiko Feldner, no. 55–72, Leiden: Brill, 2015, p. 60.
41. Om Prakash, 'The Portuguese in the Far East 1540–1640', in *Vasco da Gama and the Linking of Europe and Asia*, ed. Anthony Disney and Emily Boot, New Delhi: Oxford University Press, 2000, p. 140.
42. Ibid., p. 273.
43. Dennis O. Flynn and Arturo Giraldez, 'Born with the Silver Spoon: The Origin of World Trade in 1571', in *Metals and Monies in an Emerging Global Economy*, ed. Dennis O. Flynn, vol. 14, Great Britain: Ashgate Publishing Limited, 1997, pp. 273–94.
44. Moloughney and Wei Zhong, 'Silver and the Fall of the Ming', p. 58.
45. De Souza, *Medieval Goa; A Socio-Economic History*, p. 52.
46. John McGuire and Patrick Bertola, *Evolution of the World Economy, Precious Metals and India*, New Delhi: Oxford University Press, 2001, p. 34.

47. Ibid., p. 34.
48. Kaffir is derived from an Arabic word meaning 'non-believer'.
49. Ibid., p. 35.
50. Ibid., pp. 34–5.
51. Najaf Haider, 'Precious Metal flows and currency circulation in the Mughal Empire', *The Journal of the Economic and Social-History of the Orient*, vol. 39, no. 3, 1996, p. 303.
52. Ibid., pp. 303–4.
53. 'Tavernier makes it quite clear that these Banias were mainly bankers, who accepted deposits from the wealthy men of Isfahan on interest. These deposits were then lent out on a higher rate of interest'. Jean-Baptiste Tavernier's book *Travels in India* (Les six voyages de Jean Baptiste Tavernier, écuyer baron d'Aubonne), which was first published in French in 1676.
54. Hendrich Blochmann and Abul Fazl Allami, *Ain-I-Akbari*, vol. I, Calcutta: Asiatic Society of Bengal, 1927, p. 65.
55. Haider, 'Precious Metal Flows and Currency Circulation in the Mughal Empire', pp. 307–8.
56. 'Generale Missive: III, 36. Reporting on the great volume of the trade conducted by the Muslim and Bania merchants of Gujarat, they noted that between May 1654 and April 1655, '40 heavy ships [Cloucke Schepen] sailed from Gujarat, mostly to trade with Persia, Basra and Mocha'.
57. The Red Sea ports of Jeddah, Mocha and Aden were visited by the merchants from Cairo and Aleppo, from where the European bullion came through the ports of Alexandria. *Supplementary Calendar*, pp. 118–19.
58. M.N. Pearson, *Merchant and Rulers in Gujarat: The Response to the Portuguese in the Sixteenth Century*, London: Berkeley Press, 1976, p. 101.
59. *English Factories Records, 1665–1667*, vol. 3, Surat: Maharashtra State Archives, p. 83.
60. *English Factory Records, 1650–1660*, vol. 3, Surat: Maharashtra State Archives, p. 262.

Prominent merchants like Virji Vohra and Rustam Manockjee who invested surplus cash would compete with the Sarrafs by offering higher price for the bullion.

61. A.R. Kulkarni, 'Money and Banking under the Marathas: Seventeenth Century to AD 1848', in *Money & Credit in Indian History: From Early Medieval Times*, ed. Amiya Kumar Bagchi, New Delhi: Tulika Books, 2002, p. 101.
62. *English Factory Records, 1665–1667*, vol. 3, Surat: Maharashtra State Archives, p. 84.
63. K.N. Chaudhari, *Trade and Civilization in the Indian Ocean*, New Delhi: Manoharlal Munshi Publications, 1985, p. 71.
64. Haider, 'Precious Metals and Currency', p. 326.
65. *Factory Records of Surat, 1655–1660*, vol. 5, Surat: Maharashtra State Archives, p. 87.
66. *Supplementary Calendar, English Factories Records*, 1646–50, Surat: Maharashtra State Archives, p. 240.
67. Haider, 'Precious Metals and Currency', p. 314.
68. Ibid., p. 340.
69. It was recorded that in 1621, the number of Portuguese vessels on the Cambay run was reduced approximately from 200 to around 60 ships. This was a sign of the declining trade during the Mughal Empire.
70. Haider, 'Precious Metals and Currency', p. 305.
71. Ibid., p. 309.
72. V.B. Gupta, 'Imports of Treasure and Surat's Trade in the seventeenth century', in *Metal and Monies in an Emerging Global Economy*, ed. Dennis O. Flynn and Arturo Giraldez, vol. 14, Variorum: Ashgate Publishing Company, 1997, p. 321.
73. Haider, 'Precious Metals and Currency', p. 312.
74. James C. Boyajian, *Portuguese Trade in Asia under the Hapsburg 1580–1640*, Baltimore: John Hopkins University Press, 1993, p. 247.
75. A.D.A Silva Rego, *Portuguese Colonization in the Sixteenth Century: A Study of the Royal Ordinances (Regimentos)*, Johannesburg: Witwatersrand University Press, 1959, p. 29.

76. M.N. Pearson, 'Asia and World Precious Metal Flows in the Early Modern Period', in *Evolution of World Economy, Precious Metals Evolution of World Economy*, ed. John McGuire, Patrick Bertola and Peter Reeves, New Delhi: Oxford University Press, 2001, p. 133.
77. J.M. Campbell, *Gazetteers of the Bombay Presidency—Gujarat, Surat and Broach*, vol. II, Bombay: Government Central Press, 1877, p. 82.
78. Ibid., p. 242.
79. Rego, *Portuguese Colonization in the Sixteenth Century*, p. 79.
80. M.N. Pearson, *Coastal Western India: Studies from the Portuguese Records*, New Delhi: Concept Publishing House, 1981 p. 22.
81. If a vessel was intercepted and found to be sailing without a valid Cartaz, the ship-captain and crews were imprisoned, and the ship and cargo confiscated. In Asia, local merchants could obtain a Cartaz easily and at a modest fee, but in Europe Cartazes were generally restricted to natural-born subjects of the crowns of Portugal or Spain respectively. In Asia, specifically in coastal areas of the western Indian Ocean, Cartazes functioned similarly to safe conduct passes known as qawl (declaration, report, pronouncement) in Arabic, and permitted 'to land men and make an agreement to trade'.
82. Sanjay Subrahmanyam's *The Portuguese Empire in Asia, 1500–1700: A Political and Economic History*, Wiley-Blackwell, 2012, p. 108.
83. Mathew, 'Trade in the Indian Ocean and the Portuguese system of Cartazes', p. 243.
84. Ibid., p. 98.
85. Ibid., pp. 98–9.
86. K.S. Mathew, 'Khawaja Safar, the Merchant Governor of Surat and the Indo-Portuguese Trade in the Early Sixteenth Century', *Proceedings of the Indian History Congress*, Kurukshetra, 1982, pp. 237–8.

87. Ibid., p. 241.
88. Dennis O. Flynn and Arturo Giraldez, 'Born with a "Silver Spoon": the Origin of World Trade in 1571', in *Metals and Monies in an Emerging Global Economy*, vol. 14, Variorum: Ashgate Press, 1997, p. 272.
89. F.C. Danvers, *The Portuguese in India: Being a History of the Rise and Decline of their Eastern Empire*, vol. 2, London: Frankcass and Co., 1966, p. 115.
90. Om Prakash, 'The Portuguese in the Far East, 1540–1640', in *Vasco da Gama and the Linking of Europe and Asia*, ed. Anthony Disney and Emily Boot, New Delhi: Oxford University Press, 2000, p. 141.
91. Cottrell, *Western Power in Asia: Its Slow Rise and Swift Fall, 1415–1999*, p. 44.
92. Om Prakash, *Portuguese in India*, Vol. I, p. 281.
93. K. N. Chaudhari, *Trade and Civilization in the Indian Ocean*, p. 78.
94. Sanjay Subrahmanyam, *The Political Economy of Commerce: Southern India (1500-1650)*, Cambridge: Cambridge University Press, 1990, p. 86.
95. Cottrell, *Western Power in Asia: Its Slow Rise and Swift Fall, 1415-1999*, p. xiii.

TWO

British Monetary Concerns and the Establishment of the Bombay Mint, *c.*1661–1710

Historical Background to the Marriage Alliance of 23 June 1661

Spain's domination over Portugal ended with the Portuguese rebellion of 1640. The Spanish Empire smarting under this reversal was determined to recover its lost territory. It seemed that the Spanish would succeed unless Portugal received foreign assistance. Portugal sought help from Britain, Spain's long-standing rival. To protect their common interests, on land and seas both, a commercial treaty was signed on 10 July 1654 between Britain and Portugal. This treaty was signed during the period of the Protectorate, and Oliver Cromwell, who was the Protectorate, signed the treaty with King Afonso VI of Portugal against the Dutch.

The English monarchy was restored in 1660. A marriage alliance was struck between King Charles Stuart (Charles II) and the Portuguese Infanta Catherine of Braganza, sister of Afonso VI. This marriage took place at White Hall in London on 23 June 1661. It was ratified on 28 August 1661. As a part of his dowry Charles II received Bombay Island along with Tangiers and substantial mercantile concessions from the

Portuguese. Bombay was a collection of seven islands, namely Colaba, Old Woman's Island, Bombay Island, Mazgaon, Parel, Worli and Mahim; Bombay being the largest island. The terms of the treaty stated by Article 11 of the marriage treaty, Afonso VI, King of Portugal presented, granted and confirmed to the King of Great Britain, and his heirs and successors forever, the port and island of Bombay:

> ... with all the rights, profits, territories, and appurtenances there of ... (and) full and absolute Dominion and Sovereignty of the said port and Island and Premises with all the Royalties thereof. A secret article in the Treaty bounds the King of Great Britain 'to exert all his power to establish a solid and lasting peace between the Most Serene King of Portugal and the States, General of the United Netherlands.[1]

In case of a war between Portugal and the Netherlands, the English promised protection to Portuguese possessions in the East from attacks by the Dutch. The treaty was ratified on 28 August 1661.[2]

Articles 12 and 13 were of commercial interest. Families of Portuguese subjects were to be allowed to live and enjoy privileges and immunities, which the Portuguese themselves had enjoyed earlier before the marriage. The English could trade in the cities and towns of Goa, Cochin, Diu, Bahia de Todos-os-santos and Rio-de Janeiro as well as the other Portugal dominions in the West Indies as stated in Article 13.[3]

Resistance from the Portuguese to the Handing over of Bombay Island to the British, 1661–5

The Earl of Marlborough was despatched from England in March 1662 with five ships, namely *Dunkirk*, *Leopard*, *Mary Rose*, *Chestnut*, *Pinnacle*, and the *Convertine*, with 500 soldiers under Sir Abraham Shipman. The fleets arrived at Bombay Island in September 1662. Bombay Island was to be handed over by Portuguese Viceroy Antonio de Mello de Castro based in Goa. By special orders of King Charles II of England, Sir Abraham Shipman was appointed Governor and Commander-in-Chief of Bombay and of 'any part of the firm land in the East Indies which shall be rendered and delivered up to us'. Subjects and strangers were to be encouraged to trade, and all help was to be given to the Portuguese in the protection of their trade and navigation.[4]

The Portuguese continued to resist the transfer of Bombay Island to British. Sir Abraham Shipman received a fresh commission from King Charles II on 23 November 1663, which authorized him to receive possession for Bombay Island from the Portuguese. However, he died at Angediva on 5 April 1664, without receiving the Island.

In the year 1665, Sir Humphrey Cooke, Secretary to Sir Abraham Shipman, assumed the government in February and the islands were finally handed over by the Portuguese to Humphrey Cooke on 18 February 1665.[5] The conditions of transfer included freedom for the Portuguese to come, sell, buy, trade at their islands and countries through the port of Bombay and they were to be free from all payments. The law of Portugal would determine the rights of immovable property.[6] The Portuguese still continued to exercise the rights of Portuguese law and its control over church property and this did not prevent them from practising their religion. The English should not 'compel the inhabitants of the island of Bombay neither directly or indirectly to change their faith or to go to church and attend the sermons'. This document was signed under the Portuguese governor Antonio de Mello de Castro in Panjim on 17 January 1665.[7]

This was destined to create much friction as many of its clauses were deliberately written. By this treaty it was agreed that though the island of Bombay would be delivered to the English, the Portuguese would still retain their rights to come, sell, buy, and trade. The Portuguese ships obtained permission for entry into and exit from the island. It also stated that the fleet and boats in Bombay and Portugal were to have free egress or regress without asking for leave because a part of the bay belongs to the other islands and countries.[8] Complaints against Humphrey Cooke were many, and he was also accused of allowing the Portuguese many concessions and trading privileges. His was, however, a temporary appointment. It was Sir Gervase Lucas who took charge of the island from Humphrey Cooke. On 5 November 1666, Lucas replaced Cooke as the Governor of Bombay. In his letter to Lord Arlington on 21 March 1667, Lucas lauded Bombay Island for:

> it's magnitude as one of the most pleasurable and profitable Islands in India. Bombay island was recognised for its rich natural surroundings of safe harbour and land filled with agricultural produce. The whole Island is an *Orto (garden),* or place planted with trees which yields great profit. And if Mr. Cooke had not sullied His Majesty's title to most of the best estates in the Island, most of the inhabitant's had by this time paid His Majesty 's rent.

Lucas passed away on 21 May 1667.[9]

Lucas was succeeded by Captain Henry Garry as the next Governor of Bombay Island. A letter written by the Portuguese Viceroy of Goa, Antonio de Mello de Castro, to the King of Lisbon on 5 January 1666, in which Captain Henry Gary was criticized by the Portuguese for being 'an awful heretic named Henry Garry was a great enemy of the Portuguese nations'. During his term the revenue of the island increased from 5,214 xerafins to 6,490 pound sterling, the tavern dues (exercise) increased from 400 xerafins to 2,400 xerafins, the tobacco farm receipt from 6,000 xerafins to 9,560 xerafins and the customs receipts from 4,100 xerafins to 18,000 xerafins. Henry Gary championed the British interest and fought for the recognition of the rights of Bombay vessels for exemption from dues at Portuguese ports.[10] The Portuguese were critical of Henry Garry and termed him, in January 1670, 'very astute and an enemy of the Portuguese nation'. This statement explains that Henry Garry accused the Portuguese of not paying any boat tax in the Bombay Island but charging the English supply boats passing through their ports instead.[11] Henry Garry fought for the recognition of the right of Bombay vessels to be exempted from dues at Portuguese ports. He also championed at the Surat Council by granting passes in the king's name to the native vessels.[12]

Travellers' Accounts of Bombay Island in the Late Seventeenth Century

John Fryer, an English traveller who visited Bombay in the 1670s, recorded that the trade in Bombay was quite restricted until, under the rule of Gerald Augier, an appreciable advance was made. In 1670 the local trade was confined to bullion which was free for five years save for a custom house tax of 1 per cent on wine, tobacco, opium, coconuts and coir, while the chief imports from England were cloth, copper, lead and silver.[13]

French traveller Delon, on his visit to the island in 1673, wrote:

> At the entrance of the port of Bombay lies a rock which is stretching a mile deep into the sea makes this passage very dangerous. For this reason, we sent for some pilots who took us safely on the 12th

into that harbour which is one of the safest in the world provided you are well acquainted with the situation of the place to avoid the rocks.[14]

Dr John Fryer, among the first arrivals here in 1674, was a man of science, who expressly tells us that gold was not a product of this country. Gold was no doubt worked in India, as gold and silver were worked in Scotland before the union gave subsistence to a number of poor people.[15] John Fryer, through his lengthy letter dated February 1674, portrays the Bombay of this period. 'The most conspicuous edifices on the island', he writes, 'is the old Portuguese fort, or castle. This lies on the south-eastern side of the island and is equipped with four brass cannon and a hundred guns'. The castle gardens proved to be the most delightful in India but were 'intended rather for Wanton Dalliance Love's artillery than to make resistance against an invading Foe'. Along the waterfront overlooking the fine harbour, capable of holding a thousand English vessels, arose the Company warehouses, tiled and plastered with windows made of oyster shells, a few substantial dwellings and the low, palm-thatched huts of the natives. The population consisted of Jesuits, Hindus, Muslims, and Parsis, who carried on a thriving trade in saltpetre, raw silks and diamond.[16]

At the end of the town were a 'bazaar', where cows and buffaloes roamed, and a Portuguese church with adjoining fruit orchards. North of Bombay was Mazagon, a small village of native fishermen called 'Coolly Christian'. On the north-west corner facing the Portuguese colony on Salsette Island, stood Mahim, with its custom-house and guard-house. Fryer also recorded that the trade of Bombay was small but had advanced under the governorship of Gerald Aungier.[17] Earlier Bombay, under the Portuguese rule, was not so developed, and its trade was only confined to dried fish, coconuts, betel leaves, toddy tappers and rice. After the English took control of the Bombay Island from the Portuguese, they developed it into a commercial trading town and made it the first headquarters of the English East India Company in western India.[18]

Transfer of Bombay Island to the English East India Company

King Charles II was tired of the differences between the Governor of Bombay and the English East India Company's President of Surat. He required funds to develop his navy and to stop the increasing threats from the growing power of the Dutch naval forces which compelled him to promise the Island of Bombay to the English East India Company.[19]

The transfer of Bombay Island from Charles II to the East India Company took place under a Royal Charter dated 27 March 1668, which specified that the port and Island of Bombay were to be held 'in free and common Soccage, as of the manor of East Greenwich', at a farm rent of pound 10, payable on 30 September each year.[20] On 21 September 1668, Sir George Oxinden took charge, became the first Governor of the Bombay Island under the English East India Company on 7 January 1669 and continued until his death on 14 July 1669.[21]

Gerald Aungier's Administration of Bombay Island

Under Aungier's Governorship, the town of Surat was raided by the Maratha ruler Shivaji in 1664; Oxinden and his nephew Sreynsham defended the Company's factory in Surat. The town was again raided and destroyed in 1670 by Shivaji. It remained the presidency of the East India Company from 1612–78, and again from 1681–7, before it was finally transferred to Bombay.[22] On the death of George Oxinden on 14 July 1669, Aungier took over as the next Governor of Bombay, since he had considerable knowledge of India, having come in 1662 with the Earl of Marlborough, been a free trader and served on the council of Surat.[23] Careful schemes for its development were considered both in India and England.

After four years, Aungier recorded the imports from England, which consisted of several kinds of cloth, serge, lead, tin, copper, quicksilver, vermilion, red lead, cochineal, coral, iron and ivory, and the export from Bombay which included clothes, baftas, dungarees, portcullis, pepper, drugs and calicoes. Aungier was firmly convinced of Bombay's enormous potential for trade, and in December 1673, pointed out to the Court of Directors that an appreciable advance has been made. 'Before this time', he wrote, 'the English trade was only in Coconuts and Cairo'.[24]

Aungier played an important role in the development of Bombay Island during his term as Governor during *c.*1668–77. When he assumed the Governorship of Bombay, he exclaimed that the island is a poor hamlet at present, 'it is a city which by gods assistance is intended to be built'. And he would set it in right earnest. It was his primary aim to make Bombay a safe place for anybody to dwell and trade in.[25] He proposed that liberty be granted as a special privilege to the inhabitants of Bombay to trade in all parts of India and in the ports of the south. He also suggested the establishment of merchant societies, which could finance trade and offer funds, to those who required it, and security in both money and property. While proposing this, he cited the practice followed by the Duke of Florence in enriching the port of Leghorn.[26]

Under Aungier, the population and revenue of Bombay Island increased. He took keen interest and measures in developing the island of Bombay and ensuring its growth. He implemented new reforms, social, political, and military and monetary in nature, to improve the conditions of the island.[27] He also established a Court of Judicature (1672) to solve financial offences and guarantee the right to trade. In 1675, he set up three large courts of justice and a tribunal to decide how petty cases were to be organized, police force was to be appointed, jails and prisons were to be erected.[28]

The Bombay Mint acted as a source of money to cater to the island's financial needs. Money was required to carry out certain improvements and innovations such as erecting a post office and insurance office. All this required money; therefore, to cover up this extra expenditure, the mint developed a tax which was first imposed in 1679. A duty of half a pound was levied on all the ships anchored at the Bombay Harbour. Another tax—one rupee per annum—was charged on each shop based in the island.[29]

To carry out the management of the English East Company, the company's board of directors appointed officers to manage their financial activities. Deputy Governor Shaxton was appointed as treasurer to receive and pay all dues, maintain the military stores, pay their salaries and look into their financial needs.[30]

John Child was the accountant; James Adams, an attorney and overseer of the Garrison Company stationed at the Bombay Castle, which looked after the company's revenues. Stephen Unstick was the warehouse keeper. George Wilcox was the judge of the Court, which looked after affairs of penalty and punishment and provided justice to the innocent. These official councils of Bombay were greatly responsible for developing the island and maintaining law and order.[31]

The Bombay Mint, one of the most important institutions in the city was established under the Bombay Governor Gerald Aungier. He eased business transactions and worked towards the development of Bombay Island. A hospital was set up along with a printing press; freedom of trade was secured by installing a military garrison for the protection of its people on the island; and temples and churches were built for worship and kept free from interference.[32]

Aungier laid reforms for the policy of trade, which was meant for the protection of trade and men. He said to the Company, 'the greater force you maintain on the "Island Bombay" for its defence, the more encouragements, given to the merchants of a nation and conditions to trust their estates, families and to their ships'. He sought to protect Bombay's trade by taking up arms against any enemy arriving at Bombay and stationing a small garrison of regular troops of 200 men with the local Portuguese militia to fight enemies attacking the island.[33]

The English East India Company invited merchants and traders to the island and in return offered facilities, liberty to practice their faith and security to them and their family for them to settle there. One of the leading Gujarati merchants from Surat, Bhimji Parekh, who migrated to Bombay, was granted protection of life and property. He had even heard of the Company's large commerce, upright dealings, and justice. Some of the facilities offered to the leading merchants included the Company allotting them land or free housing and a warehouse, which could be used to store trading goods.

Merchant communities could come and trade in the island of Bombay. Parsis from Navsari too were invited to serve the Company as master weavers. Other weavers from Chaul, Thana and Bhiwandi too came to Bombay Island. These merchants and traders were granted exemption from the payments on import and export duties for the goods for five years (1670–5). All these privileges were granted to attract more merchants towards this newly acquired land to improve the economy of Bombay Island.[34]

The brahmin communities could practise their religion freely in their own houses. No other castes would live within their compound. The brahmin and his family were free from all duties and would enjoy their properties, estate, goods without any harassment. He would have the liberty to trade in his own ship to whichever port he pleases. In case he brought any goods to sell in Bombay Island within the space of a year, he could come and go without paying the anchorage duties or customs on export. In case of war or during any danger, the Company provided him a warehouse in the castle to secure his goods, treasure and his family.[35]

Aungier made his home in the Bombay Castle, where he lived surrounded by comfort and luxury. To a man of Augier's austere tastes, affairs of state were of far greater importance than the trivialities of daily life. Upon his transfer from Surat to Bombay in 1672, he attempted to solve problems that confronted him—the Marathas, Malabar and Dutch pirates, the hostility of the neighbouring Portuguese colonists at Salsette and Bassein and the treachery of the Maratha chief Shivaji, who controlled the food supply in the mainland.[36] Challenges continued to confront the British, especially diseases; one out of every five Europeans succumbed to the ravages of flux, dropsy, scurvy, gout and malignant fevers. An epidemic, known as 'Chinese death', apparently cholera, gripped the whole island.[37]

Bombay was intended to be a hub for mercantile communities where trade was pursued immensely. Since many factors were responsible for the merchants to come to Bombay Island, it was a haven. However, due to the climatic conditions such as the El Nino cycle, the periodic epidemics as well as the famines of 1682–6 devastated the entire Konkan region and parts of the Maratha region of Poona and Satara.

In 1674, irregularities in the soldiers' pay arising out of debased coinage had broken out in the island. From 1677–82, Deputy Governor Rolt guided the destinies of the young colonists. He found the Siddhis, in-charge of Aurangzeb's naval force, navigating in and out of the Bombay Harbour during their skirmishes with Shivaji.[38] Another difficult situation arose two years after Rolt was appointed Governor. While the East India Company braved drastic economies of every kind, the Bombay factory from the standpoint of dividends had been a failure for a decade or more. Repairs to the fort, salaries to the Stakeholder, and garrison and general upkeep—all of these things took a heavy toll on the London treasury.[39]

A cheque from the treasure's book revealed that at least £300,000 had been spent on the Bombay venture. Financial retrenchment, however, was met with considerable hostility by the Bombay group, whose interests lay not with the London office but with their own immediate well-being. Work on the forts was stopped, and the salaries of officials and factors were lowered. Two prominent members were destined to play an important part in the island's history—John Child, who had been made Deputy Governor, and Captain Richard Keigwin who was the naval officer and a military commander of the East India Company. Keigwin was removed from the office since he had rebelled against the East India Company in Bombay in 1683, in order for raising the salary of the military garrison in Bombay whose salaries were cut. Another important reform made by Richard Keigwin to the Bombay island was the withdrawal of the London Company's trade monopolies which was declared free and open to all during his period.[40]

Establishment of the Bombay Mint and Fulfilling Monetary Concerns of the English Company

Since the time the British acquired the island in 1665, Portuguese and other currencies had been in circulation. These included coins such as pagodas, shahis and Portuguese coins like the xeraphins and parados, valued at 9s, 4s, and 1s, 6d. These currencies remained in circulation till the mint was established in Bombay[41] in the year 1670–1 when the Court of Directors recommended that a mint be established in Bombay for minting gold and silver coins.[42]

The Court of Directors believed that the coins minted there were to be given English names designedly, 'for in this and all things else we endeavour to ensure the people and teach them the English tongue and to disuse also the Portuguese as much as we can, which will be a work of long time, because these people have been long accustomed there unto.' The circulation of English coins and the usage of English were assumed to be helpful in reducing the Portuguese influence in Bombay Island and thus help the English government.

The earliest officer connected with the affairs of the Bombay Mint was the Governor of the Bombay Island, Gerald Aungier, who commenced the process of minting coins at the Bombay Castle from 1671 AD. The first assay master to take the charge of the mint was Mr Adam Smith, appointed on a yearly salary of £60. The minting of coins within the castle continued for many years, and thereafter, a regular mint was established outside the castle. It was old and the roofs were broken.[43] Earlier the English mint would function in the Bombay Castle. Later, however, the mint was built outside the castle, which can be seen in Gorse's plan of Bombay in 1750. The map clearly shows the new mint built outside the castle. No records are available of the exact location of the Bombay Mint though.[44]

On 15 October 1676, a formal letter from King James II of England was received whose letter of patent empowered the East India Company to establish the mint at Bombay. Permission was received to coin currency in gold, silver, copper, tin, and lead. or any metal which corresponded as current in all dependencies of the Company in the East Indies.[45] Money of higher denomination coins were to be called rupees. Pices and bujuruks were names given to currency coined of copper and lead. Bombay mint was to promote trade and assert the political prominence of the British on Bombay Island.[46]

Four different types of coins were minted. Gold coins were known as carolinas, silver coins, angelinas, copper, copperoon, and tin, tinnies. Angelina was an equivalent of the rupee and copperoon, an equivalent of the pice. These samples of angelina and copperoon are available to be seen in the British Museum. These coins are rough in texture and weighing 177.2 g. and 209.6 g. respectively, the same stamp seems to have been used in both cases. There is no evidence that the carolina was ever struck. This is pointed to in William Forster's note on the first English coinage at Bombay in 1906.[47]

The earliest coins minted in Bombay Castle had inscriptions— 'The Rupee of Bombaim' in the centre and 'By Authority of the English King Charles II of England, in 1677 AD' on the obverse. The coin had a circle on the obverse and below it, the Royal Arms of England holding a shield in the centre. An inscription embossed on the coin depicts 'King of Great Britain, France and Ireland' on the reverse.[48] The earliest known coins of the Bombay Mint was the four rupee coins now kept in the museum of Bombay, dated 1676, 1677,

1678 and 1678 again, respectively. The first coin had stamps of the arms of the East India Company and the remaining three had the Royal Arms of England, that is quarterly the three lions of England, the lion of Scotland, the harp of Ireland, and the three fleur-de-lis of France. Later in 1687, in the Bombay rupee, the Company's arms re-appeared on the reverse.[49] The Bombay coin underwent many changes from the time it was first minted till it became the known currency of free India.

Difficulties in the Circulation of Money under Early Company Rule

The newly minted coins had to compete with the old Portuguese and Mughal currencies since these old currencies possessed good value and were already an established currency in the market. The Portuguese were causing hindrance to the passage of the tin coins in their territories, thus abating the value of the English coins.[50] The East India Company was responsible for these difficulties in circulation through wrong means.[51] The supply of bullion for minting was deficient. A letter dated 12 September 1676 from Surat to the Bombay Governor, Gerald Aungier, reads, 'we cannot spare so considerable a quantity of money as you desire from our great engagement of interest. If ever after you shall be in want of money, we shall duly satisfy your bills when you draw them as hitherto as we have done.'[52] A silver rupee during the reign of King James II, which was struck in 1678, bears the following on the obverse—*Pax A Deo*, written at the centre. Another in the margin is read as '*Bomaiensis Moneta 1687*', on the reverse of the coin, while at the centre a shield with the arms of the East India Company is engraved.[53]

Difficulties in Procuring Bullion Supply to the Merchants and Mughal Government

Earlier Surat was the headquarter of the English East India Company. The city had many prominent residential buildings for the Governor, the Shah Bunder, the mint master and leading merchants such as Haji Zahid Beg, Haji Kassim, Khwaja Minaz, Virji Vora and Mohandas Parek. Surat attracted a number of Armenian merchants, the most prominent among them being Khwaja Minaz. His ship, *St. Michael*, sailed to Mocha and other ports in the region. He is described in the English accounts as 'an able and well reputed Armenian merchants', who bought large quantities of broad cloth from them, and in return, sold gold and copper. He had his own agents in Gombroon and other places overseas.[54]

Note on Virji Vohra

Virji Vora was an eminent Bania merchant who traded in Surat and Bombay Island. He acted as a broker for the English Company over a long period. He lent the English a considerable amount of money. On one occasion a dispute arose over the amount to be paid for a quantity of coral and quicksilver, which Vohra had brought from the English East India Company and claimed a rebate of Rs. 2,500 on. President Blackman persuaded Vohra to return the amount and leave the decision to the company authorities in England.[55]

On 25 January 1655, Vohra wrote a letter in English requesting the rebate and signed it off in Gujarati. The letter is still available in the India Office Records. In reply to his letter, on 27 August 1655, he was informed that the matter had been carefully considered and it had been decided that no rebate was possible. However, to maintain friendly relations, they intended to send him a present.[56]

A fresh letter dated 27 March 1656, that several pieces of broad cloth and satin, two large pairs of looking glasses, and a double gilt plate of gold, engraved with the Company's arms were given as gift. The Council of State was freely granting private merchants licenses for the export of silver to the East Indies, and thus, the trade lay open to all merchants.[57]

In 1670, Nandchand Vohra, grandson of Virji Vora, bought English cloth, tin and copper in large quantities. A prominent merchant from Surat, Abdul Gaffur figures a great deal in the English records of the 1690s and 1700s, in connection with the European piracy in the Arabian Sea which had caused great damage to his ships.[58]

Another leading Indian merchant engaged in bullion trade was Rustamji Manekji. Born in Surat in 1635 to a priestly family, he was a broker to the Dutch before 1681, and later to the Portuguese and the new English Company. The Portuguese appointed him as their agent in Surat for issuing passports to Indian ships, and also to act as their attorney (*vakil*) in their relations with the Mughal government in the city.[59]

Growing political insecurity in Surat due to the Marathas and religious persecution of Aurangzeb led a number of merchants to relocate Bombay Island. Among them were Haji Zaid Beg and his son, who being despondent about the safety of the city expressed a desire to move to Bombay.[60] Prominent merchants of Surat were Tulsidas and Benidas, who were closely associated with the British from the 1640s. Their service had been recognized by the Company and they were awarded a gold medal chain worth 150 pounds. In 1668, Bhimji Parekh, son of Tulsidas sought to relocate to Bombay from Surat. In 1669, religious persecutions imposed by Mughal emperor Aurangzeb led a large number of Hindu merchants from Surat to shift to Bombay. The Parekh family belonged to the leading banias of Surat. In the year 1662, Bhimiji Parekh (1610–80), along with his three brothers Kalyandas, Kisso, and Vithaldas, were appointed as the brokers of the East India Company by Sir George Oxenden. Bhimji Parekh was a leading bania merchant from Surat and worked as the broker for the East India Company and died in 1686 and Vithaldas Parekh, brother of Bhimji Parekh continued to work as broker for the English in the 1670s and 1680s.[61]

The following details make for an interesting case study. In the 1680s, four brothers—Bhimji, Kalyandas, Kissoo (Kesav), and Vithal Parekhs—managed the private trade of Sir John Child, the English Chief at Surat. The claim arising out of the dealings with the Company was that 80,000 rupees was to be paid to the local Governor in 1688–9. This was due to Ghaffur's ship being taken by the pirates for which the English were blamed. Both Kissoo and Vithal Parekh had been imprisoned and a fine of 30,000 was imposed by the Mughal government on the English. This claim was later resolved by the Bombay Governor.[62]

Mughal Mint at Surat: Another Cause for Circulation of English Coins

An agreement was signed in the provisional convention negotiated by Sir John Child, the Governor of Surat, along with Mukhtyar Khan, the Mughal Governor, in 1688. The Company could mint their coins at the Mughal mint in Surat to impress the locals of that place and supply the currency to the Bengal market or other Mughal territories.[63]

'The Company suggested that the Coins minted at Bombay had to include gold mohurs as the Company had the Mughal's Phirman and the King's Authority to exercise this branch of delegated sovereignty'. This event became important for financial development in the island of Bombay. Through mints, payments could be made and funding could be procured.[64] Although the negotiation allowed the Company to coin money at Surat in the Mughal mint, the court preferred to act on the charter given by the authorities, which would impress the natives with the importance of the place and that, in time, they would be able to supply the Bengal market with rupees coined at Bombay. Failing this, the English hoped to exchange their rupees for those coined at Surat, which could easily pass in Bengal, Benares or any part of the Mughal dominions.[65]

The East India Company found it difficult to circulate their coins in the interior Mughal territories. The Company had to either send their bullion to the Mughal mint at Surat to mint coins or forge the Mughal coins at their own mint in Bombay. To make it legal, the Company had to obtain permission from King James II and later, mint these coins in the Mughal pattern at their own mint.[66] The Company took a decision to mint Mughal coins at Bombay without seeking permission from the Mughal emperor Aurangzeb, only relying on permission from King James II of England.[67] The Bombay Mint struck coins along the English pattern while these coins were issued in the Mughal style, with the rupee bearing the name of Bombay as well as Surat. It supervised the circulation of copper, gold, and silver coins. The mint also directed the removal of debased coins from circulation as and when it came to one's notice.[68]

In 1664–88, Bombay gradually developed into the chief centre of English commerce in western India. Considerable efforts were made in transferring the Company's headquarters from Surat to Bombay in the year 1687. A provisional convention was made where this matter was negotiated by the English Governor Sir John Child in 1688, with Mukhtyar Khan, the new Mughal Governor of Surat.

Functioning of the Bombay Mint and the Dependencies on Indian Intermediary

The records of the East India Company for a period of ten years from 1668–78 stated that a factor was appointed to investigate the matter of the mint. Sir John Child was given the post of overseer of the Bombay Mint in 1672. Another official was John Jessop, who was in charge of the mint and was to keep a check on its functioning.[69]

During the early years of the newly developed Bombay Mint, Adam Smith was sent from England to Bombay as an assay master in 16764. He had to investigate the affairs of the mint and control the quality and fineness of the coins minted. He received a salary of 60 pounds per annum. There was no uniformity of currency then as the Company's coins were only one of the many varieties in circulation.[70]

The mint undertakers were required to first produce a few specimens of the coins they proposed to mint. Then, they were to provide an estimate of the total expenses which would be incurred while coining a lakh of rupees or any other fixed sum of money. If the authorities were convinced with the estimate, they would fix a time limit for undertakers within which period they were to complete their coinage operations. If they exceeded the time limit, they were to pay interest to the authorities. Besides this, the undertakers of the mint were to follow the prescribed rates given to different types of coins while fixing their value.[71]

Money dealers played an important role in dealing with financial needs. The money dealers would be small shopkeepers, prominent brokers, bankers, money changers (Shroffs) and merchants. Several Banias too worked as brokers for the European establishments, including the English, at Surat. Their role was to grant facilities to the merchants for the transmission of drafts. Brokers and Shroffs were mediators or special correspondents, playing the role of sarrafs, to underrate the value of gold or silver content present in the bullion.[72]

Sarraf comes from an Arabic word '*sayrafi*', which refers to money-testing. These *sarrafs* played an important role in carrying out trade. Their role was to fix the value of the bullion in the market. The *sarrafs* were very secretive about the exact methods they employed in assaying and were indispensable in fixing the value of consignments. They organized commercial credits and acted as depositors, bankers, and discounters of Bills of Exchange (Hundi), which enabled them to not only supply the bullion seller with cash but also provide facilities to transfer funds from one place to another. Bills could also be bought and sold through *sarrafs*.[73]

These *sarrafs* made profits out of the purchased wholesale bullion such as gold, silver, copper, and tin. They were known for their remarkable ability to strike a good bargain, which depended on timings and auspicious days when the bargain was finalized. Sometimes, these *sarrafs* had to face their competitors who also fixed the prices of the bullion seller. The *sarrafs* fixed the bullion price and exchanged the rates of foreign coins, skilfully evaluating the cost of precious metals and adding the extra cost of minting too.[74]

The *sarrafs* were also experts in determining the weight as well as the age of the coins. They were also money-exchangers, who could change old rupees, which were less than the standard weight, into the newly coined rupees—gold mohurs into rupees and rupees into Mahmud's and dams.

The value of these coins constantly fluctuated following the fluctuations in the price of bullion prevalent at the time.[75]

Disruptions in Bombay's Trade

One of the earliest rebellions in Bombay Island took place in the English garrison when Captain Shaxton's company was overseeing the garrison in 1674. The soldiers were paid very poorly and their salary was further reduced by being paid in the local currency—bujuruks and duganis. These were coins of good value which caused huge losses to them, ranging between 18 and 30 per cent.[76]

Irregularities in the soldier's payments arose due to debased coinage. The debased currencies were used to pay soldiers, causing due loss of values in these currencies. Another cause was that the salaries of officials and factors were even lowered. Another cause for disruptions of the trade on the island was that the Portuguese refused to pay custom duties and created problems by blocking the supply of provisions coming into the island. An English traveller, John Fryer observed that the island could not provide enough provisions for a population of 60,000 people.

Various taxes were introduced and began to be imposed on houses from 1679. However, it did not suffice to defray the cost of administration. A few years after, hence, a duty of half a dollar was levied on all ships anchored in the harbour of Bombay, and a rupee per annum on each shopkeeper on the island. In 1689 Bombay was raised to the dignity of Regency, and in order to make it commercially supreme, certain improvements and innovations were proposed to be carried out; as, for instance, the establishment of a post office and insurance office. To meet this extra expenditure, it was resolved that a progressive duty should be imposed, from one shilling to two shillings and sixpence, on every house in Bombay.[77]

In March 1681, Captain Richard Keigwin was appointed by the Court of Directors to be the Commandant of the Company forces stationed in Bombay. Soldiers were ill-paid, ill-fed and made to work for more hours than justifiable, all this leading to the grievances of soldiers. Another cause was that the Bombay Governor, John Child, ordered the reduction in the salaries of the armed forces by as much as 30 per cent due to which the soldiers rebelled against him on 27 December 1683. This revolt lasted till 19 November 1684. These events affected the functioning of the Bombay Mint due to the slow supply of bullion in the island.[78] During the reign of James II, a new charter dated 12 April 1686 was granted to the Company, by which all former charters were to be renewed and confirmed the power to be passed to the Company to 'coin in their forts and species of, money usually coined by the princes of those countries'.

The Transfer of Surat Headquarters to Bombay and its Impact on the Bombay Economy

The English East India Company in Surat faced a series of difficulties with the local governors. The Mughal ruler, Aurangzeb (1658–1707), was not in the favour of the English East India Company. Observing the strained relations, the Council of Surat advised the Directors to suspend all relations with the local governors and to stop all traffic at sea. The Directors of the Company could not come to any decision without risking the Company's trade. The problems in Surat prevailed. Gerald Aungier, President of Surat, insisted that the factors at Surat act with sword in one hand and hold an olive branch in the other, signifying peace.[79]

One of the important factors responsible for the transfer of the Surat headquarters was the outbreak of the plague in Surat in 1684, killing thousands of people. Other reasons included the English Company's assessment of Surat to be in a critical state, due to the slackened commerce and the attacks from the Marathas as well the Mughals. The Mughal Governor of Surat, Mukhtayar Khan, weakened the Maratha attacks on Surat along with the counter attacks from the East India Company. Therefore, taking stock of the situation, the English government passed an order in 1684 to transfer the chief seat of the Company's trade from Surat to Bombay. This transfer came into existences only after 1687.[80]

Bombay gained the dignity of an English presidency. The mint implemented an order requiring all persons, who had access to more foreign rupees to bring them to the Bombay Mint to be re-coined. Another notice of the mint was to inform the custom master within three days, so that they could export them, and if not, their money could be forfeited when discovered. Despite such precautions taken by the Bombay Mint, offences against coinage continued to increase. The officials-in-charge were often found guilty of stealing coins and metals, which came to the mint for production of currency.[81]

The relations between the English and the Portuguese remained hostile. The Bombay Council wrote to the Boards of London in 1691 AD, which remarked that the trade in Bombay was greatly hampered by the pirates along the coast, who belonged to other nationalities. It affected the trade so much that the revenue had fallen from £5,208 to £1,416, which is approximately a dip from 52,080 rupees to 14,160 rupees in 1694.

In 1686 and 1696, there were severe outbreaks of plague in western India, which destroyed many lives and disrupted the trade there. It also affected the island trade and incurred heavy losses. The places which were the most affected by these outbreaks were Chaul, Thane, and Vasai. All of this led to the decline of trade in Bombay Island.[82] This further lowered the conditions of trade leading to severe depression from 1688–1710 AD. Thus, ten years of fair prosperity were followed by about twenty years of deep depression.[83]

Conditions of Bombay Trade in the Last Quarter of the Seventeenth Century

The British ruled over the island for nearly fifty years and the trade in Bombay Island 'flourished and increased wonderfully' during the period. The island became the centre of English commerce in western India. However, with the decision of the Company to transfer the headquarters from Surat to Bombay Island in 1687 was finalised. Between 1690–1710, the island of Bombay underwent many changes, gradually witnessing a decline. The rivalry between the London Company and the English East India Company with the other hostilities meted out by the Mughals, Marathas, and the Portuguese brought in a period of depression for the island, leading to losses for the East India Company and stagnation in trade.[84]

However, after the union of the London Company and the English Companies trading in India in 1708, trade in Bombay began to recover. John Gayer, who had moved from Surat to Bombay, assumed office on 17 May 1694. The Old East India Company refused to acknowledge him as their governor. There was immense confusion between the Surat and Bombay Governorship, with very little clarity on who the real representative of the English nation was. Later, in November 1704, Sir Nicholas Waite was made the Governor of Bombay. He found Bombay to be a 'beggarly, ruined, but fertile Island'. Mr William Aislabie was made the Deputy Governor of the Island. The row between the ruling governors created an unhealthy atmosphere for island trade.

John Gayer was the Governor and President of the English East India Company in Surat (1694–1704). In order to conduct the Company's trade and carry out official work, he sent the agent Rustam Manockji to Bombay to set affairs in order. This proposal, however, was turned down by Sir Nicholas Waite, as he refused to accept the invitation from Sir John Gayer. Later, this was reported to the Court of Directors, that the old company's servants were expelled, and yet, Sir Nicholas Waite was made the Bombay Governor in 1704, and found Bombay to be a 'beggarly, ruined, but fertile island' and thus continued to make improvements until 1708. Another reason was that all the ships, which came to Bombay Island for trade was consigned to Nicholas Waite, as the Old East India Company had given the queen of England one or two lakhs of rupees to make their peace with the Bombay Governor.[85]

The English East India Company's employee Rustam Manockji, upon returning from his visit to Bombay, informed the Governor of Surat, Sir John Gayer:

> Rustam Manockji must render protection to Sir John Gayer and to the Old Company's Servants to be answerable for the security, papers and many lacks of rupees, which the town merchants have been robbed and destroyed by the pirates, and all demands or debts yet any people may make him give satisfaction or fulfil the demand, for his master would not be answerable for anything.[86]

Another key reason for the decline in Bombay trade was the island's direct connection to the Thane Coast, where trade in grains, vegetables, fruits, animals, timber, and other precious goods took place. The trade there was also hampered by the increasing demands of the Portuguese, who levied taxes on these items. Besides these reasons, the passage of these goods into the island by the sea and land routes was also interrupted by the Mughals, Marathas, Siddhis and Portuguese. This in turn created the problem of late supply and posed a danger to life and property, resulting in slow growth, losses and uncertainty. [87]

On the financial front, the revenue earned though trade and custom duties on the ships declined during the monsoon.[88] Another cause for the decline was due to the differences in opinion between the London and the English East India Companies, which ended in 1702 and resulted in the formation of the 'New United Company'. These events culminated in a turning point in the history of the Bombay Island trade.[89]

Custom duties imposed by the East India Company on goods coming into the Bombay Island and arriving at the custom house for clearances, amounted to 2.5 per cent of taxes. An additional tax was levied on the goods which charged 1 per cent more. These additional charges were directed towards the maintenances of the island and its fortification. Special goods required special rates depending upon how valuable the goods were.[90]

Table 2.1: List of Commodities and Custom Duties

Goods	*Custom Duties on the Export Goods*
Tobacco	8%
Iron	8%
Horses	3%
Ships	5%
Cocoa	8%
Coir	8%
Dried fish	8%
Salt	8%

Source: S.M. Edwardes, *The Gazetteer of Bombay City and Island, vol-II, Bombay: Government Time Press*, 1909, p. 447.

Special goods like gold, silver, precious stones, pearls, bezoars stone, copper coins and tin were exempted from duties while being imported into the island and their export was also free. However, tobacco imported from any part of the Portuguese dominions bore a special duty of 9 per cent. Due to these reasons, the Bombay trade languished greatly and the island saw a slack in its flourishing trade.[91]

Union of the Trading Companies of London and English East India Companies in 1708

In 1708, the rivals, then known as the English Company and the London Company, merged to form the 'United Company of Merchants Trading in the East Indies', which now became the holder of the trading rights in the East.[92] This newly consolidated 'United Company of Merchants', trading to the East Indies, enjoyed a period of mutual understanding among the company's trading bodies. This paved the way for a steady commercial expansion and made the company's finances strong, enabling additional investments. By 1710, the English East India Company developed into a powerful trading body.[93]

The period 1690–1710 was a time of great economic crisis and rivalry. The Bombay trade declined due to the differences between the two companies. This union in 1708 could be attributed to the hostility of the local powers which affected the trade of Bombay Island, and it was a period of economic difficulties. It took time to recover its position in the maritime trade of the north-west and the expenses continued to grow. This remained a problem, both for the Directors of London and the East India Trading Company in Bombay.[94]

According to the Alexander Hamilton records, the trade in Bombay Island in 1696 had plummeted severely, owing to the unpredictable climate and intermittent epidemic outbreaks, which affected the economy and lives of people. One of the case studies shows, 'the Governor of Surat, Sir John Gayer, preferred a prison in Surat, where he could employ his money, which could not render any business or there was no chance of any trade.'[95] Trade in the island, at this time, did not promise huge returns and the governor of Bombay was in dire need of money to carry out such projects. Therefore, to increase the revenue of the island, they made use of all the land along the Back Bay to plant coconuts, jackfruits, and mango trees. The whole of Malabar hill was let on a lease at a yearly rent of one hundred rupees.[96]

Upon the union of the London and the English companies, a new system for the transportation of goods was introduced. The company's goods were now conveyed primarily in hired ships, and the company only kept 'some swift sailing packets and a very few trading vessels'. By 'swift sailing packets', one means the vessels which were built to carry cargoes and sail at a faster speed without being interrupted. A time limit was placed on these vessels to reach their destination.[97]

The articles which were dealt with primarily in the import trade to England included calicoes, cotton cloth, muslin, raw silk, tea, spices, drugs, and saltpetre. The official value of these exports to England in 1708 was £ 493,725, and their average annual importation for that year and nineteen years following that was £ 758,042. The company imported lead, quick silver, woollen clothes, hardware, and bullion for an average amount of £ 634,638 for these twenty years, out of which four-fifths was spent on bullion. These items were later distributed in the interior hinterlands and other places.[98]

Under the governorship of Gerald Aungier, Bombay Island underwent new changes and developments. One major development was seen in the economic conditions due to their monetary concerns. The island improved due to the establishment of the Bombay Mint. The mint helped in bringing about a dynamic improvement by introducing their English currencies and thus controlling other currencies in circulation. This led to an overall development of the Bombay Island and thus established their authority in Bombay Presidency.

During the last quarter of the seventeenth century, the trade of Bombay declined due to the indifference of the two Companies and the hostility of the local powers. Later the union of the two Companies, Trading Company of London and the East India Company in 1708 merged to form the 'United Company of Merchants Trading in the East Indies'. This mutual understanding brought in new avenues and promoted commercial expansion leading to monetary and financial improvements, thus, helping Bombay grow by erecting new institutions which resulted in greater financial stability and promoted Bombay Island trade in western India.

Notes

1. Mariam, Dossal, *Theater of Conflicts and City of Hope: Mumbai, 1600-Present Times*, New Delhi: Oxford University Press, 2010, pp. 4–5.
2. J. Gerson Da Cunha, *The Origin of Bombay*, Bombay: The Education Society Steam Press, 1900, p. 241.
3. Thomas Maynard, *Anglo-Portuguese Relations 1654–1810*, Florence: Taylor & Francis Group, 1998, p. 15.
4. Ibid., p. 47.
5. J. Gerson da Cunha, *Notes on the History and Antiquities of Chaul and Bassein*, New Delhi: Asian Educational Services, 1993, pp. 272–3.

6. Maharashtra State Archive, *Collection of Papers, Records of the Bombay Government, Received from the India Office, 1663–1675*, p. 11.
7. Shafat Ahmad Khan, *Anglo-Portuguese Negotiations Relating to Bombay 1660–1677*, London: Oxford University Press, 1922, pp. 425–7.
8. S.M. Edwardes, *The Gazetteer of Bombay City and Island*, vol. II, Bombay: Times Press, 1909, p. 56.
9. Da Cunha, *The Origin of Bombay*, p. 273.
10. S.M. Edwardes, *The Gazetteer of Bombay City and Island*, vol. II, Bombay: Times Press, 1909, vol. II, pp. 56–7.
11. Ibid., vol. II, pp. 56–7.
12. Ibid., vol. II, p. 57.
13. Ibid., p. 126.
14. Ibid., p. 48.
15. Ibid., p. 314.
16. Marguerite Eyer Wilbur, *The East India Company and the British Empire in the Far East*, Stanford: Stanford University Press, 1945, p. 162.
17. Edwardes, *The Gazetteer of Bombay City and Island*, p. 211.
18. K.K. Chaudhari, *Maharashtra State Gazetteers, Greater Bombay District*, vol. II, Bombay: Government of Maharashtra, 1987, p. 841.
19. M.D. David, *History of Bombay, 1661–1708*, Bombay: Bombay University Press, 1973, p. 84.
20. Edwardes, *The Gazetteer of Bombay City and Island*, p. 58.
21. David, *History of Bombay*, p. 213.
22. Da Cunha, *Notes on the History and Antiquities of Chaul and Bassein*, pp. 273–4.
23. Wilbur, *The East India Company and the British Empire*, p. 161.
24. Ibid., p. 127.
25. James Douglas, *Bombay and Western India*, vol. II, London: Sampson Low, Marston and Company, 1893, p. 221.
26. William Foster, *English Factories in Western India*, London: Oxford University Press, 1927, p. 92.

27. Edwardes, *The Gazetteer of Bombay City and Island*, p. 61.
28. Ibid., p. 164.
29. Edwardes, *The Gazetteer of Bombay City and Island*, pp. 278–9.
30. George W. Forrest, *Selections from the Letters, Dispatches, and Other State Papers*, vol. I, Bombay Secretariat, Bombay: Home-Series, 1887, p. 53.
31. Foster, *English Factories in Western India*, p. 7.
32. Mariam Dossal, 'Continuity and Change: The Portuguese presence in British Bombay, c.1660–1860', in *Vasco da Gama and the linking of Europe and Asia*, ed. A.R. Disney and Emily Boots, New Delhi: Oxford University Press, 2000, p. 403.
33. Edwardes, *The Gazetteer of Bombay City and Island*, pp. 279–80.
34. G.W. Forrest, *Selection from the State Papers Preserved in the Bombay Secretariat*, vol. I, Bombay: Home-Series, 1887, p. 52.
35. Ibid., pp. 55–6.
36. Ibid., pp. 163–5.
37. Ibid., p. 164.
38. Ibid., p. 164.
39. Ibid., p. 164.
40. Ibid., p. 165.
41. Teotonio R. de Souza, *Medieval Goa: A Socio-Economic History*, New Delhi: Concept Publishing Company, 1987, p. 143.
42. Chaudhari, *Maharashtra State Gazetteer*, pp. 364–5.
43. Monier Williams, 'Monetary System in British India', in *Bombay Quarterly Review*, vol. VI, October 1857, pp. 251–3.
44. Chaudhari, *Maharashtra State Gazetteer of Greater Bombay District*, p. 371.
45. Edwardes, *The Gazetteer of Bombay City and Island*, p. 275.
46. Ibid., p. 276.
47. 'Court Letter to Surat and Bombay, 14 June, 7 October 1672', *Bruce's Annals*, vol. II, p. 38.

48. Philip A.M. Anderson, *The English in Western India*, London: Smith Taylor and Company, 1856, p. 69.
49. G.R. Kahate, *The Bombay Mint*, Bombay: India Government Mint, 1986, p. 8.
50. Edwardes, *The Gazetteer of Bombay City and Island*, p. 276.
51. Ibid., p. 276.
52. Ibid., pp. 276–7.
53. George Birdwood, *Reports on the Old Records of the India Office with Supplementary Note and Appendices*, London: W.H. Allen & Co., 1891, pp. 223–5.
54. Ashin Das Gupta, *Indian Merchants and The Decline of Surat, c.1700–1750*, Wiesbaden: Franz Steiner Verlag, 1979, p. 182.
55. Ibid., pp. 182–3.
56. Foster, *The English Factories in India*, p. 16.
57. Ibid., 183.
58. Ibid., p. 183.
59. Ibid., p. 184.
60. Balkrishna Govind Gokhale,'The Merchant Prince Virji Vohra', *Surat in the Seventeenth Century: A Study in the Urban History of Pre-Modern India*, Bombay: Popular Prakashan, 1979, p. 126.
61. Ibid., p. 121.
62. Das Gupta, *Indian Merchants and The Decline of Surat*, p. 179.
63. Edwardes, *The Gazetteer of Bombay City and Island*, p. 276.
64. Ibid., p. 277.
65. Ibid. pp. 277–8.
66. *Gazetteer of the Bombay Presidency, Gujarat, Surat, Broach*, vol. II, Bombay: Government Central Press, 1887, p. 98.
67. W.H. Moreland, *From Akbar to Aurangzeb; A Study in Indian Economic History*, London: Macmillan & Co., 1923, p. 167.
68. *Descriptive Catalogue of the Public Department Diary Series, 1720–1770*, Maharashtra State Archives, vol. I, p. 14.
69. *A letter from Bombay Mint to the Court of Directors, 19 March 1677*, Maharashtra State Archive, p. 512.
70. Anderson, *The English in Western India*, pp. 132 –3.

71. G.V. Mulherkar, 'Coins of the East India Company at Bombay', in *The Bombay Explorer*, vol. I, Mumbai, 1986, p. 27.
72. Das Gupta, *Indian Merchants and the Decline of Surat*, p. 83.
73. *English Factories Records of Surat, 1665–1667*, Maharashtra State Archives, vol. 3, pp. 83–4.
74. Ibid., p. 84.
75. Ruby Maloni, *Surat: Port of the Mughal Empire*, Mumbai: Himalaya Publishing House, 2003, p. 150.
76. *Collection of Papers Received from the India Office, Records of the Bombay Government, 1673–75*, Maharashtra State Archives, vol. 6, pp. 121–2.
77. B.M. Phiroze Malabari, *Bombay in the Making*, London: T. Fisher Unwin, 1910, p. 414.
78. *Gazetteer of the Bombay Presidency*, Maharashtra State Archives, vol. XIII, pt. II, Bombay: Government Central Press, 1882, p. 481.
79. Bruce Watson, 'Fortifications and the Idea of Force in Early English East India Company Relations with India', in *An Expanding World, Warfare and Empires: Contact and Conflict between European and Non European Military and Maritime Forces and Culture*, vol. 24, ed. Douglas M. Peers, Variorum: Ashgate Company, 1997, pp. 63–4.
80. *Gazetteer of the Bombay Presidency, Gujarat, Surat, and Broach*, vol. II, Bombay: Government Central Press, 1887, p. 98.
81. J.M. Campbell, *Gazetteer of Bombay Presidency—Gujarat, Surat and Broach*, vol. III, Bombay: The Government Central Press, 1877, pp. 89–90.
82. Edwardes, *The Gazetteer of Bombay City and Island*, p. 407.
83. Edward Thompson and G.T. Garratt, *Rise and Fulfilment of British Rule in India*, London: Macmillan and Co., 1935, pp. 29–32.
84. Chaudhari, *The Gazetteer of Bombay Presidency*, p. 154.
85. Forrest, *Selection from the State Papers Preserved in the Bombay Secretariat*, p. xxvii.

The pirates who attacked the town of Surat were none other than Shivaji, who had plundered the city of Surat causing great loss to life and property. This occurred in the year 1687, therefore, the transfer of the headquarter was called for. The merchants left the city and migrated to Bombay and other neighbouring places which offered the possibility of safe trade and protection to one's life.

86. Ibid., p. xxvii.
87. Ibid., pp. 407–8.
88. *Gazetteer of India, Maharashtra State: Thane District*, Bombay: Government Central Press,1982, p. 156.
89. Ibid., pp. 156–7.
90. Edwardes, *The Gazetteer of Bombay City and Island*, pp. 436–8.
91. Ibid., p. 438.
92. James Macpherson, *The History and Management of the East India Company from its Origin in 1600 to the Present Times*, vol. 1, London: T. Cabell, 1782, p. 314.
93. H.V. Bowen, *The Business of Empire: The East India Company and Imperial Britain, 1756–1833*, New York: Cambridge University Press, 2008, pp. 278–9.
94. Edwardes, *The Gazetteer of Bombay City and Island*, p. 408.
95. Ibid., p. 407.
96. Forrest, *Selection from the State Papers Preserved in the Bombay Secretariat*, p. xx.
97. Ibid., p. xxvii.
98. Edwardes, *The Gazetteer of Bombay City and Island*, p. 407.

THREE

The Bombay Government and Merchants Engaged in Bullion Trade, *c.*1710–40

Introduction

In the early eighteenth century, Bombay emerged as the most important political and commercial centre of the English East India Company. Company merchants, Indian merchants, European merchants engaged in private trade as well as Armenian traders, Persian traders and traders from other countries contributed to the development of Bombay as an important port town.[1] Fundamental to the growth of commercial and financial importance of Bombay in the years 1710–40 were the institutions of the Bombay Mint and the Bank of Bombay. The circulation of money and the development of a banking system enabled the town's trade to flourish.[2]

During this period, the town began to recover from its economic difficulties and the trade there flourished. Improvements took place in the transportation of goods. The Company's goods were carried in hired ships; they also built 'swift ships' to carry sailing packets swiftly. These packets transported goods quickly to places where these goods were in demand or required during emergencies. These vessels were called swift trading vessels, which were of medium-built, and helped maritime trade to develop at a faster pace.[3] The improvement in navigational technology and the institution of marine garrisons boosted both trade and security.[4] Warehouses were built and fortified at places where goods were stored. Commercial offices called *kaccheri* (a fixed work centre) were built and *gumastas* (clerks or cashiers) were appointed to take care of business transactions and accounts.[5]

The value of imported goods into Bombay in 1708 was £493,725, when the average annual importation for twenty years had been £758,042, due to the rift and misunderstandings between the East India Company and the old trading company of London. This rift caused delays in the supply of goods. The Bombay government imported lead, quick silver, woollen cloth, hardware, and bullion amounting to £634,638, of which four-fifth was bullion.[6]

According to Revd Richard Cobbe, in 1715, the population of the Bombay Island increased from 10,000 to 16,000, of which Gentoos (Hindus) were traders and brokers and Koli Christians, fisher folks; Kunbis were tillers and primarily cultivators of rice field and Bhandaris were toddy-tappers. However, the commercial and the political rivalry between the British, Marathas, Mughals, and the Portuguese continued to deter the population from increasing in Bombay island.[7] Strengthening their military, the English Government promised security and invited merchants to trade safely in Bombay island. Merchants therefore continued to flock to the island and therefore the population of Bombay continued to increase.

The Role of English Company Broker—Rustam Manockji

Rustam Manockji (1635–1719) was a Parsi merchant who was very rich and influential. Rustamji served as the broker to the English East India Company and shared close business ties with the Company as well as the Mughal Court and other Europeans.[8]

He had earlier worked as the broker for the Portuguese in Surat in 1681 and later, during the English East India Company years, in 1699 and 1701. He had access to plentiful interest-free capital and control over the receipt and disbursement of large amounts of cash. He also served as the paymaster for those supplying the Company with its yearly investments and kept their records. He used to receive funds in advance, which were to be paid when necessary or when the Company was short of funds. He often paid suppliers himself and charged an average interest of 13 per cent.[9] When the Portuguese lost control over Surat, Rustam too lost his post in the Portuguese administration. Later, he began working as a broker for the English East India Company. It seems that his tenure as an English broker was short-lived as he died in 1721 and was replaced by an old Bania.[10]

There are many writers who made references to Rustam Manockji and his sons in their works. According to them, Sir John Gayer (1694–1704), was the Governor and President of the English East India Company in Surat. To carry out the Company's trade, he sent the company's agent Rustam Manockji for all the official work,but this proposal was turned down by Sir Nicholas Waite (1704–8), as he refused to accept the inivitation from Sir John Gayer. The following facts of Rustam Manockji, Sir John Gayer and his Council of Surat, are well explained and stated by Yule in his diary of William Hedges, which pertains to the period of April 1706.[11] Rustamji played an important role in the Portuguese and English administration during that period. Rustam's dealings were conducted in a rightful manner, without accepting any bribes; however, inspite of good conduct, Sir John Gayer had differences with Rustam and accused him of bribery.[12]

David. L. White, in his paper, argued that Rustam Manockji worked as a broker for the Portuguese in Surat in 1698, and from 27 December 1709 to 30 December 1714, and he also pointed out that Rustam Manockji, worked as a broker for the English East India Company till the year 1720. His position was then taken over by a Portuguese man named João Gomes Pueblos, who served as broker and attorney to the Portuguese in Surat.[13]

Role of Indian Merchants

The Indian merchants played an important role in conducting the Indian Ocean trade. These merchants were engaged in both coastal and high-seas trade. They organized maritime activities such as brokerage and lending money to buy and sell goods from nearby regions as well as distant countries. Indian merchants, namely the Gujarati Banias, Parsis, Khojas, Memons, Bohras and the others, played an important role in the Indian Ocean trade.[14]

While the Gujarati merchants controlled the trade between West Asia and the western coast of India, the trade was shared between the Arabs, Persians and other merchants from India.[15] Gujarati Bania traders formed the largest trading group in the Indian Ocean, Persian Gulf, the Red Sea as well the other South Asian countries. Other prominent merchant communities included Jains, Marwaris, and the Khatris, which formed the merchant class in northern India.[16] In south India, trade was dominated by the Chettis, Komatis, Chellabys, and Chulias. From the early times, western India was a major market for West Asian imports such as silks, carpets, brocade, dried fruits, rose-water, wines, myrrh, coffee, bullion, and horses.[17]

Among the Indian merchants who were prominent in trade in the Bombay Island in eighteenth century was Jagat Seth. The Seth family traces its roots from the Marwar region in Rajasthan. Jagat Seth was the most powerful business house in India. He was the son of Hiranand called Manekchand and the Mughal emperor Furukhsiyar honoured him with the title of Jagath Seth. He was an incredibly powerful merchant, conspired with the British in the battle of Plassey in 1757, and was responsible for the victory of the British which gave rise to the power and prestige of the English Company. Jean Law, head of French regiment at Kasim Bazar had stated that 'Jagat Seths are, I can confirm, the originators of the revolution; without them the English would never have carried out what they have'.[18]

In Surat, another important money lender, who financed business in the eighteenth century was Vishwa Shrimali, belonging to the Jain community and tracing its lineage to the Parikh family, the hereditary Nagar Seths, who could perform any occupation and would regulate the manner and methods of trading.[19]

Another group of Muslim merchants formed the next largest group to the Gujarati banias, while the Parsis and Armenians were comparatively smaller communities of merchants. One of the most prominent merchant groups were the Bohra merchants of Surat, led by Mulla Abdul Ghaffur, who was the *jamasat* of the Bohra community (head of the Bohras).[20]

Ghaffur was the most important maritime merchant during the first quarter of the eighteenth century from the Bohra community. He owned seventeen sea-vessels with a total dead weight of over 5,000 tons. Abdul Gaffur was not only prosperous but incredibly powerful too. The house of Ghaffur was an umbrella of protection for the other merchants and their mercantile prosperity. However, in his absence, there was no one to lead the merchants and safeguard their property. Abdul Ghaffur died in January 1718 and was believed to have had left assets worth 8.5 million rupees.[21] Besides the Bohra merchants, there were the Arabs merchants from Persia and the Chellabys from the Turkish community. Each of these communities had one or two leading families; among them were Mirza Muhammad Taki, a wealthy merchant with important political connections in India and Persia. Among the Arabs, it was Sheikh Hamid, a scholar of Sufiism and also a very influential merchant, who owned many ships. Turkish merchants of Surat were from the Chellaby clan in Iraq who had settled down in Surat and could also be found in western India.[22]

The position of the broker in the English East India Company was a commendable one. Brokerage played an important role while dealing in business transactions, and in the early eighteenth century, it earned goodwill and status in society. The broker made no money but his status held him in high regard. His work was primarily to manage the official English trade in the Bombay town. The brokers sometimes even participated or took charge of the private trade of the English governors or the chiefs of the English factory.[23]

Seth Jagannath Laldas Parekh was the first broker for the English East India Company. His father, Seth Laldas Vithaldas Parekh, an influential and prominent merchant, had managed the private trade of the Bombay Governor, Robert Cowan, and Company's Chief in Surat, Henry Lowther. Both these officers were engaged in private business as partners till Laldas Vithaldas Parekhs died in 1732. Seth Jagannath Laldas Parekh, was also the chief broker of the

English Company, and in return, had power over all the other English brokers who worked for the Company in Surat and Bombay. The broker carried great prestige and his family also enjoyed the hereditarily claimed position of the 'Nagar Seth'. The family belonged to the distinguished Parsi merchant Rustam Manockji.[24]

At the turn of the eighteenth century, Banwalidas Parakh was removed from the post of the broker for the English East India Company by his competitor Rustam Manockji. This position of chief broker lasted till Rustam Manockji worked at the Company. However, later, Vithaldas Parakh won the post of brokerage back from the hands of Rustam Sons in 1722 AD, and the Parakhs went on strengthening their position. Although, he could not perform as well as Rustamji and brought in losses to the English Company's trade. During his tenure, the financial situation slackened and the Company found his job to be very unsatisfactory and shoddy.

Seth Jagannath Das, who succeeded Laldas, showed the same astuteness as his father in his negotiations with the English East Company. Nowroji, the third and the youngest son of Rustam Manockji, went to England and successfully revived an old claim which was made against the Parakhs. Although the system of brokerage within the English Council at Bombay had been wiped out by the late 1730s, friends of Rustamji dominated the English Council.[25] The Parakhs were dismissed from the post of brokers for the English East India Company in 1737, and this post was reassigned to Rustamji's son Nowroji, who took the charge of managing the brokerage for the Company between 1730s and 1740s in Surat.[26]

The Monackjis and the Parakhs fought hard for their positions of brokerage at the English Company. This led hostile relations between the two families, ultimately resulting in misery for the Parakhs. The 1730s were a challenging period for the Parakhs, as their ships were seized, properties confiscated, and also their men arrested. These circumstances brought the downfall of the Parakhs and their status in society.[27]

Manakji Nowroji was the sole broker for the English Company at Surat and he helped John Lambton immensely in conducting raids against the Parakhs and seizing their trading vessels and properties. Jagannath Das could not escape from the English Company and was arrested in Bombay to assist them in the investigation.[28] Jagannath Das and Laldas were arrested while they were on their business trip to Bombay by the English East India Company as they had dues to be paid to the owner of the ship named *Jedda Merchant* belonging to the Begum of Surat which was carrying cargo to be delivered to Siam (Thailand). When the ship was anchored at the Surat port it was seized by the English Company. Therefore the Parakhs were charged with debts which had to be paid to both the merchants and the owner of the ship which Jagannath Das had hired for conducting trade. The other charges were the old debts dating to the 1680s. John Horne at Bombay and John Lambinton at Surat conspired these charges against the Parakhs with the aid of the Manek Nowroji. They belonged to the second generation of the Parakh family. Govind Das, the brother of Jagannath Das, too was arrested in Surat. However, the third brother, Manohar Das could not be arrested as he had fled and sought protection from the Marathas. Damaji Gaikewad was the Maratha Commander who rendered security to the Parakhs.

Company Merchants' Engagement in Private Trade

The English East India Company needed capital to expand their trading networks into other cities and countries.

However, in order to follow this through, the English faced acute shortage of funds from the merchant communities. To illustrate this with an example—a young William Monson arrived at Madras in 1725 and soon realized that conducting trade or investing required huge capital and financial support or credit from rich friends to build a fortune and a good life. His brother, Charles Monson sent him 20,000 ounces of silver from England between 1726–47; even this monetary support could not help William Monson to succeed in the business. Interest rates too were high during this period, as the newly opened bank needed capital for financial banking and the public did not trust the bank initially. The interest rate charged on the loan was 12 per cent per annum.[29] Another study shows that David Scott, the future Chairman of the East India Company, took twenty-five years to make his fortune in Bombay, and was still considered one of the lucky ones to be successful in the trade.[30]

Governor Robert Cowan (1728–37) was the next Bombay Governor after Governor William Phips. After taking charge of the Bombay Island. He passed an order stating that anyone who could not produce an authentic lease within six months should be dispossessed of their houses. After holding office for a short time, he began to take a pecuniary interest in the Portuguese ship *Europa* to sell her cargo at Bombay. When Governor Cowan was charged, he stated in his defence,

> I do hereby solemnly declare and swear on the holy Evangelist, so help me god, that he was ever interested or concerned, directly or indirectly, originally or latterly, in any respect whatever, or was I anyways profited or gained by the said ship 'Europa' voyage or by her touching this port island Bombay otherwise than by a present of six hams, eight dozen of French Oporto wine and a pound of snuff made me by the commander of the said ship on

his first arrival and the usual one percent on the silver belonging to the said ship 'Europa' to be coined in the Company's mint in Bombay.[31]

The foremost accusation against Cowan was that he bought coffee on his account and resold it to the Company instead of having the Company buy it first. The other accusation against him was that he had charged a private commission for the use of the Bombay Mint. Cowan availed a loan for his personal business at 2 per cent interest by stating that he was a country trader (reckoning the rupees at 216 per 100 dollars). Private commissions on coining rupees illustrate that it was a practice well established by Phips, having supplanted the Portuguese currency xerafin with the Bombay rupee, and he had worked hard to make Bombay rupee equal the Surat rupee. Governor Robert Cowan was even accused of lending money to the Indian Shroffs without taking interest in return, taking personal favours and also freighting his own ships instead of the Company ships.[32] Apparently, he made a fortune worth 0.4 million rupees. Between 1724–35, Cowan never had less than a 100,000 rupees in the account book and he also defrauded the Company of approximately £ 120,000.[33]

Governor Cowan was succeeded by the next Governor, John Horne of Bombay Island. The merchants and other principal inhabitants of Bombay presented a petition against having to pay the ground rents and quit-rent, which the Court of Directors had ordered would be levied. The masses protested that the order was contrary to the convention made with Governor Gerald Aungier in the last quarter of the seventeenth century.[34]

Governor Charles Boone's Administration in Bombay, c.1715–22

Until Charles Boone's arrival on the island, Bombay Island was frequently challenged by the European powers—the Portuguese, Dutch, French, as well as the local powers—the Marathas, Marathas and Siddis. These forces disturbed the Bombay trade and therefore, its development would be affected owing to shortage of funds and internal politics.[35]

The Maratha Admiral Kanhoji Angre took over as the Maratha Chief in 1699, fought against the English, and damaged the Company's trade between Bombay and the Malabar Coast. Angre, had captured Kolaba from the Siddis, who had infested the Gujarat Coast and created problems for the Marathas, Mughals and the English. Later, when their bases were captured, the Siddis readily settled a peace treaty with Angre on 30 January 1715. The Siddis were brought under control by the Angrias.[36]

Angrey captured two ships named *Brittania* and *Fame*, but it was challenged by Captain Mathew in 1716. The English East India Company escorted merchant ships and provided them protection. Following that, they constructed thirty-two gun ships and four grab ships, each mounting to twenty to twenty-eight guns and twenty gallivants with guns to fight against the sea-pirates as they had become very dominant in the mid-eighteenth century. Arabs from Muscat often attacked ships and looted their cargoes.[37]

Boone was made the Governor on 26 December 1715. Under his Governorship, his first achievement was to render Bombay Island safe and secure from the threat of these powers, both Indian and European. He reformed the town by constructing buildings and institutions, including the St. Thomas Cathedral. The Bombay Marine was also established to enhance the security in town further. Boone had a wall built around the town of Bombay and fortified it with strong gates on the western and northern side of the town. A large bastion with twelve cannons was also mounted to fight the enemies.[38]

To end piratical activities on the west coast, Boone successfully launched his attack against the Maratha Navy in 1717; however in 1718, he lost to Kanhoji Angrey. Later, he made a petition to King James II for naval reinforcement. Under the command of Captain Mathews, four war ships were installed to fight enemies posing a threat to the Bombay Island.[39] It could very well be said that Boone developed the defence system in Bombay.

During the Governorship of Aungier, no Court of Judicature functioned in Bombay from 1689–1718. This was soughed and rectified by Charles Boone, who proposed a new Court of Judicature on 5 February 1718. The Mayor's Court was established under his Governorship to create law and order in the island.[40] The Court was formerly established on 25 March 1718 and consisted of nine Justices with Lawrence Parker as the Chief Justice.[41] However, by the time the new charter of 24 September 1728 was ready, Mayor's Courts were established in Bombay, Calcutta and Madras. In 1728, the Mayor's Court was established to enforce commercial laws to order to help merchants as well as the trade from being exploited. The Bombay Mayor's Court proceedings give detailed and useful information about the activities conducted by the private merchants.[42] This Mayor's Court was later abolished and replaced by a Recorder's Court in 1798.[43]

The governor also settled quarrels regarding the custom dues, which had instigated the Portuguese particularly.[44] The Portuguese believed they could still use the Bombay port and easily pass without paying any customs tax to the harbour.

This affected trade in the island[45] That is because when the Portuguese had obtained possession of the island, they set up a land system there which resembled the one in Goa. They styled a system which was called *arrendamento*, i.e. hiring or renting. They had to increase the land revenue collected from the Portuguese and Siddis, a new class of tenants who held land on lease. Charles Boone, signed a treaty with the Portuguese in December 1716. Following that in 1718, quit-rent was imposed to reimburse the Company for the charges incurred for fortification.[46]

The Role of the Bombay Marine

The Bombay Marine created a semblance of protection against pirates for vessels carrying English passes and their cargoes.[47] A treaty of assistance was signed with the Portuguese on August 1721 to curb piratical attacks on sea. Boone was considered a military genius, as he brought innovations in ship-building by introducing war equipments, namely artillery, firepower, guns and landing boats.[48] The ships which ranked first were 'the fighting vessels', and the two grabs called *Restoration* and *Neptune Prize* were the first vessels in this category. The former vessel was manned by eighty Europeans of all ranks and fifty-one lascars, and the latter, by fifty Europeans and thirty-one lascars. Each of the privateers had thirty Europeans and twenty lascars, though these numbers soon diminished as the Bombay marine faced severe resistance from the pirates as the Bombay Marine was reduced due to the system of commissioning officers according to their seniority and favouritism. The result of the false economy was felt quickly and grievously. Merchants and traders fell prey to these pirates, who infested the western coast and attacked ships.[49]

The merchants of Bombay petitioned to the government to increase the number of cruisers that ran so that bankers could advance money on the security of the cargo. They brought to the notice of the government the fact that the stormy season had passed, and a boat had been equipped for the transport of merchandise and other valuable goods. On 11 September 1742, a cyclone hit Bombay which brought great devastation and losses. The records state that the gale was so excessive 'as has not been exceeded in the memory of any one now on the spot'. Together with the wind, there was rain which poured down in torrents. All ships in the harbour were forced free from their anchors. The royal ships *Somerset* and *Salisbury* suffered a lot of damages, and another vessel belonging to a Mahomedan gentleman was driven ashore from the stormy sea.[50]

The report of the Bombay Garrison states that in the years 1722–4, the small English community living within the Bombay fort felt that they were isolated in the Portuguese settlements in the north and to the south. They called for more security, and therefore, maintaining the garrison became an expensive affair. The military charges amounted to 134,991 rupees, which is almost half of the annual expenses of the Bombay settlements, the total amount being 298,457 rupees. The annual deficit for the whole presidency, with reference to Bombay and the other cities such as Surat, Broach, Tellicherry and Anjeno, was to be made up for by profits in trade and was estimated to be 300,000 rupees.[51]

In 1720, the Directors were fully aware that it would take some time before Bombay could rival Surat either in population or wealth because it was already a developed city before the English gained control over it. Bombay was gradually developing when the English seized control from the Portuguese.[52] During the early eighteenth century, relations between the towns of Bombay and Surat were marked by conflicts as well as dependence on each other for supplies as well as the trade. Once, a serious dispute arose regarding the issue of passes. The English factors at Surat issued trading passes, which was earlier the customary practice of the Portuguese; later the free passes were denied to the Portuguese by the English Company.[53] The Court of Judicature assembled in Bombay during the Governorship of Aungier until 1728, when the Mayor's Courts were established under Governor Charles Boone.[54]

The Case Study of Rama Kamati, the Leading Merchant of Bombay Island

One of the most faithful servants to the English East Company was Rama Kamati, who was considered to be the most obedient ally of the Company. Apparently, he had offered much assistance to the Bombay Council in times of stress, for in a letter to the Bombay Council on 30 June 1690, the Surat Council wrote:

> On the Island is Ramagee Comagee, (Rama Kamati), an old trusty servant of the Right Honourable Company and one who had stood by them on the Island especially during the Anglo-Maratha wars. He had been very assisting on all occasions not only in procuring men but encouraging them to fight the enemy. Those who knew him, gave him good character.

Despite this, Kamati was framed for high treason in 1718.[55]

Kamati was a Shenvi brahmin by caste. The Shenvis were among the earliest immigrants from Goa to Bombay, Bassein, and Salsett. They were once well-known as merchants and an influential class in the service of the government. They built temples of Walkeshwar, Thakurdwar, Mahim, and

Shri Venkatesh in the fort. He was in service of the British government and employed as head of the native troops.[56]

Kamati was considered to be one of the very few men who were faithful to the English East India Company and whom the Company trusted immensely. In spite of these trustworthy and good relations, he was charged with treason by the Bombay Governor Charles Boone. This was one of the blots put by Charles Boone against him. The charge was proved as the chief evidence pointed against him was a letter dated 12 October 1718. The letter was apparently written by Kamati to Kanhoji Angria, an arch-enemy of the English government. How Rama Kamati who was considered as a man who worked for the society and was looked upon which reads as follows, 'to the opulent, magnificent as the sun, valorous and victorious and always courageous the liberal, Prudent, and pillar of fortitude, the essence of understanding, the protector of Brahmins, defender of the faith, prosperous in all things, honoured of kings above all Councillors.'[57]

Some of the accusations of high treason filed against the faithful Company servant Rama Kamati, and put forth by the Bombay Governor Charles Boone and the Company of Merchants of England trading to the East Indies, were as follows.

An inhabitant of Bombay, Kamati was charged for several offences, namely advising, abetting, and assisting the enemy—Kanhoji Angria, whereby he had endangered the safety of the island. He was also accused of attempting to subvert and extirpate the English and their government subsequently, and also to jeopardize the position and safety of the Governor Charles Boone. These are the following articles which read out are as following.[58]

In 1717, the said Governor was in a treaty with Kanhoji Angria for delivering the ships belonging to Seth Govind

Das, the late broker to the company which had been recently taken over by Angria. Noticing the difficult situation, Komati apparently wrote a letter to Angria informing him that the said ship did not belong to the English or any of their dependants. Rather, it belonged to some merchants in Surat and therefore, he did not have to procure a ransom on delivering the goods. On 12 October 1718, after the war broke out, Kamati wrote another letter to Angria, warning him of the outbreak and asking him to be prepared to face the English fleet, who were ready to challenge him.

On 17 October 1718, an important letter written by the Portuguese General of the north to the Governor Charles Boone was intercepted by Kamati. This was another charge against him. It was a document, which was intimating the English about the Portuguese inclination to join hands with the English government to stop Angria's interference with the Bombay trade and caused obstacles to the merchants and the English Company. Yet another charge against Kamati was that he shared friendly relations with Angria and was party to his plot of attacking the Company. It was also proved that he had guided and counselled the enemies to attempt and invade the island with armed forces, to hold captive important men of high rank and demand a good fortune to release them and finally, take over the Bombay Island. The article also reads out that Kamati conducted unlawful trade and commerce with the enemies of the English government and this was done on several counts notwithstanding the known orders and proclamations of the Company.[59]

This is a common question which bothers people: why did the English government frame Rama Kamati—a man of high dignity, who always supported the Bombay Governor in times of stress and financial crises faced by the East India Company—of treason? How did the Bombay Governor come to accept the charges thrusted on him? This is considered to be one of the biggest faults of the Charles Boone Governorship. It is believed that Boone accepted the charges knowing fully well that Kamati had always been a faithful ally to the English.[60]

Kamati was found guilty owing to a note written in his handwriting. He was however framed by some merchants of Bombay. He shared good relations with and enjoyed special privileges from the English East India Company. He was one of the richest businessmen of his time, owning property worth lakhs. He owned a large estate and amassed a wealth of 40,000 rupees. In 1720, his house came to be used as a judicial court. Some local merchants or English officers may have envied his position in society, the business circle, and most importantly, the trust which the government posed in him. There is still no clarity on the matter of Rama Kamati's framing. His trial, however, piqued the interest of scholars towards the judicial history of Bombay and cases like this, where a man of high repute and an ally of the English government had to undergo a wrongfully motivated trial.

The Financial Foundations of Bombay's Prosperity

When the transfer of the English headquarters from Surat to Bombay took place, despite the wishes of the Court of Directors, the Company insisted that its coinage be confined to the Bombay Mint, though the bullion continued to be sent to the mint in Surat. The early English currencies had European design and their circulation was limited to certain places. The Company either purchased Mughal rupees from the Sarrafs or followed the custom of sending silver to the Surat Mint in the early eighteenth century.[61]

In 1717, the mint undertakers received a contract to strike coins in the Mughal pattern at Bombay Mint. From 1717 to 1800, the Bombay rupee was the standard currency of the island. By the second half of the eighteenth century, however, the English became a dominant power in Surat. The Nawab of Surat wished to retain his control over the Surat Mint. Therefore, the East India Company made an agreement with the Nawab stating that the rupees coined by both mints were to circulate at par within their territory and retain the standard of the rupee.[62]

The establishment of East India Company in Bombay initiated the Court of Directors in London towards seeking permission to set up a bank on the island for 'the mutual benefit and advantage both of the Right Honorable Company and the inhabitants of Bombay, by the increase of the trade and revenue thereof'. Through this letter dated 21 February 1717, the Directors accorded sanction to the Bombay establishment for setting up a bank in the following words:

> As the increase of trade has a natural tendency to increase our revenues, we shall have, in answer to the 72nd paragraph of the letter of the 21 January proposing leave to settle at Bombay, tell you that we consent thereto, provide you take effectual and constant care to secure the repayment of the money by sufficient pledges of goods or other securities and that it be lent as you propose at nine percent interest. Let us know what good effect it hath every year.[63]

The island of Bombay is considered the first banking and trading centre in India. The English East India trade developed and rose to prosperity from Bombay. The first bank in Bombay was established on 22 December 1720 after the union of the English East India Trading Company.[64]

The Bombay Mint assisted the development of the bank and the money lenders too played a key role. The agency houses in Bombay were the primary stakeholders in setting up the Bombay Bank. It was established for the welfare of the Company and the inhabitants of Bombay. Established on 22 December 1720, it had a capital stock of one lakh rupees from the Company's own treasury. The bank was under the management of the government, passed an order to the bank asking to offer interest on a deposit amount of hundred rupees or upwards for a term of six months with certainty. The payee would have a note signed and sealed for bearing interest at one *dugani* a day for hundred rupees, which is payable on demand after the expiration of six months. Interest charged on loans was 9 per cent.[65]

Bombay 14 July 1720
We promise to pay...........or order Rs. 100 current of Bombay together with the interest at one *Dugani* a day from the due date here for Rs. 100 on demand after the expiration of six calendar months for and on account of the Bank of Bombay.[66]

The Council of Board ordered, 'Messr. Walter Brown and Owen Phillips prepare and place for an office, a seal and books and ready to open the same, agreeable to the scheme, above mentioned when we see convenient for our Honourable Masters interest so to do.' For the first four years, the bank was supervised and managed by the Government of Bombay Island. However, the bank could not prosper because of its inability to provide any security to the depositor. The bank failed to transfer the properties to the customer, even after the debts had been cleared—some of them twenty years long—and the carts and houses mortgaged to the bank had begun to decay even before the settlement of accounts.[67] With this as the background, the Bombay Council at its consultation dated 30 December 1743, constituted a committee of Messrs John Morley, George Dudley and John Munro 'for examining into the bank debts and the sufficiency of the several securities'.[68] The Directors by their letter dated 20 March 1744, approved the steps adopted by the Bombay Government. The outstanding debts amounted to 100,313 rupees, out of which only 42,900 rupees could be recovered by security. In 1770, the bank developed a new system to issue notes and revise the system of loans and deposits. In order to prevent losses, regulations were passed in 1774 to tackle problems arising from debts. This first Bombay bank was shut eventually due to the heavy and irrecoverable losses it had incurred during its operation. [69]

Types of Bullion at the Bombay Mint

Bombay Castle, June 1724,

A letter written to the company, regarding the ware house-keeper, who surveyed the freight, from Bombay to Anjeno, calculated according to our resolution amounting to rupees. Six hundred ninety-two quarters and eighteen Reis, which he had collected it and directed that the same be received into the treasury. The mint master and his Hon'ble Company's silver last month where in chief, bag No. 2515, said to contain Pillar Dollars, which is found to contain the following species. They are as following.

Species	*1b.oz units*
Pillar Dollars	49–1
Mexico Dollars	1–7
German Dollars	16–10
French Crowns	5–2

A mixture of coins of baser Alloy brought loss to the Hon'ble Company of Rupees. Thirty one quarter – Ninety four and a half Reis, resolved to give our Hon'ble masters an account.

The president informs the board that one Gunnsett, who was goldsmith, native of Goa, lately came to the mint for work, for the Hon'ble Company's silver fifty-rupees, per chest more to their advantage than the present undertaker (Ragoosett), who works presently. He had directed a chest of Pillar Dollars to be delivered and to work under the inspection of Mr. Thomas Yeoman, the mint master from whose account of the produce of each now laid before us, which actually appears rupees. Fourteen Two Quarters and Sixty Reis more from the Goa goldsmith than from Ragoosett.[70]

Bombay Mint-Master Thomas Yeoman and the Goldsmith Ragoosett Gunnsett

A petition was sent to the Court of Directors regarding the quality of precious metals and its mismanagement:

Hon'ble Sir,

In obedience to your honourable command, I delivered to Gunsett, the goldsmith one chest of Pillar Dollars containing Pounds Two hundred and Ninety-eight ounces that I received by your orders from the Hon'ble Company's treasury and had it carefully coined in the mint and likewise delivered one chest of Pillar dollars to Ragoosett goldsmith quantity. £ 298 ounces of that we had coined in the mint at same time. The former produced rupees. When the latter worked with copper, lead and slag were saved and brought to Arc cot (Inferior). Eight thousands seven hundred fifty-six, one quarter and forty Reis as this Gunnisett makes Arc cot. And we have delivered it to your Honourable. A greater quantity of produce found than the Ragoosett the Hon'ble Company's former worker in this mint. I make the calculation from this amount, to know which is the most profit to my Hon'ble masters and is viz.[71]

These varieties of bullion were brought to the Bombay mint for minting and payments. When these mixture of coins of baser

Alloy, was used to convert in coins, brought a huge loss to the English Company's rupees. Thirty-one quarter—Ninety four and 1/2 Reis, resolved to give our Company's masters an account. The president informs the board that one Gunnsett, who was a gold smith, a native from Goa, lately came to the Bombay mint for work, he was paid fifty rupees, per chest more to their advantage than the present mint undertaker.

Ragooseth Gunnsett had directed a chest of Pillar Dollars to be delivered and to work under the inspection of Mr Thomas Yeoman, the mint master from whose account of the produce of each now laid before us, which appears as the rupees. Forty-two quarters—sixty Reis more from the Goa gold-smith Gunnsett than the former mint undertaker Ragoosett.[72] These were well known to the Company, that Ragoosett, the gold-smith had for years coined the Hon'ble company's foreign silver and had paid in to the treasury for each hundred ounces of Ducatoons rupees. This profit is presented to your highness.[73]

Yours Most Obedient,
Mint Master Thomas Yeoman.

Bullion Transactions in the Bombay Island

There was a great demand for a competent interpreter to be in-charge of the transaction of bullion for the English government. Biccu Sinnay was assigned to the post and promised a salary of 8 rupees a month. Vencajee Sinnay was appointed as a Sarraf (bullion dealer), of the Company's treasure for a salary of 12 rupees a month. He was recommended by the president of the East India Company as someone suitable for the honesty and diligence that the work demanded.[74]

Instruction of orders from England were given to the Bombay mint undertakers, relating to the minting of coinage, it also reads together with the reports made by Mr Davis of the sundry species of silver entered after the consultation. The mint undertakers were asked, not only to keep to the due fineness of the rupee intact but also, to coin fifteen pennies in greater weight than the standard. They were also asked to pay for the amount of silver coined in thirty days' time, unless the quantity is too large. Therefore, it was important that a proportional quantity was allowed. Coining could be stretched to eight chests of silver in a month. They were also ordered to clear off the amount of their bond immediately, once the order of minting coins were completed.[75]

When the goldsmiths came to Bombay from the Surat Mint in December 1733, they were promised favours and protection to undertake the coinage there. However, by refusing to give the exact prices for minting the coinage and also it did not allow nor could any goldsmiths in this town could state the exact value of the silver content, or even Mr Davis the assay master could'nt demonstrate by trial of 100 ozs. of silver at one time.[76]

The English East India Company invited minters and promised them favours, but the latter had to face losses during the process of minting coins and rupees of silver at the old rates from 1727–34. The president of the English Company acknowledged that the Governor Robert Cowan had promised to allow the minters the difference in value that arose while coining the silver piece as concession. However, later, Governor Cowan began making efforts to procure other undertakers, which compelled the mint undertakers, much against their will, to compensate the English Company's silver coined in 1734 at prices higher than during the Governorship of Stephen Lan Esq, John Morley, William Sedgwick, George Dudley and Thomas Marshall.[77]

Testing the Quality of the Bombay Rupee

A Bombay rupee was formerly considered to weigh 7 wt.10 qr 1/5, but through experiments made progressively and accurately, it became clear that its actual weight was around 7-h and 10-314. This was the nearest to the Surat standard of 30 vol. 56 dec. or a Bombay tola. Mr Davis who was the assay master of the Bombay mint, when he inspected the Bombay Rupee, he found that it was of several different weights. Mr Davis also found that the fineness is accurate of c.15 better than the English standard, which is only 14 ¾ less than they ought to be a difference so in considerable that the best assay masters in England couldn't conceive it's certainty. It is also pointed out that if Mr Aldines assays of England, varies one penny weight from the tower assays, as we observe they do in one place and ½ in others, it is not to be expected but that our country goldsmiths are destitute of the proper instruments and materials to work with. Therefore, we cannot help if sometimes default happens in the minting coins, which requires extraordinary heat or fire.[78]

Petitions of the Mint Undertakers—Mukensett Paddamsett and Luchmansett Ragoosett

In 1735 the petitioners wrote a letter from the Bombay Castle to the Court of Directors in London. The petitioners and undertakers of the Bombay Mint, Paddamsett and Ragoosett wrote during the tenure of John Horne, Esq. He along with his council presented the petition to the Directors of the English East India Company stating that the Company was indebted to the undertakers for a sum of 3,513 rupees and three-quarters and 35 reis. The amount was paid to the government treasury in 1734, and the 43-4-23 ounces. cwt.

qrs, of foreign silver bullion was purchased at the old rates to be minted into coins. The Bombay Governor Cowan obliged to the petitioner that they sent a notice some months ago, before the silver was delivered to them to be coined, which they could not receive on the same rates earlier decided for the country merchants, who had the consent to take the private silver, nor would they have been prevailed to the said payment if governor Robert Cowan had not promised to readdress the petitioners at the end of the seasons. All this happened in the interim, when the Bombay Governor Cowan was dismissed and when the directors applied to this successor John Horne Esqr and his council. However, they just put this matter aside by not informing the matter to the Company in England and had no consent for the petitioner; the council paid no attention, 'till they had their answer we must rest satisfied'.[79]

Malpractices Committed by the Mint Goldsmith, Ragoosett and Gunsett

Ragoosett and Gunsett accused each other of following unfair practices which he has taken some measures to prove him of his offence by Mr. Yeomans allowing thereof, that in his lead which holds the silver there was about double the quantity when separated otherwise as they avert but by throwing in some silver unobserved by them amongst his charcoal to this Gunsett had little more to reply than they should have detected him.[80]

On being ordered to withdraw, Ragoosett, the Goa based goldsmith, was required to inform the Board of Directors, what security he could give for a post that required so much trust. He replied that he would give security for whatever we they trusted him with. To this, the president informed the

Board that he had made the same promise for five month past, had not yet brought any results, and had refused when so called. Mr Thomas Yeomans being further asked his opinion of this person declared that he did not think him equal to the office, and would be confused to work with different sorts of silver, with which he already had some experience lately, which had come from Persia to the Bombay Mint. It was proved that he was at a loss, and added that they were in haste of coining silver after the ships arrived Yeomans recommended therefor that if Ragoosett paid the price for the special species. as per the Goa goldsmith, he could continue in his employment.[81]

Rating the Different Types of Dollars

The different types of dollars, dating back to the year 1726, which shows that one hundred ounces made a rupee then.[82]

Old Mexican Dollar	244	3	16
New Dollars dated since that year.	243	2	28
Old Dollars dated to the Year 1728.	247	1	39
New Dollars since that Year	244	1	39
Ducatoons 100 z will produce.	249	2	26
Lyon Dollars	195	1	41
English Crowns	245	1	37

Different Types of Bullion Used for Minting Money

The undertakers of the Bombay mint remarked on the minting of Bombay coins dating to 30 December 1737, receded by Nassau on the 5 September 1738 and humbly presented to the John Esqr, President and Governor & ca. Council of Bombay. This statement is given by the mint masters, since the minting of coins were not accurate.[83] (Mukennsett Paddamsett & Luckmidass Ragousett).

A Bombay rupee was formerly reckoned to weigh 7wt.10qr 1/5, but by experiments often and accurately made, we are convinced they do cwt-qr.dec. Actually weigh one with another full 7-10-314, which is nearest to the Surat standard of 30 vol. 56 decr. or a Bombay tola Mr. Davis the Assay master in his assay reports made here last month, says they come out upon an average of 6 or 7 different weighing of several numbers 7 qr 10 3/5 and that he found their fineness c.15 better than English standard which is only 14 3/5 less than they ought to be a difference so in considerable that the best Assay masters in England cannot conceive it's certainty.

The species of foreign silver chiefly brought in to the Bombay mint saw the influence of the English Company, which is Mexico and pillar dollars, the quantity of other sorts being very in considerable and of those only we perceive assays have been made at the tower, the Mexico is therefore said to come out by 4… cwt. dec. Trials of exactly English standard and that dated in 1729, a cwt better than English standard.[84]

Now for the readier calculation and also because of our rupee standard which is accordingly to this country way of reckoning equivalent to the 99 touch that is to say 99/100 parts of it fine silver and 1/100 part alloy, we shall bring the Mexico Dollars to the like touch and those being cwt. dec, worse than English standard, will be found equal to touch 914 then if 100 ozs. Touch silver is refined until it is reduced in to Rupee silver of 99 touches the weight remaining will be the same. The pillar dollar was found to be meeting the English standard or 92.5ouch in 1728. One hundred ounces of that species by the same rule was reduced to the rupee touch.[85] Copper too was used for minting money. Several Indian merchants dealing in bullion were as following:

1. Biccu Sinay
2. Monachjee Mody
3. Rupjee Dunjee Gopall
4. Vittuldass Kisso Ram.
5. Luchmansett Ragousett
6. Gungadass Rupjee
7. Nangurdass Lolljee
8. Sevajee Daramsett.

These bullion merchants attended the bidding auction—a procedure for purchasing these metals—for Persian copper. They were called into the chamber one by one where, after some debate, the terms of sale was agreed upon, and thus, the amount fixed had to be paid. The copper was then put up for sale. Old copper was sold at 200 Surat maunds of forty-two seers, but none of the merchant made a bid for more than 20 rupees. Hence, the sale was laid aside. The merchants then decided that the whole commodity be divided into sixteen and the following above merchants decided to take away the other lots at the rate of the following rupees and half per maund. (Maund is a weighing measurement in Asian countries, especially an Indian unit of weight where 1 maund is equivalent to 37 kg.).

The board, considering the issue, observed that the quantity was very large than the demand for copper at present. It must necessarily have been less than usual as the Portuguese used to take large quantities of copper and the Marathas were supplied in great measures because of the plunder from Salsett. The English copper was sold at the last sale for 21 rupees. However, it was paid in credit of twelve months and three per maund were allowed. Later, it was reduced to nine months without discount. The present offer was therefore preferable which is why it was unanimously accepted.[86]

Table 3.1: List of Persons Indebted for Sold Goods and the Money Lent at an Outstanding Interest on 30 November 1738

Name of Person	*Rupees*	*Reas*	*Reason for transaction*	*Due Date*	*Out-standing Rupees*	*Out-standing Reas*
Jessin Bansally	10,122	...	Woollen goods	17 November 1737.	3,793	75
Monachjee and Savajee Daramsett	230,000	64	Lead	1 Feburary 1737	57,000	Nil
Munchurjee and Bomanjee	11,069	64	Lead	31 December 1737	21	45
Munchurjee and Bomanjee	161,867	33	Woollen goods	31 December 1737	66,124	75
Nagur Lolljee	9,650	84	Lead	31 October 1737	1,970	84
Savajee Daramsett	9,390	30	Iron	31 October 1737	9,390	39
Rupjee Dunjee	9,286	68	Silver	Nil	9,286	68
Ramsett	93,366	45	Iron	Nil	9,366	5
Jeejee Mody	9,389	40	Iron	Nil	2,389	40
Monackjee Nowrojee	70,598	...	Elephant teeth	December 1737	29,598.	Nil

Source: Public Department Diary, 11/ A, 1738, Maharashtra State Archives, pp. 618-9.

Total treasure in rupees is = 189,940.271.[87]

The British developed its trading network to expand its position in order to make Bombay town and presidency as significant as Surat used to be. Bombay developed as the trading port of the Mughals as well as the English East India Company. It is difficult to analyse these changes, but through other records, especially the Cochin records of the Dutch between 1724 and 1742, it is evident that English shipping brought changes in the method of shipping by increasing the number of ships and sea-captains from seventeen to twenty eight.[88]

Bombay gradually came to be recognized as an important trading centre in the early eighteenth century, by developing links with the Red Sea and Persian Gulf. However, it was still considered an unhealthy place to live in. The small community of English servants, which consisted of thirty-five company servants, fifteen 'free merchants', and thirty country captains, some of whom were accompanied by their families who frequently saw changes in the administrative bodies of governors and councillors in the Bombay Island.[89]

The early years of the eighteenth century saw a slow growth of private English enterprise, as the local Indian trade made Surat more commercial and a great port on the western coast of India, and not Bombay.[90] As the Company made new changes in the trading pattern, trade in Bombay saw new changes in the 1720s. Two-thirds of the English trading ships at Surat were owned by both locals and other nationalities—residing in the western coast of India for trading.[91]

Bombay gradually developed into one of the most important English centres for trade, as its shipping industry saw new dimensions. It was not until 1735 that Lowji Nassarwanji Wadia emigrated from Surat to Bombay as a craftsman building ships for the English East India Company. The Wadias formed close connections with the Bombay authorities when they were invited from Surat to Bombay to become the master builders of the East India Company's dockyards in 1735. They were skilled ship builders and craftsmen of the Bombay dockyard and served the Company.[92] Gradually, the shipping industry established by the Company was the Bombay Marine stationed at the Old Woman Island. The Bombay Marine provided protection against sea pirates attacking ships carrying cargo. Thus, the Bombay Marine protected ships which carried English passes.[93]

The Parsi merchants who came to Bombay from Surat, also invested their capital to trade with the English Company rather than other European companies such as the Portuguese and the Dutch, whose maritime powers were gradually declining due to the English presence. Parsis from Navsari were also invited to Bombay to serve the English Company as their master weavers. Merchants from other cities too came to Bombay in search of safe trade and protection, which the English government indeed provided to the new settlers on the island.[94]

Sea Politics and the Role of Kanhoji Angria in Controlling the West Coast

By 1733, the Angria power declined due to the death of Kanhoji Angria and the incompetence of his successors. As a result, the foundation of the coastal Angrias' power weakened. Other coastal powers such as the Siddis tried to compete with the Marathas for coastal supremacy and control over the sea vessels passing through the western coast of India. Bombay Island in the 1740s was in a very progressive state than in the 1700s; this was owing to a new system of trading and the consolidated union of the old and new Company. These developments brought in new reforms, which helped make Bombay a prosperous trading town in western India.

It was also because of the Parsi merchant named Narsserwanji Wadia, who migrated from Surat in 1730s and built ships on the Bombay Island for the English East India Company. Later, the Bombay Marine was set up, which could not only crush the Angrias but could also keep the powers of the Marathas of Bassein and the Sawants of Wadi under control. Therefore, the English could impose their pass system along the coast and organize shipping towards China for trade.[95]

The Maratha Ditch was built in 1739, as the Maratha power extended its control over large parts of western India. The fear of attacks on Bombay loomed large. To improve security for the fortified town, a moat was dug around the fort walls in 1739. It was completed in 1743 and cost Rs.250,000. It was called the 'Maratha Ditch', to which Bombay's leading merchants contributed Rs.30,000 fearing that their business would face obstacles from enemies if additional measures were not taken.[96]

Thus, the island's revenue rose from £26,338 to £42,000 in 1744.[97] However, in the 1740s political conflicts also intensified and threatened Bombay's trade. Political and naval conflicts off the coast of Bombay contributed to the decline of Bombay's trade.

Notes

1. Laksmi Subramanian, 'Bombay and the West Coast in the 1740s', *Indian Economic and Social History Review*, vol. 19, 1981, p. 191.
2. Mildred Smith Wretts, 'The Business of the East India Company 1680–1681', *The Indian Economic and Social Review*, vol. I, 1963, p. 116.

3. Philip Anderson, A.M., *The English in Western India*, London: Smith Taylor & Company, 1856, pp. 123–4.
4. S.M. Edwardes, *The Gazetteer of the Bombay City and Island*, vol. I, Pune: The Government Photozinco Press, p. 153.
5. Ibid., p. 408.
6. Ibid.
7. Ibid., p. 153.
8. Ghulam Nadri, 'The Parsis of Surat in the Eighteenth Century', in *Across Oceans Flowing Silks from Canton to Bombay 18th–20th Centuries and No Parsi is an Island*, ed. Ranjit Hoskote, Nancy Adajania and Pheroza J. Godrej, Bombay: Marg Publications, 2013, p. 21.
9. David. L. White, 'Parses in the Commercial World of Western India, 1700–1750', *The Indian Economic and Social History Review*, vol. XXIV, no. 2, 1987, p. 191.
10. Pandurang S. Pissurlencar, *Portuguese Records on Rustam Manockji*, Bombay: Sadanand Press, 1936, p. xxi.
11. White, 'Parses in the Commercial World of Western India', p. 193.
12. Ibid., p. xxiv.
13. Ibid., p. 193.
14. Om Prakash, 'The Indian Maritime Merchant, 1500–1800', *Journal of the Economic and Social History of the Orient*, vol. 47, no. 3, 2004, p. 443.
15. Genevieve Bouchon, 'Sixteenth Century Malabar and the Indian Ocean', in *Indian Ocean 1500–1800*, ed. Ashish Das Gupta and M.N. Pearson, Oxford: Oxford University Press, 1987, p. 72.
16. Prakash, 'The Indian Maritime Merchant, 1500–1800', p. 444.
17. S. Arasaratnam, *Merchants, Companies and Commerce on the Coromandel Coast*, 1650–*1740*, New Delhi: Oxford University Press, 1986, p. 117.
18. Lakshmi Subramanian and R.K. Ray, 'Merchants and Politics: From the Great Mughals to the East India company', in

Business and Politics in India, ed. Dwijendra Tripathi, New Delhi: Manoharlal Publications, 1991, p. 45.

19. Ashin Das Gupta, *The World of the Indian Ocean Merchant 1500–1800*, New Delhi: Oxford University Press, 2001, p. 326.
20. Prakash, 'The Indian Maritime Merchant: 1500–1800', p. 441.
21. Ashin Das Gupta, *Indian Merchants and the Decline of Surat, c.1700–1750*, Wiesbaden, 1979, p. 121.
22. Ashin Das Gupta, 'The Broker at Mughal Surat, c.1740', *Revista de Cultura Review*, vol. 13–14, January 1991, p. 174.
23. Ibid., p. 174.
24. White, 'Parses in the Commercial World of Western India', p. 183.
25. Das Gupta, *The World of the Indian Ocean Merchant 1500–1800*, p. 402.
26. Ibid., p. 402.
27. Ibid., p. 403.
28. White, 'Parses in the Commercial World of Western India', p. 189.
29. Pamela Nightingale, *Trade and empire in western India 1784–1806*, Cambridge: Cambridge University Press, 1970, pp. 17–8.
30. Ibid., p. 18.
31. George W. Forrest, *Selections from the Letters, Despatches, and Other State Papers-Bombay Secretariat, Home Series*, vol. II, Bombay: Central Government Press, 1887, p. 3.
32. Holden Furber, *Bombay Presidency in the Mid-Eighteenth Century*, Bombay: Asia Publishing House, 1965, pp. 26–7.
33. Ibid., p. 29.
34. Forrest, *Selections from the Letters, Despatches, and Other State Papers*, p. 4.
35. Subramanian, 'Bombay and the West Coast in the 1740s', p. 192.
36. K.K. Chaudhari, *Maharashtra State Gazetteers*, vol. II, Bombay: Government of Maharashtra, 1987, p. 192.
37. B. Arunachalam, *Mumbai by the Sea*, Mumbai: Maritime History Society, 2004, p. 162.

38. Chaudhari, *Maharashtra State Gazetteers*, vol. II, p. 198.
39. Ibid., p. 163.
40. K.K. Chaudhari, *Gazetteers of Greater Bombay District*, vol. III, Bombay: Gazetteer Department, Government of Maharashtra, 1986, p. 52.
41. Mariam Dossal, *Theatre of Conflict, City of Hope: Mumbai, 1660 to Present Times*, New Delhi: Oxford University Press, 2010, p. 29.
42. Pamela Nightingale, *Trade and Empire in the Western India: 1784–1806*, Cambridge: Cambridge University Press, 1970, p. 17.
43. Chaudhari, *Gazetteers of Greater Bombay District*, vol. III, p. 52.
44. Edwardes, *The Gazetteer of the Bombay City and Island*, vol. II, pp. 90–1.
45. Ibid., p. 92.
46. Chaudhari, *Maharashtra State Gazetteers*, vol. III, pp. 15–6.
47. Nightingale, *Trade and Empire in the Western India*, p. 17.
48. Dulcinea Correa Rodriques, *Bombay Fort in the Eighteenth Century*, Bombay: Himalaya Publishing House, 1994, p. 23.
49. Forrest, *Selections from the Letters, Despatches, and Other State Papers*, p. xii.
50. Ibid., pp. xii.
51. *Reports of Committee of Correspondence, 1722–24*, vol. I, p. 231.
52. Ibid., p. 231.
53. Shafat Ahmad Khan, *The East India Trade in the XVIIth Century*, London: Oxford University Press, 1923, p. 421.
54. Chaudhari, *Maharashtra State Gazetteers*, vol. III, p. 52.
55. Ibid., p. 16.
56. James Maclean Mackenzie, *A Guide to Bombay: Historical, Statistical, and Descriptive*, Bombay: Bombay Gazette Steam Press, 1889, p. 302.
57. Edwardes, *The Gazetteer of the Bombay City and Island*, vol. II, p. 93.

58. Ibid., pp. 94–5.
59. Maharashtra State Archives, Public Department Diary, 1A/1720, p. 37–8.
60. Chaudhari, *Maharashtra State Gazetteers*, vol. III, p. 15.
61. John Bruce, *Annals of the Honourable East India Company*, vol. II, London: Black, Parry & Kingsbury, 1810, p. 611.
62. Ruby Maloni, *Surat: Port of the Mughal Empire*, Mumbai: Himalaya Publishing House, 2003, pp. 174–5.
63. Compilation of Standing Orders, Court to Bombay, 21 February 1717, vol. I, p. 152.
64. William J. Barber, *British Economic Thought and India: 1600–1858*, London: Oxford University Press, 1975, p. 37.

    Dugani is a copper coin = ½ pices, when a rupee was = 192 pices.
65. B.M. Phiroze Malabari, *Bombay in the Making*, Bombay: T. Fisher Unwin, 1910, pp. 345–6.
66. D.R. Almadi, *The Beginnings of Banking on Bombay Island*, Maharashtra Archives Bulletin no. 12, Bombay: Government of Maharashtra, 1979, p. 5.
67. Edwardes, *The Gazetteer of the Bombay City and Island*, vol. II, p. 289.
68. *Public Department Diary, Court's Letter to Bombay, 20 March 1744*, vol. III, Maharashtra State Archives, 1742–51, p. 72.
69. Chaudhuri, *Maharashtra State Gazetteers*, vol. II, p. 388.
70. *Public Department Diary, Letter from the Mint Master, Thomas Yeoman to the Court of Directors, 2A/1724*, Maharashtra State Archives, p. 134.
71. Ibid., p. 134.
72. Ibid., pp. 134–5.
73. *Public Department Diary, A letter by the Mint Master, Thomas Yeoman, to the Court of Directors, Regarding the Company's Servant Ragooseth and Gunnseth, and the Profits, 2/ A, 1724*, Maharashtra State Archives, pp. 135–6.
74. V.B. Gupta, 'Imports of Treasure and Surat's Trade in the Seventeenth Century', in *Metal and Monies in Emerging*

Global Economy, ed. Dennis and Arturo Giraldez, vol. 14, Hampshire: Ashgate Publishing, 1997, p. 353.

75. *Public Department Diary, Reports Sent by Mr. Davis Regarding the Silver Coinage, from 1727–1734, 11/ B*, Maharashtra State Archives, pp. 335–7.
76. *Public Department Diary, 11/ B, 1738*, Maharashtra State Archives, p. 612.
77. Ibid., p. 357.
78. *Public Department Diary, Mr. Davis Report to the Court of Directors, Regarding the Function of the Bombay Mint, 10 / A, 1737*, Maharashtra State Archives, pp. 472–3.
79. *Public Department Diary, Petition Given by the Mint Undertakers to the Court of Directors, Regarding the Amount to be Paid, 14/B, 1741*, Maharashtra State Archives, p. 283.
80. *Public Department Diary, 2A/ 1724*, Maharashtra State Archives, p. 136.
81. Ibid., p. 136.
82. *Public Department Diary, 14/B, 1740–1741*, Maharashtra State Archives, p. 284.
83. *Public Department Diary, 11 B/1738*, Maharashtra State Archives, p. 609.
84. Ibid., pp. 609–10.
85. Ibid., p. 611.
86. *Public Department Diary, 11/ A, 1738*, Maharashtra State Archives, pp. 134–6.
87. Ibid., pp. 618–9.
88. Holden Furber, *Bombay Presidency in the Mid-Eighteenth Century*, Bombay: Oxford University Press, 1965, pp. 70–1.
89. Ibid., p. 71.
90. William Foster, *English Factories in India*, Oxford: Clarendon Press, 1908, p. 41.
91. Ibid., pp. 41–2.
92. Asiya Siddiqi, 'The Business World of Jamsetjee Jejeebhoy', in *Trade And Finance in Colonial India 1750–1860*, ed. Asiya Siddiqi, New Delhi: Oxford Unversity Press, 1995, p. 187.

93. Foster, *English Factories in India*, p. 43.
94. Ruby Maloni, 'Surat to Bombay: Changing Definitions of a Port City', *Surat: Port of the Mughal Empire*, Mumbai: Himalaya Publishing House, 2003, p. 165.
95. Ashin Das Gupta, *India and the Indian Ocean World: Trade and Politics*, New Delhi: Oxford University Press, 2004, p. 141.
96. Dossal, *Theatre of Conflict, City of Hope*, pp. 32–3.
97. J.M. Campbell, *Gazetteer of the Bombay Presidency—Gujarat, Surat and Broach*, vol. II, Bombay: Government Central Press, 1877, p. 50.

FOUR

Trade, Finance, and Politics in Mid-Eighteenth-Century Bombay, *c.*1740–80

Introduction

This chapter focuses on the sea politics connected to trade and political power—the control over all the trading vessels carrying valuable commodities. Both local and foreign powers contested to control the island of Bombay, strategically located on the west coast of India. By the 1740s, Bombay had become rich and prosperous. This was mainly due to the protection rendered by the Bombay Marine and the active participation of English and Indian merchants in the trade there. After the 1740s, however, the trade in Bombay gradually declined due to the disturbance on the west coast by the enemies, namely the Portuguese, the Dutch, and the French. This period saw constant naval attacks from Indian and foreign powers. The local powers included leaders such as Kanhoji Angria of Kolaba, Khem Sawant of Malwan, and the Siddis from Janjra region. Angria commanded the Mahratta fleet and his primary station was greater Kolaba—an island off Alibag, a little to the south of Bombay. He held districts in the Concan as far as to the south as Vingorla. Angria's key opponents were the representatives of the English East India Company.

The town of Bombay used to be threatened by sea-pirates, both belonging to the Indian as well as the foreign nationalities. Their piratical activities brought huge losses to the merchants and their trade which resulted in slow economic decline, wealth loss, and the delay of bullion supply to Bombay. Therefore, to tackle such threats, numerous changes were introduced in the town by the English government in the 1740s. Owing to its political and maritime strength, the English East India Company controlled the trade on the western coast of India. After the 1740s, however, the scene on the western coast changed. The influence of the Marathas, Mughals, Siddis and other foreign powers often created conflicts with the English government. In order to control these offences, the English government established the Bombay Marine, through which law and order was to be established.

Politics in Bombay in the Mid-Eighteenth Century

'The assessment of Bombay town during the 1740s was highly discriminating factor, since Bombay town was in the culminating phase of growth and development of Bombay's political influence.' The west coast, especially Bombay, faced many dangers—from the Angrias, the Marathas in the Konkan, and the Khem Sawant, the chief of Sawantwadi. However, the English East India Company in Bombay refused to submit to such political blackmail or 'depredations' as they called it.[1]

The town came under the threat of enemies prying to take the control of this geographically located natural harbour and town. Therefore, the Bombay Marine was established in 1753 leading to a stability of law and order in the city, such that trade be carried out smoothly without being interrupted by enemies. The political influence on Bombay though showed signs of greater danger to the trade as the traders continued to be captured and looted on the west coast. The English East India Company had to reckon with forces such as the Marathas and the Konkans and from areas such as Chaul and Bassein, where the Bijapur Sultan, Adil Shah had exercised a hereditary monarchy. Through these developments, the Deshmukhs got an opportunity to free themselves from the control of the Sultans. Thus, the downfall of the Bijapuris made the Marathas combat the Portuguese, the English and the Siddhis effectively.[2]

As a result, the Marathas had become very powerful and notorious against the English and tried their best to exercise supremacy along the west coast of India. The step taken by the Marathas led to many malpractices, including passes which were granted to the traders and their sea-vessels in return. To collect these passes, one had to pay money. If any vessel passed the port without taking the pass, it was confiscated. All of this caused many inconveniences to the ship as well as the owners and traders such as loss to one's property, inability to deliver goods on time, and even danger to one's life if they revolted against these malpractices.[3] The establishment of the Bombay Marine brought the downfall of the Angrias as well the Marathas of Bassein, Malwan, and Sawantwadi.

Khem Sawant was the leader of the Sawants of Sawantwadi. He was a staunch opponent of the English Company and did not toe the line of the East India Company. The English government, therefore, termed him a sea-pirate, as he acted as a hindrance to the English Company as well as the trading merchants. He participated in activities with another pirate from Malwan, the chief of Ratnagiri. Both of them together attacked and captured booties from these trading vessels and detained boats and vessels carrying goods.[4] His activities can be well explained from his account, dated 21 April 1742, that vessels captured by Khem Sawant and Kanhoji Angria were seized, their case was presented to the Bombay Council, and a lengthy petition was filed against them by the merchants.

The Bombay merchants pressurized the English Company to compensate them for their losses. On 18 March 1743, these pirates paid 7,388 rupees as compensation to the merchants and promised to pay the remaining debt within two months. The total sum to be paid was 9,751 rupees. Another case of piratical attack made by Khem Sawant in 1743 was filed by the merchant, whose goods worth 120,000 rupees were lost. The English government failed to recover the goods but were successful in procuring the amount from Khem Sawant and the Malwans.

The English Company's Response to the Piratical Attacks

The English Company believed it was its responsibilities to protect the merchants and traders as the governing body of the western coast and the rulers of Bombay and the adjoining port-towns. Thus, they stepped in to keep these pirates under control and to help the merchants seek compensation for their lost goods. The local merchants, who came to Bombay for trade, found it very difficult to trade and protect their goods because of the pirate infestation in the western coast. Increasingly, the coastal sea politics became a serious offence, bringing huge losses to merchants and their goods, seen in the Bombay Public Proceedings. The English East India Company forcefully introduced a system of issuing passes for all trading merchants, so that they could have control over maritime trade activities on the western coast and at the same time, earn good revenues by establishing their custom houses. They wanted to adopt the same business conduct as the Portuguese during their rule over western India. The passes in return helped the merchants protect their goods and vessels. Sometimes, these pirates too bribed the Company officials and paid loyalties to the English Company.[5]

The most influential Konkani merchants were Babla Kamat, Vencat Kamat, and Ghar Naique, who worked as agents from Bombay. Naique was a brahman Konkani merchant who conducted his trade from Bombay. In 1733–4 he set up his own trading centre and traded with other ports on the western coast of India.[6] Noticing his flourishing trade, the English government refused a trading licence on the Bombay Island.

To challenge the English government's decision, Naique filed a petition on 25 September 1741. It was a petition to allow him to continue his trading ventures, which was turned down. This makes clear the political supremacy which the English were exercising on the coast and the traders. They seized three vessels on 21 April 1741, namely *Sulematy*, *Goruh*, and *Morradon* at Surat. These vessels were being escorted by the English. The vessels were intercepted by Khem Sawant as he shared good relations with these merchants, Ghar Naique and Sancar Sinay. Khem Sawant did not attack their vessels, as he was in fact given money to guard their vessels from the pirates.[7]

There emerged a development in the commercial sector of Bombay. The Banias began paying special attention to their trade. Bullion was an important item of trade required in the town and other hinterland ports to conduct trade and finance and for minting coins.[8] The Bania merchants from Surat, Poona, and Aurangabad came to Bombay and set up their trade after the transfer of Surat factory. These Banias were led by Roopjee Dhanjee, Vithaldas Kesouram, and Vrindavandas, who immediately brought to their notice the losses that have been incurred:

Your Company and Board of Council are sensible that though these freights are at first no more than consignments to us from these merchants to the north ward, yet from your petitioners returning them such goods as they want, this money is still kept in Bombay and greatly lends to the keeping up a currency of trade, which is equally advantageous to the public as well as to your petitioners, whereas if there is any opportunities missed of bringing bullion and other valuable commodities on this freight, those people would cause their money to be brought at once in to their own hands and they would then have no tie upon them to send their boats to us for collecting cargoes. This beneficial trade to the Bombay town from the north ward would be lost. The Bombay town of not being supplied of the yearly sum, we fear will cause such an extreme scarcity of money in Bombay. It appears to us that an advantage accrues to the Company on this money from Mocha of three freight and coinage. Your petitioners humbly pray that your honour will continue the method of sending one of the honourable company's vessels to Mocha to bring treasures so necessary for the public use and in return bring relief to your petitioners.[9]

The Bombay traders received financial support from the private agents, brokers, and political patrons. Although the trade was controlled by the Court of Directors and the Governor of Bombay, they could not control their enemies and had to participate in the political game of bribing them to secure their acceptance. The financial support rendered to the merchants and traders of Bombay Island gave a tremendous impetus to not only the trade promoters but also the commercial bodies and agents.

The British position in India was established through the exchange of bullion for Indian goods. The institution that was created to maintain this trade after the company reduced its import of bullion was essential to the mechanism of the empire in India and an important element in the domestic British financial structure. The disruption of the traditional trade declined due to the shortage of bullion metal. Indo-European relationship did impact the Asian trade, which later changed the Indian trading pattern between 1757–1860. It was mainly due to the changes in the global sphere, which affected the Indian trade, especially Bombay particularly.

This was because Bombay was the most important commercial centre of trade and finance.[10]

To consolidate their power, the Britishers in Bombay entered political arrangements with the Portuguese and the Angrias to prevent them from coming under the control of the Marathas.[11] The English East India Company also maintained friendly relations with the Marathas, who had become very powerful under the leadership of Kanhoji Angria and Khem Sawant of Malwan. They were considered the foremost power on the west coast in the mid-eighteenth century. These local powers were the enemies of the English government and disturbed the trading activities on the western coast. Therefore, to protect the merchants and traders on the island, the English Government issued passes and even granted protection to these merchants. These passes were very similar to the Portuguese Cartaz system. Those ships which had this sailing licence in the Indian Ocean were given protection by the English. This system of protection forced the merchants to buy passes from the English. The Portuguese too created trouble by interrupting the coastal trade. Due to this, the merchants and traders looked forward to Kanhoji Angrey and Khem Sawant of Sawantwadi, active in their pursuit to control sea trade by capturing trading vessels from local as well as the foreign traders carrying valuable goods.[12]

The English East India Company acted politically as well as commercially to secure their supremacy on the western coast of India. The Bombay Governor established the Marine

Garrison to keep a check on the enemies, and the island became one of the most important commercial centres for trade, military and marine navy in India.[13] Trading items were purchased and financed by merchants in Bombay and they maintained trading connection with other ports on the Konkan-belt as well as Surat, Mocha, and other ports of West Asia. Bullion was traded and transported to Bombay from Europe, West Asia, and Africa. Later, it began to be supplied even in the interior hinterland for financial transaction and minting money.[14]

In 1742, Bombay suffered great loss due to the orders of the Bombay Council to abolish the post of Marine Admiral, resulting in the poor care of the large mercantile fleet, open to pirate attacks. Another cause for the decline of Bombay trade was the declaration of war between England and France in 1744, and it was inevitable that two French privateers would be hovering around Bombay to intercept company officials and the only solution was to adopt protective measures to send alarm to any English vessels entering the Indian shores and resuming the post of Marine Admiral. During these critical years of warfare between France and England, the Bombay Marine ships were constantly engaged in co-operating with the Royal Navy and took swift action against the pirates which had infested the Persian Gulf and the western coast. [15]

The Operation of English Custom House on the West Coast

The English East India Company observed strict measures while issuing and maintaining company's passes to all traders trading in the island of Bombay. The granting of these passes was an important act to be observed. Vessels trading without these English passes were detained, searched, and seized.[16] The Company also used the Bombay Marine as an instrument for the maintenance of law and order. This system of sea licensing, enforced by the compulsory act of the English Company, created distress among the Marathas, Mughals, and the merchants. The local powers had earlier enjoyed privileges from the merchants in guiding their ships and earned good revenues from their vessels. This also explains the supremacy of the local powers along the west coast before the granting of passes and protection offered to these traders.

The English Custom House was instituted to impose laws and policies on traders and merchants and to earn revenues in return. The body also sought to manage the economic condition of Bombay due to the political instability among the Marathas, the Mughals, the Portuguese, and the pirates, both local and foreign in origin. The English were well equipped to protect the traders and created awareness about their military strength and operations.[17]

A duty of 3.5 per cent was levied towards all imported goods on the island and the funds were directed towards the building of the custom house. Convoy duty was collected for small vessels which paid 10 rupees, while the bigger ones paid 20. Freight account too was carried out; freighted goods such as gold and silver belonging to black merchants brought on the Company's vessels from Persia or the Red Sea carried a duty of 2 per cent, while the Company's covenant servants paid 1 per cent. The Company encouraged merchants to ship their money to the island, like silver, which was freighted in the Company's vessels to be coined at the mint. In return, the Company earned freight duties.[18]

In 1744 a set of orders for the guidance of the Bombay Custom Master was published, which stated that all merchandize imported by Europeans, subject to certain exceptions, should pay a duty of 4.5 per cent, of which 1 per cent was allocated to the town-ditch and a half per cent to the new custom house. Goods imported by the local merchants in the three masted vessels paid 4.5 per cent, but when imported in the smaller vessels, an additional 2 per cent was added towards the cost of building town walls. Grain and timbre exports by local Indian merchants entailed a duty of 5 per cent.[19]

In 1747, the Court of Directors wrote to the Bombay Governor requesting the abolition of these duties in cases where the merchant goods did not land on the island. He also added that the shibars, gallivats, and small boats, which supplied basic goods such as timbre, rice, fruit, and cattle provisions to the island, should not be charged.[20] In 1752, a special duty of 1 per cent was levied ad valorem of all goods imported and exported at Bombay and Surat in ships hired by the Company and all country ships and vessels, which were entitled to the Company's protection and also bore the English colours. In 1765, the Bombay Custom Master was likewise ordered to oblige all merchants not under the Company's protection, bound from the southern to the northern ports, which came in at Bombay for the benefit of convoys, to deliver an account of their cargo upon their arrival. On the cargo, the Customs Master was ordered to levy the duties valued at 10 per cent under the market price.[21] The customs collected at Bombay during 1778–89 fluctuated between Rs.157,000 (in 1761–2) and Rs.325,000 (in 1777–8) and averaged to about Rs.201,000 in the first ten years and about Rs.284,000 in the last nine.[22]

Francis Pym, an English Civil Servant, and His Flourishing Private Trade

Francis Pym was a civil servant of the East India Company stationed at Bombay, and his accounts spanned between May

1746 to March 1751. Pym invested in private trade, lent loans, and earned interest on it. With these profits, Pym decided to invest in a big commercial venture. He joined hands with a Parsi merchant and bought copper in November 1748. Another associate named Lawrence Sullivan was offered a loan of Rs.20,000 by Pym in December 1749. It was in the form of a respondentia bond to Captain John Watson for a voyage to Mocha. This is how Pym earned interest on the money lent; he even received Rs.10,000 from a Parsi household on Sullivan's account.[23] Sullivan had many contacts, and he used them to help Pym widen his business.

In January 1750, he was given a post in the Company's factory at Surat, which undoubtedly was the best place in the Bombay presidency for trade. His dealings with Parsis, Muslims, and Hindus multiplied, and even the English used him as their agent. Among them were Thomas Hodges, Charles Crommelin, and Lawrence Sullivan, who was a factor of Bombay in the year 1741 and returned with a good fortune to England in 1752. Pym's diary gives a detailed account of his active enterprises—he invested in respondentia (loan taken by the owner), provided ships with cargoes from other merchants and agents for ships, financed voyages, and sold goods. He and his associates traded in ships, captains, foreign coins, dollars, crowns, venetians zelotas, pearls, tutenag, and cochineal. He entered partnerships with Sullivan (1713–86), who became the East India Company Chairman in 1758, Captain Samuel Hough, and later David Scott and John Forbes, who worked as ship officers before joining private trade and establishing agency houses.[24] It was these men who were the real entrepreneurs of the English private trade

The private economic power in Bombay, thus, came into very few hands, particularly those who were ship-owners, merchants, and bankers. Francis Pym became the real entrepreneur of the English private trade in the mid-eighteenth century. In 1753, 'Grosse, who was in the Bombay town, witnessed that the inhabitants in the town had multiplied' due to Surat's declining prowess. The merchants and traders flocked to Bombay as it opened new avenues for them. Many traders from other cities like Poona, Kolhapur, and Aurangabad also came to Bombay to try their luck. They invested their money in new banks which had opened in the town to lend financial support to the traders. The traders felt especially secure in Bombay because of the protection rendered by the English government.[25]

In 1755, the Angrias were crushed down by the Marathas and the English in collaboration, as Kanhoji Angria's maritime strength was creating problems for the English government. Making use of the opportunity, the Marathas offered their support to the English government and in return sought benefit from the English, who became more powerful than the Angrias and could control the west coast.[26] The year 1755 was significant for the Marathas as they established friendly relations with the English government and received a considerable amount of money for joining them in their expedition against the Angrias. The amount which was paid to the Marathas needs to be examined as it was paid in bullion for fighting the war against the Angrias. But in 1757, for both the English and the Marathas as they succeeded in defeating Kanhoji Angria.[27]

Bombay merchants witnessed the defeat of sea pirates, who had given tremendous blows to merchants and ships in carrying trade via the coast as well as the sea. An English traveller named Edward Ives, who was in the Bombay town in 1757, observed that Bombay was prospering in those years. In his words, Bombay was the most flourishing town in the world—'the grand store-house of all Arabian and Persian commerce'.[28]

On 30 July 1765 in the Bombay Castle, some biscuits, coconuts, and old Copper were reported to be unserviceable. Following this, the military paymaster and the superintendent were ordered to do a survey. An extract from Mr Robert Sandy's letter dated 30 July 1765 was read out. In this letter, a proposal for the introduction of gold coins was made owing to the shortage in supply of silver in Bombay and leading to the minting of gold coins. The introduction of gold currencies created too much of agony for minters and traders since the value of silver and gold coins differed extensively.[29]

The Bombay government had put up a notice in the town that made it forbidden to entertain strangers beyond a particular time after which a notice would be in the diary. Several merchants attending on strangers in the town would have to pay for any inconvenience caused by them. This can be explained by an example—the number of these visitors varies with the demands of the markets island and the supply of articles for which they are often obliged to wait for the arrival of ships.[30]

Artisans and traders were encouraged to migrate from the interior hinterlands. Among the ones who did migrate were the Bhandaris from Chaul, cloth-weavers from Gujarat, and communities of goldsmiths, ironsmiths, and others such as Bhatias, Banias, Shenvi brahmans and Parsis. The most noteworthy members among the Parsis were Rustom Dorabji, Patels of Bombay, and Lowji Nassarwanji Wadia, the master ship-builders of the Bombay Dockyard.[31] The Wadias were master ship builders and craftsmen of the Bombay dockyard, served the East India Company, built and maintained ships for the Royal Navy and also constructed many ships for private merchants. Between 1767 and 1791 twenty-seven ships, ranging between 300 tons and 1,000, tons ships were built at Bombay town.[32]

Muncharji Jivanji, a wealthy Parsi merchant and ancestor of Sir Cowasji Jehangir, came to settle in Bombay from Navsari in Surat in 1744. Two other communities, of whom special mention is made during this period, were the Vanjaras—inhabitants of the ghat country, who brought large amount of money to buy goods in the island during the fair season—and the Bhatias and Banias, especially those of the Kapol division, who played an important part in the commercial development of Bombay during the nineteenth and twentieth centuries. The Kapol Banias came from Gogha and Surat with their leader Shet Rupji Dhanji in 1756. Slaves recruited from Madagascar and Zanzibar were brought to Bombay for recruitment as soldiers and to work in the dock.

Development of the Bombay Harbour

The Governor of Bombay began to develop the maritime industry for carrying out commercial activities and planned to expand the harbour and dock for enhancing the naval power. The first Bombay Docks foundation was laid by the Parsi merchant Lowji Nusserwanji Wadia, the master carpenter who was brought down to Bombay from Surat in 1735 to construct ships at the naval dockyard. Along with him, ten other Parsi carpenters came to Bombay too and throughout the British rule, they were engaged in building new vessels for the Company. Nusserwanji utilized his skills using European technology and Indian raw materials to produce good quality vessels. The dock was well planned and built to carry trade and dock ships and local and foreign ships. It started functioning in 1748, however, the plan of building the dock was conceived in 1686. The Bombay Marine was one of the most important developments after the Bombay Mint. The engineer assigned to build the dock was Captain de Funck, a Garrison engineer who imported the pier dock which came into existence in 1742. He improved the conditions of the pier which could not hold for long because 'of the continual washing of the sea'.[33]

By 1748, Bombay Marine was strengthened and had three ships consisting twenty-eight guns, twenty-eight gun-grabs, and eight gallivats. These ships were built to fight the pirates and protect cargoes. The Company spent as much as 50,000 rupees annually for the maintenance of this dock. By the end of 1750s, the Marine participated in combat operations and grew into a disciplined service force.[34]

In 1753, the Naval Dockyard was opened, which remains the oldest dock in the city. The shipping industry boomed in the island of Bombay. The safe accessibility of the Bombay harbour throughout the year and its connections with the other parts port-towns on the western coast of India made it an immediate attraction. The Bombay harbour was controlled by the Bombay Governor William Wake, who used this port to build the economy and conduct trade with other ports on the western coast. Governor Wake exercised his supremacy on matters concerning the harbour. It soon became the most active trading port, not only for the Company but also to local Indians and foreign merchants who frequented the harbour to trade in the island. The Company exported its goods from England into the harbour and disposed their manufactured goods such as woollen clothes, glassware, ammunition, medicines, rosewood, and bullion there. Annually, goods worth around 14 lakhs were imported to Bombay and it was later distributed in the hinterland of western India.[35]

The harbour under the English Trading Company also saw developments in the domain of maintaining and building new ships. The Bombay Dock became an important centre for trade and ship construction, which through its revenue from trading licences strengthened the economic conditions of the town. The English granted passes to those who traded under the English Governorship. They engaged in exclusive trade of Indian commodities with the Marathas, including cotton, which was supplied to Bengal and China from Bombay Dock. The trading activities in the harbour brought in lakhs of rupees annually—a huge profit—and in return, strengthened the power of the English East India Company on the island of Bombay.[36]

The maintenance of the Bombay Marine was one of the key responsibilities of the Company. This ensured a steady supply of revenue from the harbour. Bombay would soon become a winning settlement of nearly eight lakh people and render a difference of £ 250,000 to the Company annually. This dock was built in such a way that it could accord assistance of all kinds to a squadron in the time of war and protect the commerce on the western coast. These were the leading motives of the Bombay government to pay attention to the dock.[37]

From 1759–1829, the Bombay government appointed a captain of the Bombay Marine each year as commodore of the Surat squadron, following the footsteps of how the 'Mughal Admiral' controlled the piracy. Therefore the English squadron too continued a regular patrol and kept a check on the pirate infested areas to capture or destroy piratical activities which had become common on the western coast. The Bombay Marine even escorted trading vessels through the pirate infested areas.[38] A regular ferry boat was also introduced between Bombay and Thana in 1776.

Emergence of Bombay as a Powerful Military Base under the English Government

The Court of Directors announced stringent orders against gambling and oath-taking. In 1760, regular uniform consisting of blue frock-coats and yellow waistcoats, with gold lace for higher grades, were made mandatory for the marine garrisons. A set of disciplinary orders, the first batch of official regulations ever published for the marine service, was imposed on commanders.[39]

After 1771, the Bombay town, under the Governorship of William Hornby, saw a dynamic change in its military strength. John Watson, the Superintendent of the Bombay Marine, made strenuous efforts to keep the enemies under check. The payment of salary to the seamen, who had earlier demanded exorbitant wages, was regularized. The year 1772 also witnessed the first survey expedition undertaken by the Bombay Marine. This survey was conducted under the command of Lieutenant Robinson, who managed to explore the coasts of Sind, Kathiawar, and parts of Arabia and Persia.[40]

In 1771, the Board of Directors appealed strongly against the export of naval stores from Europe to Bombay on the grounds that it led to an increase of the naval forces of the Marathas, as the merchants of Bombay traded in this commodity and supplied it to the Marathas. The supply of warfare commodities to the Marathas was considered to be very much against the interest of the English Company.[41]

Speculations by Travellers in the Bombay Island in the Mid-Eighteenth Century

John Fryer, an English traveller in Bombay recorded 10,000 people living in the island in 1661 and it increased to 60,000 in 1673 according to Fryer's report. According to Niebuhr, the population of Bombay was 140,000 in 1744, and increased to the total population of 1,13,726 in 1780.[42] This rise in population was due to the development of Bombay's trade and also the drought which forced people to migrate to Bombay Island. People from all over the mainland flocked to the island, and with their contribution succeeded in making Bombay a flourishing centre of commerce. Provisions and supplies were plentiful, but prices soared, becoming double of what they used to be earlier.

Abraham Parsons, describing the Bombay town in 1765, remarked that:

> Between the two marine gates is the castle properly called Bombay castle, a very large and strong fortification which commands the bay. The works around the town are so many and the bastions so very strong and judiciously situated, and the whole so defended with a broad and deep ditch, as to make a strong fortress, which while it has a sufficient garrison and provisions, may bid defiance to any force which may be brought against it.[43]

Another important English traveller of the time was James Forbes, who described the port during 1766–70 as:

> The harbour is one of the finest marts in India, employing large number of vessels, accessible at all seasons and affording a safe anchorage during the tempestuous monsoons. The merchants carry trade with all the principal sea-ports and interior cities of the peninsula of India and extend their commerce to the Persian and Arabian Gulfs, the Coast of Africa, Malacca, China and the Eastern islands.

There were three excellent docks and a spacious marine-yard, where teak ships of all sizes were made by skilful Parsis, the exact imitators of the best European models.[44] Parsons commented on the name of the Bombay town in 1775, 'it was first called so by the Portuguese, which literally in English "Good Bay", which it is in all respects being so very capacious as to be capable of receiving any number of ships of any size or draft of water with room sufficient to moor clear of each other in safety.'[45] 'Each year brought fresh and wealthier settlers, and every sea breeze wafted into the crowded harbour of Bombay ships of every port from China to Peru.'[46]

Policies of Coin Circulation

In 1744 England declared war against France and Spain, which lasted till 1762. The war disturbed the channel which ensured the flow of bullion to western India and affected the supply of bullion to the Bombay Mint.[47] During the first half of the eighteenth century, Governor William Wake passed orders to confiscate coins which were being circulated in the Bombay town to be confiscated. A considerable quantity of silver rupees of varying coinage and alloy and of a value inferior to the standard of the Bombay and Surat rupees was being brought to the Bombay Island. In 1741, an overwhelming scarcity of copper forced the local authorities to coin tutelage pice for the value of Rs.2000, which continued till 1773. The authorities dictated that there should be people appointed in the land pay office to exchange rupees for pice at the rate of 80 pices for a rupee.[48]

Pice became one of the most important currencies in Bombay. Where were the silver, gold, and copper currencies? It could either be that there was a low supply of precious metals or the supplying countries found it difficult to export them. Another order to be followed at the mint in 1743 was to curb the minting of copper, and whatever the Bombay mint had, had to be collected in the treasury. This was due to the introduction of large quantities of pices, much less in

value than the Bombay pice, from the Maratha dominions.[49] In 1744 orders were issued for the coining of gold rupees of the same fineness as that of a Venetian, but with a weight of 40 vals (instead of 38 vals) and the same impression as that in the silver rupee. This was done so that they could make some profits and still retain the real value as they were to pass for 15 silver rupees as before.[50]

John Spencer, the Mint Master of the Bombay town, presented a letter to the Board of Directors stressing on the capacity and attention of the present undertakers at the mint; stating that if the incapacities are not timely remedied, it may create loss in the English East India Company's revenue. Large quantities of silver annually came to the Bombay mint for minting of coins. The Bombay mint undertakers took into the consideration on 25 March 1748, that the present undertaking was to prevent a large balance of silver dust which remained in the furnace after being utilised in the process of minting. From the above consultation letter, it is understood that advances would apply to the keepers of the Company's cash chest for the requisite silver Arcot rupees or gold pagodas. Most of these coins were fresh from the company's own mint, whether the visitors could adjourn to see the European assay master and the Indian mint contactor at work with their attendant goldsmiths and coiners who worked in the mint. In his consultation report, the assay master Spencer made notes of many problems in the mint which required urgent remedies. He focussed on the condition of the mint and its operation. The method of minting coins required a thorough inspection of the mint to ensure good quality. He also pointed to the residual balance of silver, use of gold powder and the problem of mismanagement at the mint.[51]

In 1751, the Council, in want of gold to pay for the pepper to be contracted from Kanwar, directed the chief and factors at Surat to purchase 10,000–15,000 venetians at the most reasonable terms so that they could send them to Bombay. In 1757 the need for smaller currency led to the coinage of half and quarter pices for the value of 10,000 rupees. In 1765, the scarcity of silver led to an eventual introduction of the gold currency. Two years later the rupee currency was regulated by the issue of a publication requiring that Bombay rupees whether cracked, broken, chopped, with holes with full weight (100 gunjas make a rupee) be used at full value. 'All Mahmud Shaw and Amund Shaw Surat rupees, whether broad ones, cracked or even chopped if full weight, be received and passed as current at the full value of 80 Pice the rupee'.[52]

The Gold-Silver Ratio: Objectives of the East India Company

The new responsibilities of the English government in India raised two enormous problems—firstly, they were to establish the authority of the parliament over the East India Company at the political front. One of the important steps taken towards this direction was the passage of the Regulating Act of 1773. The second step was to create a system of effective administration in India.[53]

During the first half of the eighteenth century, a considerable quantity of silver rupees of varying coinage and alloy and of a value inferior to the standard of the Bombay and Surat rupees used to be brought to Bombay from other cities. People were appointed at the land pay offices to exchange rupees for pices at the rate of 80 pice for a rupee.[54] Due to the scarcity of copper, the local authorities coined tutelage pice for the value of 2,000 rupees. This coin was, however, discontinued in 1773. The search for small currency led to the minting of half and quarter pices for the value of 10,000 rupees.

Another important issue that Bombay faced was the great scarcity of silver in the middle of the eighteenth century which led to the establishment of gold currency in 1767. The resolution passed in 1767 equalized the standard of Surat rupees with that of Bombay rupee. In 1774, the rupee coined at Broach (now known as Bharuch) was admitted as currency in Bombay. A year later, owing to the demand for silver currency, gold was coined for an amount of 60,000 rupees in pieces of the value of one silver rupee each; they were to be in fineness exactly equal to other gold rupees in circulation and one-fifteenth of the weight of a gold rupee. However, in 1778, the coinage of gold was stopped.[55]

The old Bombay rupee was identical to rupees coined at Surat under the Mughals. It weighed 178.314 grains and contained 1.24 per cent of alloy. As the Nawab of Surat did not observe the agreement made with the Bombay government, all the Bombay rupees were carried to Surat to be re-coined and the Bombay Mint ceased to coin silver for more than twenty years. In the beginning of the eighteenth century, the government had ordered the Surat rupee to be struck in Bombay and since then, the rupee was produced in a manner that it weighed 179 grains and contained 7.97 per cent of alloy.[56]

In 1766, the East India Company tried to establish bimetallism or fixed legal ratio between gold and silver. Gold Mohurs were at first valued at 14 Sicca rupees. But the new gold Mohurs of 1769 were declared equivalent to 16 Sicca rupees, though the market price of gold was less. The facts remain that in 1773, there was 139 kinds of gold Mohurs, 61 kinds of gold Hun or south Indian gold called pagodas by 214 kinds of foreign coins.[57]

Another important issue which emerged in the last quarter of the eighteenth century was that the coining of gold rupees was eventually stopped. The troops suffered due to this as they were paid in gold currencies and charged an additional tax of 3 per cent. An export duty of 3 per cent was imposed in 1770 on all unwrought silver and foreign coins exported from Bombay and Surat, except when destined to China, Batavia or other presidencies, 'small gold coins have been stamped and issued from the mint of Bombay equal in value to one silver rupee which gold coins. It is hereby declared will be in all payments at the treasury of Bombay and of Surat and in all payments of revenues or purchases, etc. which bears Surat impressions'.[58]

During the first half of the eighteenth century, a considerable amount of silver rupees of 'varying coinage', meaning the purity of the rupee or coin and the amount of alloy present in them, were brought to India. These monies were brought to the Island from other foreign nationalities. Officials were appointed at the land pay office to exchange rupees for pices at the rate of 80 puce for a rupee. Due to the scarcity of copper, the local authorities coined Tutelage Pice to the value of Rs. 2,000. These coins were later discounted in 1773.

A similar crisis had occurred during the Mughal bureaucracy. With the shifting of silver rupee to gold rupees, there was a change in the mode of payment to the military sector serving under the Subhedar Regiment which was paid in gold in 1676. And this change is seen again in the year 1780, from silver to gold. The crisis clearly shows the extent to which the money supply in the Mughal market in the seventeenth century. This crisis was again seen in the 1780s, when the value of gold was substituted for silver and gold acted as a credit to offer a new currency. The precious metals saw differences in the value and the ratio between gold and silver coins, as they changed from time to time. Calculations were made in rupees; though gold rupees worked up to 1818, when it was ordered to be displaced by the East India Company's silver coinage.[59]

Private Business Ventures of Bombay Governor William Wake (1744–1803)

The Bombay Governor William Wake was known as the country trader during war time, as he had participated in private trade. He introduced regular measures to reduce charges and increase revenues. However, from 1760–1803, no worthy measures were taken to keep the revenues up in a way that it meets their expenditure. As a result, the Bombay government faced financial difficulties while waging the Maratha and Mysore wars.[60] William Wake's role as a private trader in the economic history of Surat and Bombay is well known. Wake and his private trading give us a deep insight into the economic conditions and trade in mid-eighteenth century Bombay and Surat. William Wake acted as a free merchant and supercargo of several country ships in 1720s before he rose to become the Governor of Bombay in 1742.

Wake's private trade was handled by a merchant named Mulna Fakkruddin, the grandson of Mullah Abdul Ghafur, known to be the wealthiest merchant in his times. Wake hired ships from Fakkruddin and employed at least two sea-captains, if not more.[61] Fakkruddin enjoyed the same fortune as Wake and migrated to Bombay in 1745 due to the crisis in Surat.[62] He complained to the English Governor William Wake about his protection but was compelled to pay Governor William Wake one and half lakh rupees in

1744. The amount was considered to be less due to which he was imprisoned and an additional sum of 25,000 rupees was demanded from him at Surat.[63] In the trading season of 1747–8, Wake employed sea captains to venture his cargoes for his private trading business. The captains commanding his ships were Josiah Holmes and Thomas Purnell. Thomas Purnell was often appointed as the sea captain for merchant Mulna Fakkruddin, who owned many ships.[64]

On 10 July 1747, a ship named *Fackiero Mirachub*, commanded by William Wake's friend, Thomas Purnell, a resident of Batavia, sailed for Bombay and Surat, carrying a cargo invoiced at 46,019 Rix dollars or 73,360 rupees. It consisted chiefly of powdered sugar, sugar candy, some wine, ivory, iron, camphor, porcelain, velvet, and sandalwood. After a forty-one-day voyage from Batavia to India, the ship made an entry on Indian shore on 21 August 1747. Captain Purnell carried Dutch freight and passport which belonged to Mulna Fakkruddin. Enroute Captain Thomas Purnell allowed a Parsi merchant Manekjee Nowranjee to board the ship against a charge of 20,000 rupees in silver without William Wake's knowledge. *Fackiero Mirachub* sailed to Surat on 25 August and was seized two days later by the French forces. Purnell was accused of having ransomed the ship for 40,000 rupees at Goa, which he denied. Wake had hired this ship from Mulhna Fakkirrudin for 10,000 rupees for eight months. Later, however, this ship was taken into Goa as a prize of war.[65]

Important Letters of William Wake Concerning the Bombay Mint

Bombay Castle, 5 January 1744
To,

The Governor of Bombay, William Wake Esqr,
President and Bombay Council.

Having duly agreed some need rupees of the coinage and Silver of the king William the 17th. The silver was used for the coinage, which had fineness of the Bombay standard weight.

Most obedient humble servant,
William Davis.[66]

Bombay Castle, 1 March 1744
Treasury
To balance of last month......................179539.3.7
Foreign silver received in part of 6 chests delivered to be coined on 29th November............7000.
Rupees 186539.3.7
Bombay Castle, 28 February,
Error Excepted,
William Wake,
John Morley.[67]
FOREIGN SILVER,
Ramsett Luckmonsett and Mint Undertakers delivered them to be coined 20, chests New Philip dollars being of remains of the Shaftesbury's Silver.

5313.4
1455.4
Total = 20346.8. [68]

BOMBAY CASTLE ON 25 OCTOBER 1763:

The board took the decision to repay back the sale of the remaining copper, which being put up, sold to the under mentioned persons as follows.
Copper fine per ship lord Mansfield.[69]

Name of the Person	*Copper Square Sheets*	*Metres*
Nattu Mohammad	25---------------------75	23.8
Gorrobjee Manick	25------------------------	23.8
Hirjee. Naye	25---------------------75	23.8
Nil	25---------------------75	23.8
Padmonjee Luckmonjee	25---------------------75	23.8
Vittal Janojee	25---------------------75	23.9
Gorrobjee Manick	25---------------------75	23.9
D	25---------------------75	23.9
D	25---------------------75	23.9
D	25---------------------75	23.9

Bullion Supply from Mocha to Surat and Bombay

It was the bullion from Mocha that helped finance the trading and commercial ventures of Bombay merchants, something which helped Bombay's trade to prosper in the mid-eighteenth century. The Company imported bullion from Mocha to Bombay.[70] The Mocha-Bombay-Surat connection came to life in 1747, when the town faced difficulty with the delivery of freight and the merchants of Bombay and Surat faced losses. Mocha was an important trading town for the supply of silver and other goods. The value of this bullion trade can be seen in the consultation of Mocha Factory Records of 1752.[71] The Surat merchant Nangar Lackmidass, Monackjee Naurojee, and Bhawani Sankar, and the growing importance of Bombay which absorbed the treasure from Mocha came to be utilised by the Bombay merchants to finance their trade and other activities for the development of Bombay.

The First Anglo-Maratha War (1775–1782)

The British occupied Salsette in the year 1774, which was earlier ceded to the British East India Company by the Treaty of Salbai, signed in 1782. The province of Salsette was taken over by the Marathas from the Portuguese in 1737. Other towns like Bassein, Karanja, and Bandora too were later ceded to the Marathas in 1739, but it was taken over by the British in 1774.[72]

The first collision between the Marathas and the British took place in 1774 when a civil war broke between Raghuba and the ministry which acted as a proxy for the child Peshwa, Madhav Rao II. Hearing of the Portuguese expedition for the recovery of Salsette, the Bombay government seized the town of Thane. The Bombay Council signed a treaty of alliance with Raghunath Rao in 1774 and agreed to aid Raghuba in return for the cession of Salsette, Bassein, and certain parts of Guzerat districts in 1775.[73]

The capture of Thane also accompanied the fall of Salsette and other smaller towns occupied by the Bombay troops. Raghunath Rao had become a fugitive. The Poona ministers retaliated by blocking the English coastal trade and stopped supplies from reaching Bombay. Raghunath Rao took the most drastic step by sending his agents to Pune in October 1774 and Robert Gambier, president of Surat along with Mallet, an agent of the English factory, instructed the British workers to extend hospitality towards Raghunath Rao. Soon after, on 7 March 1775, the long-deferred treaty between Raghunath Rao and the Bombay government was signed at Surat.[74]

A contingent of 2,500 men, including 700 Europeans with sufficient artillery, was to be placed at the disposal of Raghunath Rao, who was to bear the expenses of one and a half lakh rupees every month in advance. Six lakhs rupees or its equivalent in jewellery were to be deposited with the English, and in addition, Raghunath Rao was to cede all the islands of Bombay including Thane, Vasai, Salsette, and the talukas of Jambusar and Oplad near Surat, to the English in perpetuity. Observing the political chaos, the English and the Marathas came to an understanding to form an agreement. In pursuance of this agreement, the English force under the command of Colonel Keating left Bombay for Surat. This naturally led to the fermentation of the war between the English Governor-General and the Marathas.[75]

Political strife in Bombay became so acute that diplomatic negotiations between the two groups had to take place. The discussion happened between Raghuba and Fathesingh, for which Raghuba secured help from the English East India Company. Under these circumstances, the Bombay government proved that they were the shrewdest of merchants. It exploited the opportunity fully to overthrow Raghuba and his men. Taking control of the situation, the English demanded a huge sum of money from Fathesingh, to defeat Raghuba, a powerful Maratha who actively disturbed the trade and imposed its malpractices on the people. Therefore, four drafts were prepared to sign the treaty between the English and Fathesingh. Unfortunately, these drafts were considered unsatisfactory and therefore rejected.[76] The fifth and the final draft, which came to be known as the Surat treaty, was signed between the Maratha leader Raghunathrao and the English East India Company government on 7 March 1775. Later in the same month, over 1,900,000 rupees was secured for the English on 16 March 1775. It was a stupendous amount, especially if it is taken into consideration that it represents the interest at 5 per cent on the capital of 380,000 rupees.[77]

The Gaikwads refrained from participating in these diplomatic negotiations since they were not informed earlier about these developments and enjoyed no political power. They were not even consulted, though they were expected to make great financial sacrifices. One of the six articles in the Surat treaty states, 'Raghoba also engages immediately to procure from the Gaikwads, a grant to the English Company forever with all the necessary Sanads of their share in the total revenue collected by the Gaikwads in the town and Parganas of Broach.' This article brings a mutual understanding between the British and Raghuba against the Gaikwads. The government attained a military victory on 17 February 1775, and had they been able to gain this success prior to the signing of the treaty, it would have led to the reconsideration of their status.[78]

The Governor General however concluded the treaty of Purandhar with the Poona ministry in 1776. The treaty read out certain terms and conditions which were as follows. That Raghuba was to be pensioned off while Salsette and Baruch were to be left in the hands of the British. However, these conditions gave rise to newer disputes and there was also a looming threat of a French invasion which prompted the Bombay government to send Raghuba towards Poona. Madhava Rao Sindhia was the first to come to terms with the treaty in the year 1781, and some months later, Nana Fadnis also agreed to the treaty of Salbai in 1782. For twenty years from 1782–1803, the British and Maratha governments remained at peace.[79] The decade of 1780 thus witnessed the debut of Bombay as a military power and its garrison was greatly strengthened on the advice of Lord Clive and General Lawrence. Their suggestion was that Salsette and its outpost should be placed with a military force to check the enemies and help the merchants and the Bombay mint to get its supply of bullion without any delay or loss.[80]

The Population of Artisans in Bombay Town in 1780

Communities of Artisans	*Number of Members*
Goldsmiths	316
Ironsmiths	48
Coppersmiths	145
Weavers	151
Carpenters	125
Shoemakers	63
Pot-makers	62
Washermen	63
Tailors	228

The total Population of Bombay Artisans Communities = 1200.

The population of Bombay Island in 1780s had increased to at least 113,726.[81]

Edward Ives stated that the inhabitants of Bombay were numerous and made up of almost every nation in Asia.This increase was due to improved conditions and safety to life encouraged communities to come and settle on the town.[82]

An Estimate of Local Communities in Bombay

A special committee for the Bombay census was set up in 1780 to regulate its increasing population. The population of Bombay comprised of artisans and ethnic communities who had come to the Bombay town to trade and were also invited to develop the town with their skills. They were mostly craftsmen who contributed greatly in accelerating economic growth as well as development. Bombay's population was estimated to be nearly 113,726. George Edward Ives of Kent, who had come to Bombay in a mercenary service of a surgeon under Robert Clive, recorded that the inhabitants of Bombay were numerous and made up of almost every nation in Asia. Each year brought fresh and wealthier merchant settlers, who settled in the island of Bombay. Ships from every port, from China to Peru, could be found in the Bombay port.[83]

By 1780s the town of Bombay was populated with a number of Parsi businessmen and artisans, who had come to Bombay from Surat and invested their capital in the trade in Bombay. The town of Bombay developed, and Bombay agency houses were established in the last quarter of the eighteenth century. Large ships were built to promote trade with South-East Asian countries such as Japan, China, Malacca, Sumatra, Java, and Ceylon. Bombay under the presidency of the English power had to develop trade and earn good revenues as the government was interested in building larger vessels. This happened with the shift of Parsi traders and their capital from Surat to Bombay, adding more financial strength for trading and investing. Establishment of agency houses brought a revolution in the commercial sector of Bombay and helped in boosting the trade. This change helped in giving western India a dominant position in European and Asian trade, but the economic power in Bombay was concentrated in a few hands, especially the ship owners, merchants, and bankers.[84]

According to *Forbes* in 1783, the population of Bombay had increased dramatically since 1774.

Notes

1. G.W. Forrest, *Selection from the State Papers Preserved in the Bombay Secretariat*, Maratha Series, Bombay: Government Central Press, vol. I, Bombay, 1887, p. 83.
2. Lakshmi Subramaniam, 'Bombay and the West Coast in the 1740s', *The Indian Economic and Social History Review*, vol. XVIII, January–March 1981, pp. 190–2.

3. Ibid., p. 190.
4. *Public Department Diary*, Maharashtra State Archives, 15/B, 21 April 1742, p. 321.
5. *Public Department Diary*, Maharashtra State Archives, 14/C, 1741, p. 199.
6. *Public Department Diary*, Maharashtra State Archives, 14/C, 25 September 1741, p. 241.
7. *Public Department Diary*, Maharashtra State Archives, 15/C, 1742, p. 297.
8. Ashin Das Gupta, *The World of the Indian Ocean Merchant 1500–1800*, New Delhi: Oxford University Press, 2001, p. 315.
9. Subramanian, 'Bombay and the West Coast in the 1740s', pp. 212–13.
10. Asiya Siddiqi, 'The Business World of Jamsetjee Jeejeebhoy', in *Trade and Finance in Colonial India 1750–1860*, ed. Asiya Siddiqi, Delhi: Oxford University Press, 1995, p. 196.
11. Subramanian, 'Bombay and the West Coast in the 1740s', p. 196.
12. Das Gupta, *The World of the Indian Ocean Merchant 1500–1800*, pp. 330–1.
13. Forrest, *Selection from the State Papers Preserved in the Bombay Secretariat*, p. 243.
14. Subramaniam, 'Bombay and the West Coast in the 1740s', p. 193.
15. S.M. Edwardes, *The Gazetteer of Bombay City and Island*, vol. II, Bombay: Time Press, 1909, p. 280.
16. Ibid., pp. 193–4.
17. Ibid., p. 194.
18. Ibid., pp. 448–9.
19. Ibid., p. 450.
20. Ibid., p. 450.
21. Ibid., p. 450.
22. Ibid., pp. 450–51.
23. Pamela Nightingale, *Trade and Empire in Western India, 1784–1806*, Cambridge: Cambridge University Press, 1971, pp. 18–9.

24. Ibid., pp. 18–20.
25. *Gazetteer of the Bombay Presidency: Thana*, vol. XIII, Pune: Government Photozinco Press, 1882, p. 89.
26. Subramaniam, 'Bombay and the West Coast in the 1740s', p. 197.
27. Ibid., p. 497.
28. Ibid., p. 499.
29. *Public Department Diary*, Maharashtra State Archives, 45/I, 1765, p. 56.
30. *Public Department Diary*, Maharashtra State Archives, 15/I, 1741–2, p. 67.
31. Edwardes, *The Gazetteer of Bombay City and Island*, vol. 1, pp. 154–5.
32. Maharashtra State Archives, *Public Department Diary*, vol. 100, Bombay 1792, p. 21.
33. Forrest, *Selections from the Letters, Despatches and Other State Papers Preserved in the Bombay Secretariat*, p. 256.
34. Ibid., p. 274.
35. Ibid., p. 275.
36. Radha Kumud Mookerjee, 'Indian Shipping and Maritime Activity from the Earlier Times', *The Journal of Asian Studies*, ed. B.B. Mishra, vol. XX, November 1960, p. 129.
37. Forrest, *Selections from the Letters, Despatches and Other State Papers Preserved in the Bombay Secretariat*, p. 282.
38. B. Arunachalam, *Mumbai by the Sea*, Mumbai: Maritime History Society, 2004, pp. 166–7.
39. *Public Department Dairy*, Maharashtra State Archives, 34/1760, p. 156.
40. Ibid., pp. 156–7.
41. *Selections from State Papers*, Maratha Series, Maharashtra State Archives, 1885, p. xi–xii.
42. Edwards, *The Gazetteer of Bombay City and Island*, vol. 1, p. 155.
43. K.K. Chaudhari, *Maharashtra State Gazetteers*, Bombay Presidency, *Greater Bombay District*, Department of District Gazetteers, pp. 216–17.

44. *Gazetteer of the Bombay Presidency: Thana*, p. 500.
45. Edwardes, *The Gazetteer of Bombay City and Island*, vol. 1, p. 49.
46. Ibid., pp. 155–9.
47. Chaudhari, *Maharashtra State Gazeetteers*, p. 205.
48. *Public Department Diary*, Maharashtra State Archives, 16/1743, p. 19.
49. *Public Department Diary*, Maharashtra State Archives, 14/1740–41, p. 6.
50. *Public Department Diary*, Maharashtra State Archives, no. 65, 1774, pp. 421–3.
51. Ibid., pp. 68–9.
52. *Public Department Diary*, Maharashtra State Archives, no. 48, 28 April 1767, p. 294.
53. Chaudhari, *Maharashtra State Gazetteers, Greater Bombay District*, p. 363.
54. *Gazetteer of Bombay Presidency: Thana*, vol. XIII, Maharashtra State Archives, Pune: Government Photozinco Press, 1882, p. 50.
55. *Public Department Diary*, Maharashtra State Archives, 45/I, 1765, p. 56.
56. 'Bombay Mint, 150th Anniversary Celebrations', 1 May 1982, Bombay, p. 12.
57. Jadunath Sarkar, *Economics of British India*, Calcutta: Kunta Line Press, 1913, pp. 260–1.
58. Edwardes, *The Gazetteer of Bombay City and Island*, p. 282.
59. Najaf Haider, 'Precious Metal Flows and Currency Circulation in the Mughal Empire', *The Economic and Social History of the Orient*, vol. 39, no. 3, 1996, pp. 354–5.
60. Edwardes, *The Gazetteer of Bombay City and Island*, vol. II, p. 444.
61. *Public Department Diary*, Maharashtra State Archives, 14/1740–41, p. 68.
62. Holden Furber, *Bombay Presidency in the Mid-Eighteenth Century*, Bombay: Asia Publishing House, 1965, p. 53.

63. Subramanian, *Bombay and the West Coast in the 1740s*, p. 208.
64. Furber, *Bombay Presidency in the Mid-Eighteenth Century*, p. 54.
65. Ibid., pp. 56–8.
66. *Public Department Diary*, Maharashtra State Archives, 18/I, 1745, p. 31.
67. *Public Department Diary*, Maharashtra State Archives, 24/1, 1751, p. 87.
68. Ibid., p. 13.
69. *Public Department Diary*, Maharashtra State Archives, 41/II, 1763, p. 670.
70. Subramanian, 'Bombay and the West Coast in the 1740s', pp. 210–11.
71. Ibid., p. 214.
72. Forrest, *Selection from the State Papers Preserved in the Bombay Secretariat*, p. 256.
73. *Selections from Papers*, Maharashtra State Archives, Maratha Series, vol. II, 1885, p. xvi.
74. Chaudhari, *Maharashtra State Gazetteers*, p. 211.
75. Ibid., pp. 211–12.
76. J.H. Gense and D.R. Banaji, *The Gaikwads of Baroda*, vol. II, Bombay: D.B. Taraporevala Sons & Co., p. xvi.
77. Ibid., p. xiv.
78. Ibid., p. xiv.
79. *Imperial Gazetteer of India, Provincial Series-Bombay Presidency*, Calcutta: Superintendent of Government Printing, 1909, pp. 30–2.
80. Edwardes, *The Gazetteer of Bombay City and Island*, vol. II, p. 118.
81. Ibid., p. 156.
82. Ibid., p. 157.
83. Pamela Nightingale, *Trade and Empire in Western India; 1784–1806*, pp. 23–4.
84. Edwardes, *The Gazetteer of Bombay city And Island*, vol. 1, pp. 157–9.

FIVE

Bombay's Bullion Trade with Europe, China, and Japan, *c.*1780–1820

Bombay Town in the Last Quarter of the Eighteenth Century

Alexander Hamilton, an English official, provided valuable information on Bombay's trade in the 1780s. Merchants of Bombay traded with all the principal seaports on the west coast, namely Chaul, Surat, and Bhatkal, as well as the other interior towns of India. They extended their trading networks to the Persian Gulf, the African coast, Malacca, Singapore, Indonesia, other ports of South-East Asian countries such as China and Japan, and Europe. Through the Bombay port, trade was carried out by Indians and the British in these countries in the 1780s.

Bombay had three excellent docks and a spacious marine-yard, where teak ships of all sizes were made under the skilful supervision of Wadia master builders. The ship, *East Indiaman Earl of Balcarres*, built by the Wadias in 1810 in Bombay, weighed 1417 tons. Such ships carried cargoes between India and China.[1] During the last quarter of the 1780s, Bombay emerged as a port town of considerable significance with a population of more than 100,000 people. James Forbes (1766–83), author of the four volumes *Oriental*

Memoirs, described the town with its natural harbour, landing bay, and docking sites as 'one of the finest marts in India [which] employed a great number of vessels in its extensive commerce'. Ships could find safe anchorage even during the most tempestuous monsoons.[2] In 1766, *Forbes* recorded that Bombay's trade had greatly increased in the decade 1774–83. The political uncertainty in the mainland had brought people to Bombay. Provisions and supplies were plentiful, but prices were high and they doubled in a decade. The town had developed with the mushrooming of houses, and even vegetable and fruit gardens had sprouted in and around it.[3]

It had been remarked that Bombay's population had increased due to the flourishing commerce. The great famine of 1802–04, which resulted in the increase in population in the Bombay town by more than 160,000 people and approximately 200,000 in 1806, was due to merchants and traders pouring into Bombay town from the nearby areas and villages in search for food and relief from the famine. Bombay was prosperous city at the time and the people came with their goods to seek better opportunities as Bombay city was better developed.[4] Another reason for the increase in population in Bombay during 1806, was that the British colonial government had established relief camps in Bombay for the famine stricken areas and therefore people flocked to Bombay to take this relief provided by the British government.

The town of Bombay in the last quarter of the eighteenth century was considered an important financial trading centre of western India under the British government. Surat was an important supporting port for the trading operations at Bombay. It was mainly concerned with the trade with China. Ships were built at the Bombay port for carrying trading activities, especially long-distance trade, and the sizes of the ships were around one thousand tons, much larger than the ships which had dominated the fleet of India around the turn of the eighteenth century. Bombay Marine too was in control of the coastal waters, and the private English vessels carrying the English pass were well-protected.[5] The Arabs of Muscat, prominent in the Arabian Sea, were adept at navigating down the coast of Africa. So were the other Arabs from the Gulf and port of Hadhramaut.[6]

Bombay's Connection with Other Trading Towns in the Early Nineteenth Century

The trade in Bombay was connected directly to all minor and major ports on the western coast of India. These ports included Janjira, Shriwardhan, Harnai, Dabhol, Chaul, Bhatkal, Raigad, Ratnagiri, Vijaydurg, Malvan, and Panaji on the Konkan coast; Karwar, Mangalore, Calicut, Cochin, and Tuticorin on the west coast; and Madras and Calcutta on the east coast. The international trade carried through the Bombay port constituted almost two-thirds of the foreign trade from Bombay in totality. Modern-day Myanmar, Sri Lanka, Pakistan, Bangladesh, African countries, Australia, New Zealand, Canada, Far Eastern countries, United Kingdom, United States of America, Russia, West Germany, and many other American, Asian, and European countries were a part of the trade.[7]

Trade during the first decade of the eighteenth century, was at its peak. This increase in trade can be attributed to several factors. Bombay was located strategically on the west coast, allowing efficient trade with Europe and the Middle East. Many policies were introduced to promote trade and commerce in Bombay town. Bombay trade was confined chiefly to Asian countries in the first half of the nineteenth century. For several years, Bombay had passed into the possession of the East India Company and the internal trade in the island was hampered by lack of capital, external warfare, and naturally occurring epidemics.[8]

Maritime historian such as Blair and James Robertson, in their collection of primary sources, estimated that at least 50 tons of silver (2 million pesos) would be passed over the Pacific annually. Manila traded in silver and silk while Japanese silver flowed into China in exchange of Chinese gold. Over-issue of paper money in China had reduced the value of this fiduciary medium. Regular commerce required a medium of exchange to replace the worthless paper money, and hence, silver evolved as the metal of choice. Gold was too valuable for most ordinary transactions, but copper coinage was a candidate for monetary pre-eminence.[9] Geis explains how silver defeated copper in a passage worth quoting at length.

> The value of the coins lay in the metal, not in the mint. In that respect Copper coins were hardly different from silver; each was valued as a piece of precious metal. While silver could, if necessary be assayed for purity, Copper coins could not. To assay a copper coin entailed its destruction. The only way to ascertain the copper content was to melt the coin, and this would defeat, the purpose of coining money, but with coins of varying weight and metallic content in circulation, setting a price in copper coins became a tricky business. The rice merchants would have to specify what kind of copper coins he had in mind, each had a different value in the market place, and the price of the merchants rice depended on the type of coin offered in payment. How much simpler to set the price in silver, and that in fact is what happened. Silver came to be the preferred medium of valuation and exchange.[10]

Presence of Parsis in the Trading Activities of Bombay Town

The Indian mercantile community in Bombay in the early nineteenth century was dominated by the Parsi community as it appears and they played a very significant role as brokers to the British and contributed to the development and building of the economy of Bombay.

The Parsis were the largest land owners of Bombay and Salsette and many had acquired their property as inam grants in the eighteenth and early nineteenth centuries. They also received rewards in wealth and Prestige for their service to the Company. Besides being prominent land owners, they were also the leading merchants of Bombay and worked as a guarantee brokerage of European merchants, in the banking commission business and also had interlinked overseas trade activities as ship owner and ship agency and insurance.

The Court of Directors of the East India Company considered the Bombay port as one of the most important trading destinations and financial centres in western India. Charles Forbes described the Parsi merchants of Bombay as 'great traders', who traded with foreign countries and made profits.

During the eighteenth century, a very large number of Parsis immigrated to Bombay due to the development of the Bombay port and its trading connection with other port towns. In the 1780s the number of Parsis in Bombay was 3,000. In 1790, however, Gujarat underwent serious famines due to which a large number of people migrated to Bombay. Parsis became rich there and prospered as ship-builders, ship-owners, businessmen and also as property-holders in the nineteenth century. By 1811, their number increased to 10,000.[11]

The Parsis assumed dominance in the trading world and primarily conducted trade with China from the principal ports of Bombay, Daman, Calcutta, and Karachi. Hirji Jivanji and his brother Manekji are acknowledged to be the first Parsis to visit China in 1756. The duo established a firm in Canton, the only port open to the foreigners. Peston Coswaji Sethna established Cowasji Pallanji & Co. in 1794, one of the first Parsi firms in Canton, and he died in Macao in 1842. Chinese trade, of which opium consisted the greatest proportion, offered financial foundations for many of the major Parsi businessmen in the nineteenth century.[12]

The Wadias were the master-builders of the Company ships. Nusservanji Manockji Bomanji (1766–1814), Pestonji Bomanji (1754–1816), and Hormusji Bomanji (1766–1826) belonged to the third generation of Wadias. They were the first to take to trading and worked as an agency for the British Company Forbes & Co.[13] Under the British, Bombay became the chief maritime province and trading route for commodity movement prior to exportation. The town also had an excess of imports over exports.[14]

The most noteworthy members of the Parsi community were Ruston Dorabji, the Patels of Bombay, and Lowji Nassarwanji Wadia, the master-builder of the Bombay dockyard.[15] Dadabhai Pestonji Wadia (1802–85) is counted among the greatest merchants of his times. The family of Manakji Nassarvanji Petit traded with China and Britain. By the early nineteenth century, the property owned by Dadabhai Pestonji Wadia earned almost 125,000 rupees every year as rent from his landed property.[16]

Jamshetji Jejeebhoy (1783–1859) was one of the most prominent Indian merchants of Bombay and earned the title—the most prosperous Parsi merchant in Bombay. Jamshetji Jejeebhoy was the first Parsi trader who made five personal trips to China in 1807 and established a commercial family business empire from the trade. In 1814, he purchased his first ship named *Good Success*, followed by six more ships and the chartering of others as the volume of his trade increased.[17] Jejeebhoy traded in cotton from Madras and opium from Calcutta to China. He had trade relations in Canton and urged his agent, James Matheson, who controlled the most powerful agency houses at Canton to send sycee—ingots of Chinese silver—in payments. On the other hand, Jamshetji began exporting Chinese tea and silk to London.[18]

Establishment of European Agency Houses in Bombay and other British Presidencies

The engagement in private trade by the Company's employees was prohibited in the 1780s. These employees belonged to both Indian and foreign nationalities. Prohibition on these employees in 1780s against the Company's monopoly threw open the entry for the private merchants of London and other participants to join this venture.[19] The European traders, trading either on their personal or Company's account, were greatly dependent on Indian intermediaries—Shroffs or financiers and *gumastas* or agents—who procured goods from the interior, often by financing production through the putting-out system. Procurement of prices were often fixed before the sale took place.[20]

Agency houses or private Europeans firms which dominated Bombay's Asian trade included Bruce, Fawcett & Co., Forbes & Co., John Leckie & Co., and S. Beaufort & Co. The business proved to be extremely lucrative, particularly where firms were themselves in ownership of ships which carried goods.[21] In Bombay, David Scott was a private trader who had made a fortune through the agency business. Another important private businessman was Charles Cockerel from Calcutta who supported the growth of the empire in India. However, later, he went against the Company's rule and was not in favour of the Company as a regulator of trade. Charles Forbes was one of the founders of the Bombay firm or agency house known as the Forbes. The credit of having the first agency house in India belongs to John Forbes as he founded his Forbes & Company Ltd, in 1767.[22] It remained the only European mercantile firm in western India until 1790, when Bruce Fawcett & Co., another agency house, came into existence and both firms worked closely with each other and joined hands to monopolize the trade in certain commodities such as cotton and opium. The main operations of Forbes and Co., were agency business, shipping, moneylending and general trading.[23]

The European merchants held the key post in the Government of Bombay; Patrick Crawford Bruce and Henry Fawcett, senior partners of Bruce, Fawcett & Co. were Accountant General and Mayor of the town of Bombay.[24] Bruce and Fawcett & Co., was founded in 1790 and later, Forbes and James Campbell spent the better part of their careers as politicians in Britain fighting against the monopoly charter. The founder of Paxton, Cockerel & Co. was William Paxton, a soldier and mariner by profession who joined the Company's service as an assayer of gold and silver. Paxton joined Charles Cockerel as a partner and made large amounts of money, culminating their careers as prominent merchant-bankers in London. Paxton was the great grandfather of Archibald Wavell, one of the last Viceroys of India. Palmer & Co., the largest agency house in 1830, was established by William Palmer, a Company officer and a contemporary of Hastings.[25]

Agency houses were established with the support of Indian merchants and entrepreneurs. The firm had numerous Parsee brokers who helped the agency house in its transactions with Indian and foreign merchants. Brokers and agents also looked after the firm which was located in China, which dealt in the opium business and this trade in opium was very profitable and most of the mercantile firms in Bombay traded in it in some way. Charles Forbe was against this lucrative trade in principle and thus opium never became a major commodity of trade of the Forbes trading operations.[26]

In Bombay, Jamshetjee Jeejeebhoy formed a partnership with Charles Forbes and became the chief agent of Jardine-Matheson, the agency house of Canton. It was not only merchants who came to India to trade after 1813 but other skilled professional workers like artisan-entrepreneurs too came. A number of tanneries and glass works, iron smelting, and carpentry workshops too were established. In Bombay, Madras, and Calcutta, artisans and manufacturers of almost every trade could be found. These developed into centres of artisan enterprise, which grew into factories after 1850. For example, in Howrah, shipyards and warehouses had begun to develop even before the jute factories.[27]

Bullion and Financing of Trade in Bombay

Throughout India, silver was the chief measure of value, and the silver rupee came to be commonly exchanged as currency. Many traders engaged in the practice of debasing coin and rulers issued rupees of different measuring weights and fineness.[28] It is seen that the Bombay rupee was in great demand throughout western India. From Sind to Travancore, nearly all business was done using the Bombay rupee, of which the sterling equivalent in the 1780s was two shillings and three pence. In Bengal, the dominant coin was the sicca rupee, worth keeping in their books in terms of an imaginary coin; the current rupee, of which the sterling equivalent was about two shillings, was defined as 16 per cent below the standard of the sicca rupee. This indicates the superior quality of the sicca rupee. Madras was the land of the Arcot rupee, however, so many other rupees were also in use in south India.

In 1784 European enterprises were doing business very differently. It was carried out using gold coins—which is a 'star' pagoda valued at about eight shillings. The intrinsic values of sicca rupee, Bombay rupee, and 'star' pagoda in terms of sterling were 24.5659 pence, 24.4745 pence, and 84.5304 pence respectively. Samples of these coins were regularly sent to London for assaying.[29] The suppliers received an advance, which would apply to the keepers of the East India Company's cash chest for the requisite silver Arcot rupees or gold pagodas. Most of these coins were fresh from the Company's own mint; the visitors could adjourn to see the European assay masters or the Indian mint contractors at work with their attendant goldsmiths and coiners.[30]

During the ten trading seasons from 1783–93, the invoiced value of goods exported from India to London by the English East India Company amounted to £10,284,479. The invoiced values of goods exported on the Company's ship was in 'private and privilege'. This meant that the company had the exclusive rights to trade in certain goods or in certain areas, and had the priviledge to charge higher prices for those goods. Some items were for personal consumption and were priviledged and exempted from custom duty as they belonged to the East India Company officials. It included Chinese items with Indian items but was separated from the total and invoiced values which shared the same relationship between sale values and invoiced values. Items such as gold and silver are known; they were imported in India by the Company. The figures for goods and base metals and for bullion were £2,208,979 and £721,914 (in silver) respectively. These base metals, a little less expensive, included copper, tin, iron, and zinc, as opposed to valuable and expensive bullion and noble metals such as silver and gold.[31]

Bullion Used for Carrying Out Warfare Campaigns

The outbreak of war between Tipu Sultan of Mysore and the British forced the import of bullion into India, in order to buy warfare materials and pay soldiers.[32] The second Anglo-Mysore War began in 1780 and continued till 1792. Consequently, the demand for bullion in the country increased. In 1790, silver, valued at £70,000, was removed from the Company's China-bound ships at Madras to ensure that the war against Tipu Sultan was not impeded. This happened again in 1805–6 when Lord Cornwallis was seeking an 'extraordinary resource' that would enable him to pay his troops. In 1805, Lord Cornwallis ordered that 789,768 ounces of silver, invoiced at £202,281 and destined for Canton, be removed from the Company's ships at Madras; in the following year, 505,298 dollars were removed from another China-bound ship at Penang in Malaysia and sent to Calcutta.[33]

The dispatch of silver to India after 1785 was intended for commercial purposes. For instance, in 1786, 1803, and 1804, the directors ordered that shipments sent to Bombay be directed towards Canton for the purchase of raw cotton. Consignments were sent to other locations because wars in India created the need for bullion. Thus, the Company was in acute shortage of silver. In 1793 it was reported that the Company's treasure in Calcutta had no silver due to the Governor General Richard Wellesley's (1798–1805) involvement in the Anglo-Mysore war and Second Anglo-Maratha war, which required large sums of bullion to pay the Garrisons and therefore silver had to be transferred from London. In June 1799, £200,000 of silver had to be divided between Madras and Bombay for purposes of commercial investment, and £700,000 in gold had also been sent for general use due to the shortage of silver as it was being used to finance military warfare.[34]

Between 1802–5, the total amount of silver sent to India amounted to almost £3.5 million. The Court of Director of the East India Company acknowledged that the new Governor General, Lord Cornwallis, was facing great difficulty while paying the large number of regular and irregular troops employed in his campaigns in the second Anglo-Maratha war. The funds were scarce, and the Company had to find measures to fulfil this acute shortage. As a result, consignments of silver amounting to £500,000 were sent to Bengal in 1806. Exports of silver ceased after 1808 due to the war strategy adopted by Wellesley and the heavy maintenance of military expenditure during the third and final Anglo-Maratha War of 1817–8.[35] During this financial crisis, Forbes and Co., jointly with Bruce Fawcett & Co., supplied huge sums of money to the East India Company government at low rates of interest during the period of wars with the Marathas from 1799–1806.

European activity in 'country trade' unquestionably stimulated an excess of exports in silver and goods from India to China after 1770. After this period, exports of bullion almost ceased. The factors responsible for the slowing down of bullion export from India are too many. The most important reasons for the decline of bullion were the French

Revolution and the American Revolution, which broke out in the last quarter of the eighteenth century. Following these developments, silver began to flow back from China to India.[36]

Scarcity of Silver Supply and the Suspension of the Bombay Rupee during 1780–1800

The silver rupee coins minted at the Bombay Mint were very popular as they contained more silver and less alloy than the coins minted at the Surat Mint. The Bombay rupee weighed 178.314 grains of silver and contained 1.24 per cent of alloy. In comparison, the Mughal rupee coin minted at the mint of Surat contained alloy of 15 per cent. These differences in the minting of rupees led to many crimes such as debasing of coins and forgery. Some people made large profits by melting Bombay rupees and getting them minted at the Surat Mint. To curb this malpractice and on account of scarcity of silver in Bombay, causing problem at the Bombay Mint, the Bombay rupee was suspended from 1780–1800.[37]

The twenty-year-long suspension of the Bombay rupees in Bombay town introduced the gold rupees and coins for circulation. The scarcity of silver was clearly a consequence of India's new role as the principal clearing house for Britain's international payments. Bullion flow was an important trading item in the late eighteenth and early nineteenth centuries, as it was required for international monetary transactions as a direct medium of payments. The transfer of bullion was often necessary to carry out business transaction. Moreover, the value of bills was always reckoned in terms of its actual return in bullion. 'Bullion', thus declared the prominent merchant and banker, John Horsley Palmer, 'is the regulator of every description of trade throughout the world.'[38]

The English Company began to ship silver from Bengal for the purchase of its cargoes of tea and silk in China, in addition to supplying silver to its establishments in Madras and Bombay. For the Bombay government, silver shortage thus created major problems in finding a medium to receive the revenues and to pay its servants and garrisons. Therefore, a gold currency was introduced in the town of Bombay. The introduction of overvalued gold coins aggravated the scarcity of silver. Undervalued silver coins began to be melted down and exported. It became evident that the over-valuation of the old coin would cut into the Company's finances.[39]

A measure was already taken in 1792 to tackle the scarcity and extend the circulation of the sicca rupees. The English government put a restriction on the absorption of gold. Later in 1806, silver was declared the uniform standard value in India. Twelve years later in 1818, the gold pagoda, which was made the principal coin of the south India, was withdrawn and silver rupee was substituted and legally declared as currency.[40] The next reform in the currency was introduced in 1835 as the Company's rupee of 180 grains.

British Private Exports of Silver to Asia, 1791–1806

Silver was exported on private account by the ship commanders, crew, and passengers on board, especially East Indian men who had the opportunity to carry silver legally and illegally to Asia for their own use. For example, Major General Claude Martin, the remarkable French officer in the East India Company who was in the service of the Nawab of Awadh at Lucknow, exported large amounts of indigo through his agents, William and Thomas Raikes & Co., in London. He settled his accounts by sending quantities of silver in return from London in 1793. Martin received 31,314 ounces of silver from London, and in 1795–6, he acknowledged the receipt of 70,000 silver dollars which came in twenty-four chest boxes.

In 1803, Archibald Hamilton carried over 37,000 Spanish dollars valued at £8,058 to Bombay. Two years later, he shipped nine chests of silver dollars to Bombay that had been purchased for £10,000. On the first occasion, Charles Forbes & Co. paid Hamilton a sum of Spanish dollars that was equivalent to £10,742; and on the second, the leading Parsi merchant and ship builder, Pestonji Bomanji paid him a sum equivalent to £12,458. This transaction makes it evident that there was a steady flow of private silver from Britain to Asia. A considerable export of silver from London to Bengal, Bombay, Madras, and Canton took place between 1791 and 1806.

Imports and Exports in the East India Company's Trade

According to Sir John Shore's testimony in his famous fifth minute (1787), 'The Company is Merchants as well as Sovereigns of the country.' The earlier English merchants which traded with the Persian Gulf and the Far East, would in return bring large quantities of bullion such as silver and gold. B.N. Ganguli, an eminent economist, raised the following question—if India was prosperous as a sink of precious metals before the period of the British rule, how could she be in the face of the inflow of bullion after 1801? The import of bullion was chiefly attributed to commercial and financial necessities.

European ships carried cargoes between India and ports of Europe, China, Japan, and South America. Bombay developed in the last quarter of the eighteenth century as one of the most important centres of trade and ship-building.

The Bombay Marine was created by the East India Company to meet the early threats from the Portuguese and Malabar pirates. Moreover, Bombay was the most suitable centre from where the commercial activities could be controlled and marine operations at the Gulf of Cambay, the coast of Konkan, and the Malabar region could be supervised. Since the Surat dock was taken over by the British and transferred to Bombay, it became the most important English base to check piracy and piratical menaces.[41]

The Charter Act of 1813

When the Charter of the East India Company was renewed in 1813, an allocation of a portion of its budget for the revival and improvement of the East India Company Charter was undertaken.[42] The Charter Act had initiated an era of free trade result of which Bombay became an international entrepot with its trade thrown open to the world. Governor Mountstuart Elphinstone promoted the expansion of Bombay's trade which was then mainly in cotton.[43] During the period between 1801–63, the net imports of bullion was £234,353,686. The period 1864–69 saw net imports of bullion amounting to £101,123,448. The coinage in India between 1801–69 was about £266 million. Bombay became an important maritime province and terminal point in the routes of commodity transportation; its strategic location connected it to many other different parts of the world.[44]

The Company looked for a suitable base which would protect its China-bound ships passing through the Straits of Malacca, a vital bottle neck for trade with East Asia. Another powerful competitor—the Dutch—had disrupted the passage to Sumatra through the Strait which was the shortage connection to other Asian trading ports in 1784.

The port of Calcutta, which had trade relations with Ache, was also disrupted by the French as they had the permission to use the port of Acche. Calcutta was under the East India Company's rule while Acche was controlled by the French, who through Acche sought to control the Bay of Bengal during the monsoon.[45]

The English East India Company won the contest for India, which was denoted by the signing of the Treaty of Paris between the United Kingdom and United State of America, Holland, and Spain on 9 April 1784. This treaty made Britain the only major European power in Asia. The English East India Company's trading activities in China earned them sufficient silver to sustain the balance of payments with China's trade and made India a base for opium supply to China.[46]

Dr Asiya Siddiqi has rightly pointed out the contrast between the policy of encouraging gold absorption till 1792 and discouraging it thereafter. Thus, duties were imposed on the import of gold in 1792, and later in 1800; the weight of the Bombay gold coin was also changed in order to bring it to parity with the debased silver rupees. In 1801, the same presidency issued low-denomination gold coins to supplement the silver currency.[47]

In 1800, the English government ordered the Surat rupee to be struck in Bombay, and since then, the rupee was maintained at an equal value in the mints of Surat and Bombay. It weighed 179 grains and contained 7.97 per cent of alloy. The purity of the rupee was considered to be far superior as it had fewer alloys in it. In the year 1806, the dispatch was in favour of a single standard value of silver. 'We are by no means, desirous of checking the circulation of gold currency, but of establishing a gold coin on a standard fitted for general use. This coin in our opinion should be called gold rupees'.[48]

Gold Coins Minted in Various Presidencies in the Early Nineteenth Century

Table 5.1: Gold Coins Minted in Bengal, Madras and Bombay in the Early Nineteenth Century.

Year Range (May–April)	*Location*	*Value of gold (in £s)*	*Percentage of coinage by value*
1802–9	Bengal	93,220	0.88
1810–18	Bengal	1,063,315	6.04
1819–20	Bengal	90,077	1.46
1821–30	Bengal	1,2,785	8.55
1808–9	Madras	171,515	16.04
1810–11	Madras	453,600	40.00
1812–17	Madras	608,323	30.33
1818–20	Madras	855,937	43.46
1802–10	Bombay	744,961	56.92
1811–14	Bombay	1,041,266	52.73
1816–20	Bombay	383,970	52.90
1823	Bombay	36	1.46

Source: Bombay Mint, 150th Anniversary Celebrations, Bombay: published by Bombay Mint, 1 May 1982, p. 366.

Asiya Siddiqi contends that during the crisis of the Napoleonic wars, Britain was in the most advantageous position of being able to draw on the bullion resources from the East; it was also resourceful in bringing in the precious metals. On the other hand, Britain focused its attention on the Napoleonic wars, as the French regiments were very competent and challenged the English supremacy. The consequence of the Company's monetary policy was that the silver continued to be absorbed in India, while gold imports were induced to England at a time when the reserves of gold were very low and conditions had been fostered to divert it from India. This was done with the intention to control the bullion market. It was mainly to put a halt on gold payments by the Bank of England in the years 1797–1821, a period when gold reserves were being observed with great anxiety. This anxiety was particularly acute when bank notes became scarce after 1816; the Bank of England was enlarging its bullion reserve in order to resume gold payments.[49] Siddiqi further explains that India was supporting the British bullion market and helping the British to strengthen their economy and trade in various commodities.

Table 5.2: India's Bullion Trade: Annual Average Value (in pounds)

Year Range	*Exports*	*Net Imports*
1802–10	26	2493
1811–18	84	2456
1819–20	543	5883
1821–26		
1826–7		
1830–3		

Source: Srinivas Ambiraj, 'Political Economy and Monetary Management: India, 1766–1914', The Economic History Review, vol. 39, vol-1, Cumbria: Wiley, 1986, p. 154.

The above table reflects a crisis in the period between 1830–3. During the years 1825–6 and 1826–7, India was a net importer of bullion to the value of £4,996,000, while its total exports to all other countries came down to £791,000.[50]

The following table exhibits the scheme of the British Indian monetary system as it exists currently. Although the gold coins and copper anna form the subdivisions in the scheme of the

British Indian currency, the coin denominated 'pie' had no place in the monetary system of India prior to 1827.[51]

Crisis in the Minting of Bombay Rupees

The Bombay Governor, Jonathan Duncan passed an order in 1800 stating that the mint of Bombay would mint coins containing 15 grains of silver each, which represented one coin of gold. However, a year later in 1801, a shortage in the Bombay rupees was noticed due to the shortage in the supply of silver in the town of Bombay. This crisis resulted in the introduction of new gold coins to be circulated. In 1815, the English government ordered the abolition of the Surat mint and the coinage of the English presidency came to be conducted at the mint of Bombay. In 1827, copper pie was introduced in Bombay, and it weighed 33.5 grains, equal to one twelfth of an 'anna'.[52]

The process of coinage in India was made uniform in 1835. The English East India Company's rupee was ordered to take the place of the Mughal sicca rupee of Surat, but there was a considerable difference between the Company's rupee and the sicca rupee. The latter contained 8 per cent more silver than the former. In 1841, a two-anna silver piece was introduced, and a proclamation was made to regulate the minting of gold coins, making it compulsory to bear on the obverse the face of Queen Victoria and on the reverse, a figure of a lion and a palm tree with the designation, 'The East India Company'. This proved that the English East India Company was the most influential and powerful body among the European powers, particularly superseding the prominence of the Portuguese.

Another change in the Bombay Mint took place in the year 1844; this pertained to the minting of copper coins.[53]

These changes in Indian coinage became a subject of debate, and many reconstructions came to be suggested in the following years—1812, 1827, and again in 1869. When decimal coinage was at its peak, the rupee still remained the medium of exchange and constituted the legal money in which all payments were to be made in this realm. Every rupee loan which the government of India contracted and every currency note which was issued were promises to pay the owner in silver rupee.[54]

The following table represents the Bombay currency alongside with the imaginary coins which existed in 1802:

Table 5.3: Value of the Imaginary Coins which Existed along with the Bombay Currency in the Year 1802

Imaginary Coins	*British Currency*
2 reas	1 urdee
4 reas	1 doganey or single pice
6 reas or 3 urdee	1 dorea
8 reas or 4 urdee	1 Fuddea or double pice
3 1/8 Fuddea pice	1 anna
12 ½ pice or 4 annas	1 quarter rupee
25 pice or 8 annas	1 half rupee
50 pice or 16 annas	1 rupee
5 rupees or 80 annas	1 pauchea
15 rupees	1 mohur

2 Reas, 1 Anna and 1 quarter-rupee were imaginary, in accounts the coins were confined to the following
100 reas = 1 quarter
4 quarters = 1 rupee.

Source: Dennis O. Flynn and Arturo Giraldez, 'Born with a "Silver Spoon": The Origin of World Trade in 1571', Metals and Monies in an Emerging Global Economy, ed. Dennis O. Flynn and Arturo Giraldez, An Expanding World, vol. 14, USA: Ashgate Publishing Company, 1997, pp. 269–71.

Accounts were kept in rupees, quarters, and reas. The Indian currency then was of exactly the same denomination and value as at present. The East India Company's rupee was ordered to take the place of the sicca rupee in all contracts under the orders issued in 1795. The East India Company's rupee thus became the current medium. The difference between the sicca rupee and the company's rupee was that the former contained 8 per cent more silver than the latter.[55]

Bombay Mint in the 1850s

Coins of various sizes were minted for use in the territories of the East India Company until 1835, when an order for universal coinage in gold and silver was issued. This uniform coinage was introduced for all the English possessions to have uniformity in coins having the name and images of English monarchs so that they could succeed in eliminating all the Mughal coins which were still in circulation in the English territories. This order was undertaken by James Princep, the then Assay Master of the mint in Benares and later, Calcutta Mint. The silver rupee coin of 1835 had a portrait of the English King William IV, who was on the throne of the United Kingdom of Great Britain and Ireland. Although the East India Company came to an end in 1858, the coins continued to bear the designs and title of the Company till 1862.[56] The rupees minted in Bombay were of pure silver and bore the portraits or busts of the English sovereign. When silver rupee was short in supply, gold rupee was minted in its stead. The Bombay Mint was the only place in the country where gold was refined. Therefore, bullion was imported to Bombay from other countries for minting, jewellery-making, and financial transactions.[57]

English Trading Company in Canton (China)

Silver was used as a medium of monetary exchange and also as a repository of wealth in China from the beginning of the imperial epoch. This white metal was in high demand which was noted by nearly all foreign commentators of the Chinese world from the sixteenth to eighteenth centuries. Manuel de Comarda de Noronha, a Captain General of Macao in the 1630s, recorded, 'when the Chinese smell silver, they will bring mountains of merchandise.' It was believed that silver became a craze for the people of China, especially at the turn of the seventeenth century.[58] 'The Chinese are very skilful in judging at sight the finest silver, and are scarcely ever deceived'. This was quoted by a traveller and Jesuit father, Jean Baptiste Du Halde who was in China in the late seventeenth and early eighteenth centuries.[59] Thus, silver and copper came to be used as mediums of exchange in China under the Ming dynasty. Silver was also the preferred currency of travellers and traders. It was also considered to be a stable currency, less susceptible to inflationary pressures.[60]

China became the global centre for silver under the Qing dynasty (1644–1911). After the decline of Potosi silver from the Andes mine, the demand came to be fulfilled by the Peruvian mines in 1640s and accounted for 60 per cent of world's silver production in the late sixteenth and seventeenth centuries. Europeans played an important role in the Sino-Japanese silver trade, and Japan soon emerged as the main supplier of silver to China. It established a commercial capitalism in Asia due to its rich silver mines and earning huge profits by exporting to other regions, especially China.[61]

Chinese trade destroyed the financial stability of the Ming emperors (1368–1644). Formerly, the Chinese paid their taxes in rice which was later converted to a fixed quantity of silver payable to the government. This created an upheaval among the poor agricultural peasants since paying taxes in silver resulted in a decline in their purchasing power. The new policy thus contributed to the overthrow of the Ming dynasty. The poor conditions of living must have affected the Chinese people, having to lead lives marked by depression and poverty. This in turn led to the increased use of opium in an attempt to forget about their debts and sorrow. This is how opium contributed to the Chinese social life by ensuing an addiction among people. It also played an important role for the British government in earning revenues. Opium was shipped from Bombay and Calcutta in exchange of tea, silk, porcelain ware, and jade.[62]

The Portuguese, while going from Macau in China to Japan, carried white silk, gold, musk, and porcelain in order to bring silver in return. They would fill their ships with the chest of white metals almost above 6,000 cruzados (approximately 17,000 kg.) and use this metal to strengthen the country's economy. By 1638, the economy under the Ming dynasty underwent disastrous consequences. China faced an insurmountable shortage of silver because of the rapidly decreasing copper-silver exchange rate. Many people in China faced immense difficulties in paying taxes and rent, repaying loans, and the general incapacity to buy basic necessities, even food, all due to the scarcity of silver.[63]

The British traded with China in commodities such as tea, silk, porcelain, imports of bullion, especially silver, woollen textiles, and opium from Bengal in India.[64] Current-day Guangzhou, formerly known as Canton, was the first trading port open to Europeans. The trade in China was commissioned by the Chinese government; a group of Chinese merchant families was formed to act as brokers superintending the foreign traders. Their responsibilities were to look after European ships and to be their security merchants. These merchants formed a guild called the *cohong* ('hong', referring to trading firms).[65]

In the 1780s, Britain was running up a serious trade deficit while the Chinese government was busy celebrating the addiction the British developed to their tea; the Chinese seemed to want very little besides silver in return. From 1780–90, the trade profit between India and China failed to make even a dent of £2 million out of £28 million. Between 1752–1800, 105 million silver dollars (approximately £ 26.25 million) flowed into China while 384 million travelled in the opposite direction to London.[66]

Opium and Chinese Silver: British Trading Payments

A major interest in the trade of opium was taken by the agency houses in the early quarter of the nineteenth century. Opium, especially, was used by the English Company to pay its bills in India or London. Specially designed ships were used for opium transportation. The sellers either drew bills against silver or paid for opium. By drawing bills in Canton, the merchants could safely remit their money to Bombay or London, whereas the Company received silver which was then used to buy Chinese tea. Ships sailed from Bombay to China carrying opium and cloth and carried silk, tea, silver, and porcelain wares in return. Therefore, the pirates in the Indian Ocean became interested in the precious metals that these ships often carried.[67]

Chinese consumers increasingly developed a taste for Indian opium over the preceding couple of decades. Between 1752 and 1800, a net of 105 million silver dollars (approximately £26.25 million) flowed into China, while between 1808 and 1856, 384 million travelled in the opposite direction. The balance apparently tipped by booming opium imports. From 1800–18, the average annual traffic held steady at around 4,000 chests (each chest containing around 140 pounds of opium); by 1831, it was nearing 20,000 chests. After 1833, when the free trade lobby terminated the East India Company's monopoly on the tea trade, the market was flooded by private merchants hungry for tea and profits. The greater part of the profits fell into the pockets of the British government, whose agents in India controlled the opium production and helped in transporting the drug to China. The British government succeeded in the accumulation of silver and its diversion to India, thereby making profits at the cost of India and China.[68]

The Company washed its hand off the policy, letting private merchants sail for the Chinese coast, where they anchored off the Island of Linton. Eager Chinese wholesalers would then use silver to buy certificates from private trading offices in Canton and exchange them for opium. This silver would then secure tea for the English market. The threat posed by opium to political stability was thus intensified by the government's financial worries. The early decades of the nineteenth century was a period of rising opium consumption. The Chinese empire seemed to run out of silver, which was apparently vanishing. The independence movement, both in India and China, caused an estimated decline of 56.6 per cent in the silver production relative to the 1790s.[69]

As long as both Indian cloth and Chinese tea were paid for with silver bullion acquired in Spain, India and China trades did not directly interact. But when the flow of silver became uncertain during the American War of Independence, the Company needed to find ways of paying for tea with Indian goods. By the end of the eighteenth century, Indian opium provided a solution to the British government through its exports from Malwa, Daman, and Diu via Bombay port to China. This is how Bombay became the most important trading port, carrying trade across the Indian Ocean to other countries.[70]

From 1801 until the close of the East India Company's reign in 1858, commerce persisted between Bombay and China. Opium played an important role in the bullion transfers too, primarily silver and gold, which gave rise to 4 million rupees in the first decade, 22 million in the 1840s, and then fell to 17 million in 1850s. After the British victory, Bombay received the bulk of recorded bullion shipments. However, things changed dramatically in the 1820s as Bombay increasingly surpassed Calcutta in bullion remittances.[71]

This suggests that the greater part of private returns from the opium trade went to the mercantile communities in western India. The bullion financed profits and investments in opium for the next season in that region. The profits were used to buy silver which flowed from Canton to London sent by British trading firms such as Jardine Matheson and others. By 1830, these shipments had reached 6.7 million Mexican silver dollars per year. These rising bullion imports were more important than it appeared. The opium trade gave India a new source of precious metals and was, in fact, its primary source of gold and silver in the early nineteenth century. North American silver flowed through China to India. India's silver rupee coinage relied heavily on shipments of bullion from China to offset the outflow of bullion as a tribute to Britain. From the days of Robert Clive, British rule reversed the usual flow of precious metals in the world economy. During the early years of the nineteenth century, India was maintaining a positive balance of trade and services with China, which was one of the repositories of the new world precious metals. Europe paid bullion for Indian goods in return.[72]

The mid-eighteenth-century conquest of Bengal in 1757 gave access to an enormous quantity of precious metals. It was not necessary any more to ship coins and bullion from England to Bengal for the purpose of buying goods for export. The revenue from Bengal alone now could provide the funds necessary for this purchase. At the same time, the East India Company started carrying silver from Bengal to avail the supplies of tea and silk in China.[73]

The East India Company could stop importing precious metals to pay for its commercial purchases and use state revenues instead, but Britain extracted tribute from India that was eventually settled in flows of precious metals to England. For example, in the year 1828–9, India shipped 3.1 million rupees of bullion to Britain as payment of the Company's obligation to remit private British savings and to transfer the investment profits. This is reflected in the Indian debt which rose from £15.6 million in 1800 to £67.5 million in 1857.[74]

Economic historians such as K.N. Chaudhari, Tapan Raychaudhuri, and C.A. Bayly maintain that India had entered an economic slump by 1820, which culminated in the financial crisis of the early 1830s. This can be assessed from how the credits were tight, the prices slumped, and the production fell. Throughout the nineteenth century, Chinese bullion strengthened India's monetary reserves, improved its liquidity, and paid a part of the costs of empire to Britain. Silver from China fed the Indian mints as they turned the metals into millions of rupees, each containing 165 grains of pure silver (in a *tola* of 180 grains).[75]

China, an Important Trading Centre of the English Company

During the eighteenth century the Qing Empire of China was ruled by the Qianlong emperor (1736–95). In Qianlong's reign the economy appeared to be thriving. Commerce was well developed and Guangzhou emerged as an important Chinese maritime port. By the eighteenth century, the most important participant in the trade was Great Britain. The British trade was monopolized by the East India Company—it handled the tea trade, China's most substantial export. The British trade with China compromised the exchange of Chinese tea for British woollen and metal goods.

By the 1760s the value of tea exports greatly exceeded British imports and the balance had to be made up with silver metal. In 1784 the British government passed the Commutation Act, which cut tea duties sharply. Consequently, the demand for tea increased and tea duties continued to provide a large proportion of the British government's revenue. To balance the trading deficit, raw cotton was exported from India to China on 'country ships' owned by private British merchants.[76] Maritime trade was confined to Guangzhou, and the participation of Chinese people was restricted only to groups of merchants known as *cohong* to Westerners. As they were responsible for the debts of foreign merchants, they protected themselves by setting aside a share of their profits in what was known as the *consoo* fund. Foreign traders were subjected to various regulations such as they could not bring guns and women to the city and could only reside in Guangzhou during the trading season.[77]

Relations between British and Chinese merchants were friendly until an incident in 1784 disturbed the peace and strained the relationship. A British merchant ship, *The Lady Hughes*, fired a salute, accidently killing two Chinese officials and wreaking havoc. Later, the smuggling of opium into China by the British created an interest in the Chinese to trade with them. With the import of lower priced Bengal opium into China, by the 1820s, the value of this opium was so high that the balance of trade was paid off in silver metal. It became a cause for concern for the Chinese government as the silver being drained out from China caused the poor peasants trouble in paying their land tax in silver. [78]

William Jardine was one of the most notable opium traders in China. British private traders like him managed silver imports from Japan, silver production in Latin America, copper cash production in China while tackling debasement, hoarding, and world trade depression simultaneously. Under the Guangzhou system, the East India Company and its private traders like William Jardine, Matheson & Co., importers of opium, began to export tea and silk as well.[79] Five important ports were opened to conduct this opium trade; they were Xiamen, Fuzhou, Ningbo, and Shanghai, along with Guangzhou and Nanjing.[80]

Opium was sold at official British auctions in India and later exported to China by private British officials and Indian traders under certificates issued by the English East India Company until 1858. Opium sale at Guangzhou paid for tea shipped to London via Bombay. Thus, it can be called a triangular trade between Guangzhou, Bombay, and London. The draining of silver to pay for the ever-increasing imports of opium began to alarm the Qing administrators, as the decline of silver was causing people to use copper coins to buy silver for tax payments. This threatened the government's revenues as well as the livelihood of people.[81]

Lord George McCartney took scientists and artists on a 66 gun man-of-war and two escort vessels loaded with British manufactured goods, with an entourage of hundred people to penetrate in the Chinese port. The Chinese Emperor Qing labelled the British merchants as a 'tribute from England', sent to China to seek permission or negotiate a treaty of commerce for their government in order to open new markets in China. Later another official Lord Amherst led a British diplomatic mission in China to meet the Chinese emperor Qianlong in 1816, to establish formal trade between Britain and China. However, the mission was unsuccessful and the emperor Qianlong refused to accept Lord Amherst and the gifts which he had brought for the emperor and he was also not allowed to enter in the Chinese port of Canton.[82] Another factor was that imperial China's foreign trade played a key role, although subordinate in manner, as a source of imported silver as well as a market to stimulate production for export.

Japanese Copper Trade with the Portuguese and Dutch

At the beginning of the eighteenth century, English and Portuguese traders engaged in copper trade between Chinese and Indian ports. According to Dutch records at Malacca, cargo ships halted at the port of Malacca, where non-Dutch European traders re-exported Japanese copper from Amoy and Canton in China, Tonkin in Vietnam, and Ayutthaya in Siam via Malacca and transported copper to Madras and Surat in India.[83]

As pointed out by Holden Furber, the large inflow of European copper by the English East India Company and British private traders lowered the price of this much demanded metal copper in the South Asian market and further lessened the profits per unit of the Dutch East India Company (Vereenigde Oost Indische). Japanese copper was preferred over European copper in South Asia. The metal was used in Asia to manufacture copper coins. Copper was also widely used by common people across Asia, especially for storing water, as utensils, and for making statues. Inter-Asian competition for Japanese copper began in the eighteenth century; however, by the mid-eighteenth century, the English East India Company brought large amounts of European copper to South Asia. 1 picul = c.60 kgs, a unit used for measurement in South East Asia, especially in Java (Indonesia), by the Dutch.[84]

Last Quarter of the Nineteenth Century: Japan's Trading Connection with Bombay

Japan's external trade was dominated by the British, Dutch and American trading companies, but its trade with Chinese had been long established. Japanese raw silks, silver, tea, handloom textiles, paper, copper, coal, and iron were exported, while Chinese, American, and Indian cotton yarn, mill-made cloth, woollens, and other basic manufactured goods were imported into Japan. In 1858, the United State of America demanded its entry into Japanese markets and ports which resulted in the signing of the first treaty known as the Treaty of Amity and Commerce on 29 July 1858 and the opening of ports at Nagasaki, Yokohama, Kobe, and Shimada for foreign traders.[85]

Bombay's business firms like the Tatas and the two Sassoon companies and other small merchants too had connections with the Chinese trading ports of Canton, Shiouz, and Hong Kong, which came under direct control of the British in 1842. This trading connection of Bombay merchants in Canton further extended their networks to Japanese port towns. E.D. Sassoon & Co. of Bombay was among the first to open a branch in Yokohama soon after the treaty of trade was signed between America and Japan.[86] In 1893, Jamsetjee Tata negotiated a collaboration with Nippon Yusen Kaisha (NYK), a shipping company, which plied two cargo ships (*Annie Barrow* and *Lindisfarne*) on the Bombay-China-Japan route, both flying the Tata Lines flag.

The Japanese presence in Bombay was connected through trade in South Asia, especially the trading exchange between Bombay and Kobe-Osaka which was made possible with the businessmen—Jamsetjee Nusserwanji Tata in Bombay and Andrew Yule of Calcutta, who were business partners. The first Japanese trading firm to be established in Bombay was Mitsui Busan or Mitsui Trading Company (1893). A cotton trading company, Toyo Menke Kaisha Ltd (Japan Cotton Trading Ltd.), entered the business in the 1890s. This prompted an association between Indian merchants and Japanese cities such as Kobe and Nagasaki.[87] Singapore and Hong Kong too played a vital role in conducting the import trade from Japan and transporting the supply to Bombay.

Last Quarter of the Eighteen century: Trade in Bombay and the Economic Conditions

The year 1795 marks the continuous movement of native traders from Surat to Bombay. After 1795, a steady increase was noticed in external commerce as attributed in Lord Melville's report for 1802–3, causing the reduction of custom duty from 6 to 2.5 per cent. Later in 1813, Lord Melville passed a bill which destroyed the commercial character of the English Company and threw open the trade of India to the merchants of Liverpool, Glasgow, and other important trading centres'.[88]

Table 5.4: Bombay's Export in 1858–9 and Import in 1833–4 (in Rupees)[89]

Goods	*Exports, 1833–4 (in rupees)*	*Imports, 1858–9 (in rupees)*
Merchandise	2,667,403	116,942,181
Horses	644,425	2,615,000
Treasure	11,990,127	64,248,229

Source: Victor Pursell, *South and East Asia since 1800*, Cambridge: Cambridge University Press, 1965, p. 12.

The trade in Bombay fell short of 700 lakh rupees.

The debates regarding the flow of bullion among the recent historians have emphasized on the contribution of indigenous credit in the expansion and consolidation of the British Empire during the second half of the eighteenth century and the first half of the nineteenth century. Maritime historian, Lakshmi Subramanian strongly argues that the British Empire in Indian relied heavily on the support rendered by the Indian bankers and merchants; Kumkum Chatterjee contends that it was a relationship encompassing collaboration and conflict. C.A. Bayle has rightly argued that the English East India Company depended heavily on Indian corporate institutions for their own commercial interests and warring strategies to finance wars in western and southern India.

Table 5.5: Bombay Castle Report on the Treasures Imported and Exported from Bombay

Treasures	*Imported*	*Exported*
Merchandise	40,588,135	143,644,235
Horses	251,190	–

Source: Victor Pursell, *South and East Asia since 1800*, Cambridge: Cambridge University Press, 1965, pp. 495–6.

Report of Bombay Castle, 25 August 1813: Statement of the treasures imported and exported from Bombay and subordinates for the month of July 1813.

Total Imports of Penang & Ca, Bassein & Co Goa & Konkan,

Bombay	8,430	4,224	3,206	1,000
Surat	"	"	"	"
Rupees	8,430	4,224	3,206	1,000
Subordinates				
Bombay	Surat	Guzerat		
"	"	"		
"	"	11,050 treasure in silver.		

Treasure In gold Rs. 4032

In silver Rs. 4398

Total = 8430.

Exports To

Bombay 24,295, Surat 24,295.

Bombay Mint Master's Letter to Secretary Newnham

A Letter from the Mint Master of Bombay to Secretary Newman dated 1814:

To Mr. Secretary Newman,

I have the honour to enclose for the information of the Governor in council and for transmission to the Court of Directors statements of the coinage at the mints of Bombay and Surat for the last 13 years, which is from January 1st, 1801 to December 31st 1813. This statement gives the record of revenues derived by the Company which contracted with each mint during that period. As these statements exhibit separately the amount of bullion coined on account of the honourable Company and that on account of private merchants, the court will be enabled to form a tolerably correct Judgment of the regards to the buildings and the necessary implementation of coinage conditions. This became important to check the whole coinage of this presidency without the intervention of a contractor.

There are altogether five enclosures, they are as follows

(*1ST Enclosure*), I have the honour to enclose for the information of the Governor in council and for transmission to the Hon'ble Courts of Directors statements of the coinage at the mints of Bombay and the Surat for the last 13 years. From 1 January 1801 to 31 December 1813 together with the statements of the actual revenue derived by the Hon'ble Company contracted with the expenses of each mint during the same period.

(*2nd Enclosure*), As these statements exhibit separately the amount of bullion coined on account of the English Company and that on account of private merchants, the Court will be enabled to form a tolerably correct judgment of the expediency of placing the mint of Bombay in a state of efficiency both in regards to buildings and the necessary implements of coinage, conditions which it would seem indispensably necessary to be complied with to enable Government to carry in to execution the repeated orders of the court to conduct the whole coinage of this presidency without the intervention of a contractor.

(*3rd Enclosure*), It will appear by statement no.1 that the cross revenue on coinage at the mint of Bombay for 13 years amount to Rupees 653,209 that is (six lacs, fifty three thousands, two hundred and nine), on a private merchant bullion including the profit on Copper Coinage. It is from this sum be deducted Rupees 289, 570, out of which the Company's mint establishment has been paid to the contractor to cover the expenses of coinage and of course to leave a profit but in what proportion to each it is obviously impossible from the nature of the agreement for me to ascertain.

(*4th Enclosure*), I have also the honour to stand up agreeable to the orders of the Hon'ble Court 24 gold Mohurs, promiscuously taken from the various coinages which have taken place at the mint since the receipt of their late orders in the proportion of nearly one piece in every thousands and which I trust will give satisfaction as to the purity of the Coinage.

(*5th Enclosure*), It was fully my intention to have transmitted by the present dispatch as full and satisfactory a reply to the Hon'ble Courts late communication of the subject of the mint as the materials I possess and the information I have been able to procure would admit of and to which my attention has for some times been devoted. The importance of the subject and other professional avocations and I may add considerably proportion of ill health. There is however one point to which in my opinion the Hon'ble Court seem to attach a greater degree of importance than it deserves regarding the machinery necessary for establishing a good and sufficient coinage to answer the demands of this presidency and as it may be the means of saving a considerable expense and expediting the object which the Court have in view. I think it right to state that after giving the subject much consideration, I am fully satisfied that the only articles of machinery which cannot be procured here in the degree of perfection required are laminating rollers of steel of sufficient power to reduce the precious metals to a proper degree of thinness for the purpose of coinage.

I am therefore induced to recommend to the Court of Directors to order a sufficient supply of there both for gold and silver (say three pairs of each sort with spare pieces to provide against accidents), by the earliest opportunity. With these I feel every confidence that a coinage may be established which cannot be imitated by the native coiners and will effectually do away the endless frauds and vexations, the inconveniency of which has been so often felt by Government.

Signed R. Stuart,
Bombay Mint Master
Bombay, Mint Office, 26 December 1814.[90]

The English East India Company eventually won the contest for India by making India free from the burden of war responsibilities of France. The treaty of Paris between the United Kingdom and the United States, along with related treaties ending wars with France, Spain, and Holland, left

Britain as the major European power in Asia in 1783.[91] The Directors of the East India Company in London were of the opinion that wars cost a lot of money and were cutting down their profits. Therefore, they wanted to incur no further responsibilities of the government and the burden of war with France at the turn of the eighteenth century.[92]

Factors Responsible for the End of the English East India Company's Trade

In the early years of the nineteenth century, Bombay town saw a drastic change in climatic conditions, which resulted in epidemics, famines, and huge fires and caused an imbalance in the trade of Bombay.[93] The English Company also lost its trade in Bombay due to the local political instability of the Marathas which drove the Bombay presidency into a fiscal crisis in the last decades of the eighteenth century. The beginning of the opium trade with China, thus, brightened the prospects of the port city.

The Anglo-French rivalry as well as the second Anglo-Maratha war cased more damage to the English business. The defeat of the Marathas by the British in the third Anglo-Maratha War in 1818 led to a change in the political re-organization of western India and the creation of Bombay Presidency, with Bombay as its capital. The city was now under complete sovereignty of the British. The Bombay Presidency, with its sizeable and growing hinterlands, along with the two other presidency towns, Calcutta and Madras, came to serve an increasingly important function within the British colonial order.[94]

Tea became the chief Chinese export to England in 1810. Records show that the British East India Company purchased 27,000 pounds of tea[95] and the commodity emerged as its main business generator. As long as Indian cloth and Chinese tea were both paid in silver from Spain, Indian and Chinese trade had no occasion to interact. But when the silver flow became uncertain during the American War of Independence, the Company needed to find ways of paying for tea with Indian goods. The end of eighteenth century onwards, Indian opium began to offer itself as a solution. In my opinion, the bullion which was hoarded was used to make payments. The English lost the textile business in India after the decline in the textile trade of 1800s as the Industrial Revolution gained momentum. 'Before the profitable trade of War...gave a mortal check to honest industry, the loom furnished a great and flourishing Commerce,' wrote the Welsh naturalist, Thomas Pennant in 1798. The more serious check came from the invention and rapid spread of machine-spinning of yarn. A reverse flow of yarn into India began from the early 1820s, ending a 200-year long trade in Indian textiles.[96]

After the 1820s, Bombay's outlook as a city changed and it progressed into developing stronger business ties with China. It exchanged opium with bullion, especially white metal (silver) and cotton. This business and capital were owned and controlled by the British and Scottish traders primarily. During this period (1862–7), Bombay town was under the Governorship of Sir Henry Bartle Edward Frere. Under him, the Bank of Bombay collapsed due to the commercial crisis in 1866, for which he was partly responsible. The Chinese emperor Qing ended trade relations with the British in December 1839 due to the minor accident caused by the British sailors. This led to a declaration of war by the British. Following this, the Chinese ships were outmatched since the British navy was known to be the most powerful force in the world. True to its reputation, it launched swift attacks on the cities of Canton and Tianjin, as well as other sites along the coast.[97]

The 1830s witnessed a rapid increase in the opium trade. The East India Company's monopoly on the trade in China ended. When Charles Elliot (1801–50), the British Superintendent of Trade with Chinese merchants refused 21,000 chests of opium and handed them to Lin Zexu (1785–1850), an anti-opium crusader, to combat the consumption of this illegal commodity, he destroyed the chests completely. Lin Zexu had also written a letter to Queen Victoria regarding the import of noxious substances into China while the British received tea, rhubarb, porcelain, and silver from China. Another able governor, General Qishan (1786–1854) was regarded as a remarkable diplomat, who upon assessing the situation ceased the signing of a treaty in January 1841 where he and Charles Elliot agreed that the British would receive Hong Kong as a monetary indemnity and attain permission to open trade in Canton, Xiamen, and Fuzhou. The British succeeded in attacking these ports and they captured Nanjing, the capital city for the first Ming emperor, in 1842. Witnessing the fall of Nanjing, the Qing emperor agreed to signing the Treaty of Nanjing.[98] Opium trade did great damage to China and millions suffered and died of addiction in the nineteenth century. Finally in 1907 Britain agreed to stop the supply of opium to China. Both the First Opium War (1839–42), and Second Opium War (1856–60), brought significant changes in China and had deep consequences where China paid a heavy price and called the nineteenth century an era of humiliation thereby forcing the Britain to stop the export of Indian opium into China.[99]

The British had by now achieved their goal and were successful in controlling the island of Hong Kong and other ports of trading and arranging compensation for the opium destroyed by Lin Zexu. The British compelled emperor Qing to abolish the *cohong* and to grant them permission to trade with any and all merchants in China.[100]

Bombay continued to trade and saw new developments in the banking institutions, money market and thus continued to see its growth into a financial capital which is discussed in Chapter 6.

Notes

1. Gulam A. Nadri, 'The Parsis of Surat in the Eighteenth Century', in *Across Oceans Flowing Silks from Canton to Bombay 18th–20th Centuries and No Parsi is an Island*, ed. Ranjit Hoskote Nancy Adajania and Pheroza J. Godrej, Mumbai: Marg Publications, 2013, p. 97.
2. S.M. Edwardes, *The Gazetteer of Bombay City and Island*, vol. I, Bombay: The Government Photozinco Press, 1909, p. 49.
3. Mariam Dossal, *Theatre of Conflict, City of Hope: Mumbai, 1600 to Present Times*, New Delhi: Oxford University Press, 2010, p. 50.
4. Ashin Das Gupta, *The World of the Indian Ocean Merchant, 1500–1800*, New Delhi: Oxford University Press, 2001, p. 201.
5. Ibid., p. 201.
6. Ashin Das Gupta, *India and the Indian Ocean World: Trade and Politics*, New Delhi: Oxford University Press, 2004, p. 142.
7. Ibid., p. 495.
8. Dennis O. Flynn and Arturo Giraldez, 'Born with a Silver Spoon: The Origin of World Trade in 1571 AD', in *Metals and Monies in an Emerging Global Economy*, vol. 14, USA: Ashgate Publishing Company, 1997, p. 262–6.
9. Edwardes, *The Gazetteer of Bombay City and Island*, vol. I, p. 194.
10. Nadri, 'The Parsis of Surat in the Eighteenth Century', pp. 41–3.

11. R.A. Wadia, *The Bombay Dockyard and the Wadia Master Builder*, Bombay: Privately Published by R.A. Wadia, 1957, p. 87.
12. Nadri, 'The Parsis of Surat in the Eighteenth Century', p. 46.
13. Asiya Siddiqi, 'The Business World of Jamsetjee Jejeebhoy', in *Trade And Finance in Colonial India 1750–1860*, ed. Asiya Siddiqi, New Delhi: Oxford Unversity Press, 1995, p. 186.
14. James Maclean, *A Guide to Bombay*, Bombay: Bombay Gazette Stream Press, 1877, p. 63.
15. Siddiqi, 'The Business World of Jamsetjee Jejeebhoy', Ibid., p. 190.
16. Dwijendra Tripathi, *The Oxford History of Indian Business*, New Delhi: Oxford University Press, 2004, pp. 79–80.
17. Nadri, 'The Parsis of Surat in the Eighteenth Century', p. 44.
18. J.R.P. Moody, *Jamsetji Jejeebhoy: The First Parsee Baronet*, Bombay: 1959, p. 163.
19. H.V. Bowen, 'Investment and Empire in the Later Eighteenth Century: East India Stockholding, 1756–1791', *Economic History Review*, 1989, pp. 231–2.
20. Mariam Dossal, 'The Call of the Sea: Maritime Mumbai, c.1660–2000', *Ports, Towns, Cities: A Historical Tour of the Indian Littoral*, ed. Lakshmi Subramanian, Mumbai: Marg Publication, 2008, p. 132.
21. Ibid., pp. 133–145.
22. Pamela Nightingale, *Trade and Empire in Western India: 1784–1806*, Cambridge: Cambridge University Press, pp. 24–5.

    Sycee was made of indigenous Chinese silver which contained an average of 12 grains of gold per pound of silver, whereas Mexican silver contained about 4 grains.
23. Tirthankar Roy, *The East India Company*, New Delhi: Penguin Group, 2012, pp. 195–6.
24. Holden Furber, *John Company at Work*, Cambridge: Harvard University Press, 1948, p. 26.
25. Ibid., p. 26.
26. Holden Furber, 'Asia and the West as Partners Before Empire

and After', *The Journal of Asian Studies*, vol. XXVIII, no. 4, 1969, p. 713.
27. Dwijendra Tripathi and Jyoti Jumani, *The Concise Oxford History of Indian Business*, New Delhi: Oxford University Press, 2007, p. 24.
28. Siddiqi, 'The Business World of Jamsetjee Jejeebhoy', p. 192.
29. John King Fairbank and Merle Goldman, *China: A New History*, Cambridge: Harvard University Press, 2006, p. 191.
30. Tripathi and Jumani, *The Concise Oxford History of Indian Business*, p. 25.
31. Furber, *John Company at Work*, pp. 306–8.
32. S.B. Singh, *European Agency House in Bengal*, Calcutta: Firma Mukhopadhyaya & Co., 1966, pp. 32–3.
33. H.V. Bowen, 'Bullion for Trade, War, and Debt-Relief: British Movements of Silver to, around and from Asia, 1760–1833', vol. 44, no. 3, *Modern Asian Studies*, 2010, p. 463.
34. H.V. Bowen, *The Business of Empire: The East India Company and Imperial Britain, 1756–1833*, Cambridge: Cambridge University Press, 2006, pp. 237–8.
35. Bowen, 'Bullion for Trade, War, and Debt-Relief', p. 460.
36. Furber, *John Company at Work*, pp. 309–12.
37. G.V. Mulherkar, 'Coins of the East India Company at Bombay', *The Bombay Explorer*, vol. 1, July 1986, Mumbai, pp. 25–8.
38. Ibid., pp. 26–8.
39. Siddiqi, 'Money and Prices in the Earlier Stages of Empire', pp. 232–3.
40. Tripathi and Bowen, *The Concise Oxford History of Indian Business*, p. 25.
41. Siddiqi, 'Money and Prices in the Earlier Stages of Empire', p. 235.
42. B.N. Ganguli, 'Dadabhai Naoroji and the Mechanism of "External Drain"', *The Indian Economic and Social History Review*, vol. II, no. 2, 1965, pp. 89–91.
43. Murali Ranganathan, *Govind Narayan's Mumbai: An Urban Biography from 1863*, London: Anthem Press, 2008, p. 6.

44. Teresa Albuquerque, *Bombay, a History*, New Delhi: Promilla & Co., 1992, p. 7.
45. Ganguli, 'Dadabhai Naoroji and the Mechanism of "External Drain"', pp. 98–101.
46. Arthur Cotterell, *Western Power in Asia: Its Slow Rise and Swift Fall, 1415–1999*, Singapore: John Wiley & Sons, 2010, p. 98.
47. Ibid., p. 87.
48. Siddiqi, 'Money and Prices in the Earlier Stages of Empire', p. 339.
49. 'A Return of the Bullion, That is Gold and Siilver Imported in, to, and Exported from Each Presidency', *Parliamentary Papers*, vol. 1, Great Britain, 1864, p. 309.
50. Siddiqi, 'The Business World of Jamsetjee Jejeebhoy', p. 10.
51. Ibid., p. 14.
52. Williams Monier, 'Monetary System of British India', *Bombay Quarterly Review*, vol. VI, October 1857, p. 251.
53. Morris Rossabi, *A History of China*, UK: Wiley Blackwell Publishing, 2014, pp. 293–5.
54. Ibid., p. 295.
55. K.K. Chaudhari, *Maharashtra State Gazetteers, Greater Bombay District*, vol. II, Bombay: Gazetteers Department, Government of Maharashtra, 1987, pp. 364–5.
56. *Bombay Mint, 150th Anniversary Celebrations*, published by Bombay Mint, 1 May 1982, p. 366.
57. Edwardes, *The Gazetteer of Bombay City and Island*, vol. I, p. 282.
58. Srinivas Ambiraj, 'Political Economy and Monetary Management: India, 1766–1914', *The Economic History Review*, vol. 39, no. 1, 1986, p. 154.
59. G.V. Mulherkar, 'Coins of the East India Company at Bombay', *The Bombay Explorer*, vol. I, Mumbai, July 1986, pp. 25–28.
60. Clive Dewey and C.A. Bayly, 'Rulers, Townsmen, and Bazaars: North Indian Society in the Age of British Expansion 1770–

1870', *Economic History Review*, ed. E.H. Hunt, vol. 38, 1985, p. 431.

61. Brian Moloughney and Xia Weizhong, 'Silver and the Fall of the Ming: A Reassessment', in *Metals and Monies in an Emerging Global Economy*, ed. Dennis O. Flynn and Arturo Giraldez, An Expanding World, vol. 14, USA: Ashagate Publishing Company, 1997, p. 167.
62. Ibid., p. 168.
63. Flynn and Giraldez, 'Born with a "Silver Spoon": The Origin of World Trade in 1571', pp. 269–71.
64. William S. Atwell, 'International Bullion Flows and the Chinese Economy, circa 1530–1650', in *Metals and Monies in an Emerging Global Economy*, ed. Dennis O. Flynn and Arturo Giraldez, USA: Ashgate Publication, 1997, pp. 144–5.
65. Ibid., p. 162.
66. John King Fairbank and Merle Goldman, *China: A New History*, Cambridge: Harvard University Press, 2006, p. 195.
67. Jean Baptiste Du Halde, *The General History of China*, vol. II, London: Watts, 1736, p. 7.
68. Jullia Lovell, *The Opium War*, London: Picador, 2011, p. 2.
69. Ibid., p. 2.
70. Bowen, 'Bullion for Trade, War, and Debt-Relief', p. 341.
71. Ibid., pp. 2–5.
72. Ibid., p. 36.
73. Tirthankar Roy, *The East India Company*, New Delhi: Penguin, 2012, p. 190.
74. John F. Richards, 'The Opium Industry in British India', *The Indian Economic and Social History Review*, vol. 39, no. 2–3, 2002, p. 168.
75. Ibid., pp. 168–9.
76. Rusheed Wadia, 'Trade and the Raj', in *Across Oceans of Flowing Silks from Canton to Bombay 18th–20th Centuries and No Parsi is an Island*, ed. Ranjit Hoskote, Nancy Adajania and Pheroza J. Godrej, Mumbai: Marg Publications, 2013, p. 80.

77. Richards, *The Opium Industry in Britain India*, pp. 168–9.
78. Ibid., pp. 169–70.
79. J.A.G. Roberts, *A History of China*, New York: Palgrave Macmillan, 2011, pp. 161–3.
80. Ibid., p. 163.
81. 'Cohong' meant trading firms which formed the security Guild; Cohong and Hoppo were expected to tax the foreigners for their imports, especially tea and silk.
82. Roberts, *A History of China*, p. 163.
83. Fairbank and Goldman, *China: A New History*, p. 198.
84. J. Mason Gentzler, ed., *Changing China: Readings in the History of China from the Opium War to the Present*, New York: Praeger, 1977, p. 26.
85. Fairbank and Goldman, *China: A New History*, Press, p. 198.
86. Roberts, *A History of China*, p. 163.
87. Shimada Ryuto, 'The Golden Age of Japanese Copper: The Intra-Asian Copper Trade of the Dutch East India Company', *Intra-Asian Trade and the World Market*, ed. A.J.H. Latham and Heita Kawakatsu, London: Routledge, 2006, p. 32.
88. Ibid., pp. 31–2.
89. Kaoru Sugihara, 'Japan as an Engine of the Asian International Economy, *c.*1880–1936', *Japan Forum*, vol. 2, 1990, p. 211.
90. Sifra Lentin, 'Imperial Japan's Trade with Bombay', *Gateway House*, Bombay, 23 March 2019, pp. 1–2.
91. Ibid., pp. 2–3.
92. Edwardes, *The Gazetteer of Bombay City and Island*, vol. I, p. 416.
93. Ibid., pp. 153–4.
94. Ibid., pp. 161–5.
95. Arthur Cottrell, *Western Power in Asia: Its Slow Rise and Swift Fall, 1445–1999*, Singapore: John Wiley & Sons, 2010, p. xiv.
96. Victor Pursell, *South and East Asia since 1800*, Cambridge: Cambridge University Press, 1965, p. 12.
97. Ibid., p. 495.
98. Ibid., pp. 495–6.

99. Rushed Wadia, 'Trade and the Raj', in *Across Oceans of Flowing Silks from Canton to Bombay 18th–20th Centuries and No Parsi is an Island*, ed. Ranjit Hoskote, Nancy Adajania and Pheroza J. Godrej, Mumbai: Marg Publications, 2013, p. 81.
100. Arthur Cottrell, *Western Power in Asia: Its Slow Rise and Swift Fall, 1445–1999*, Singapore: John Wiley & Sons, 2010, pp. xiv–v.

SIX

Bombay's Emergence as the Financial Capital of India, from Bombay Mint to the Reserve Bank of India, *c.*1820–1935

Introduction

This final chapter of the book deals with the growth of Bombay town after 1820s until the founding of the Reserve Bank of India in 1935. The growth of Bombay town happened due to its commercial trading commodities such as opium and cotton textiles for bullion, which created favourable trading networks. Besides the prospering of businesses in Bombay, it also resulted in the establishment of banking and financial institutions. One of the most important institutions in Bombay in the seventeenth century was the establishment of the Bombay Mint which played a pertinent role in building Bombay's commercial front and developing it into a cosmopolitan city. From Bombay mint to banking institutions, Bombay paved its way in creating the money market which, in turn, impacted the expansion of Bombay as the financial capital of India in the twentieth century. The establishment of the first bank in Bombay in the early eighteenth century gave an impetus to banking in India, and its implications on the economy played a fundamental role in the money market of Bombay and other colonial port cities of British India. This chapter will also recount the journey from the setting up of the Bombay Mint to the opening of banking and financial institutions in Bombay in the early nineteenth and twentieth centuries, thereby creating capital for the mercantile communities to carry out their financial needs for conducting business in Bombay.[1]

The Bombay town also emerged as the centre for business transactions in the nineteenth century which led to the development of new banks, textile industries and railway lines. Banking communities too played an important role in funding companies and profits were determined on the basis of bazaar rates. The hysteria regarding shares from 1861–5 brought in a period of business speculation in Bombay. Alongside, many new projects were initiated in an effort to beautify Bombay under the Governorship of Sir Bartle Frere. These new ventures led to the growth of India as a financial centre and laid the foundation of the first central bank in the country called the Reserve Bank of India. It was established to provide financial help to local banks as well as to aid Indian businessmen and English merchants in their business ventures. The help provided to businesses created conditions for the growth of trade, promoted the economy, and controlled the prices and monetary fluctuations in the nineteenth and early twentieth century.[2]

The Role of the Bombay Mint and its Operation in the Mid-Nineteenth Century

The Bombay Mint is one of the oldest English mints in the country dating to the last quarter of the seventeenth century. The mint gives us an interesting insight into how the British coinage was introduced in India under the Bombay Governor. Later, the mint underwent a few developments between the years 1824–30 to accommodate the growing demand of coinage. However, an incident was reported on 28 August 1821 claiming that the Assay Office of the Bombay Mint was robbed. Following the investigations, a small fraction of the stolen wealth was discovered in the water tank which formed the northern boundary of the mint. In the same location, a twenty-eight storied tower of the Reserve Bank of India stands today.[3] The Assay Department was as old as the Bombay Mint. Its function was to monitor the quality of the coins manufactured in the mint and maintain the correct legal standard of the coinage in the country. The assay master also gave advice on the selection of metals and the quantity of alloys present in the metals and their impurities. The problems arising from the process of minting were investigated by the assay master and without his acknowledgement, the coins would not be circulated.[4]

Captain Hawkins built the new mint on 7 September 1824. 'The nearest part of the new mint is located outside the Bombay Castle where the old mint was established'. The exact location of the Old Mint stood between the Reserve Bank of India and the Bombay Castle (presently I.N.S. Angre). Captain John Hawkins from the Bombay Engineers completed the Town Hall, and after his demise, it was taken over by Colonel Thomas Cowper.[5]

The Bombay Mint underwent a renovation due to its faulty condition in the years between 1824 and 1830. Captain John Hawkins, an engineer by profession, undertook the project of constructing a new mint. On the completion of the Bombay Mint, the committees set up during the process of constructing the Bombay mint were abolished and Mr James Farris was appointed as the new Mint Master on 4 January 1830. Changes were introduced in the Indian coinage system—a subject of debate within the committees and the Company. Later, in the year 1835, the coinage system was made uniform. The two important proclamations issued by the Bombay Mint in 1832 were related to the gold and silver currencies and an order to introduce copper coinage at the mint.[6]

Based on three steam engines in the Bombay mint, the daily count of minted coins was around 150,000. In 1863, Colonel Ballard became the next Mint Master. He was also the most popular British Mint Master during his service of seventeen years. In his tenure, the Company's old coinage was discontinued and the new coinage bearing the effigy of the ruling monarch was introduced in the country. Ballard delivered on the heavy demand of minting at the Bombay Mint. He also served as the Commissioner of Currency Issue for the Bombay office from March 1862 to September 1870 and Colonel Ballard also reclaimed the land from the sea which is now known as Ballard Estate; the name was given in rememberance to his memory. There were two printing security presses at Mumbai and Nashik attached with this mint and which continued till the year 1876 under the control of the Bombay Government.[7]

In 1879 Lieutenant Colonel White became the next Mint Master, and under his tenure, technical probes were carried out to ensure better efficiency of the Bombay mint and to monitor the mechanical process. The bullion used for minting coins was first tested by cutting small pieces of silver from the corner of the bars which were then sent to the assay master for a report on the accurate valuation of the bullion. In 1890 Colonel Riddle took over the charge of the Bombay mint. He carried out an experiment to ascertain whether gold could profitably be separated from the silver that existed in good quality. The result obtained from this experiment was that the rupee coinage of the years 1835–73 contained seventeen tons of gold. Several of these currencies were later sent to London for treatment by the bullion brokers of the Bank of England.[8]

Until 1876, the Bombay Mint was under the administrative control of Bombay government. In 1876, the mint was transferred to the Government of India by the Finance Department Resolution no. 247 dated 18 May 1876. The operation of Indian mints was regulated by Coinage Acts of XVII 1835, XIII 1862, and XXIII 1870 until 1893, by the order of the Coinage Act. Under the new Indian Coinage Act of 1906, amended from time to time, a coin could be minted up to a denomination of one thousand rupees.[9]

One of the important activities at the Bombay Mint used to be the manufacturing of reference—the secondary and working standard of weights and the working standards of capacity. Each of these standards played a vital role in the work of the state governments by ensuring that the weights and measures used in the trade and commerce were of required accuracy. During the British rule in 1870s, a bill was passed making the metric system uniformly applicable all over the country. Accordingly, the Bombay Mint would manufacture standards of weights and measures and supply them to various states governments notwithstanding the changing laws for weights and measures. It can thus be argued that the significant progress in weights and measures could be possible because of the advances made by the Bombay Mint. Since 1958, the Bombay Mint has been supplying references, the secondary and working standards sets, after checking against our accurate standards authenticated, calibrated, and approved by National Physical Laboratory of India, in New Delhi.[10] The Assay Laboratory of India, Government Mint at Bombay is the oldest laboratory in the country. It was established by the British in 1829 and continues to be in business for testing the value of precious metals. Throughout this long period, the Assay Laboratory maintained its integrity in testing without fear and favour. This laboratory has testing facilities for gold, silver, ferrous and non-ferrous alloys, and coin metal.

Emergences of New Banks in India and its Role

Table 6.1: Establishments of Various Banks in India and its Foundation Years

Names of Banks	*Year of Establishment*
Bank of Bombay	1720 (origin of banking in Bombay)
Bank of Bengal	1809
Bank of Bombay	1840
Bank of Allahabad	1865
Punjab National Bank	1894
Canara Bank	1906
Bank of India	1907
Bank of Baroda	1908
Central Bank of India	1911
Bank of Mysore	1913
Union Bank of India	1922
Imperial Bank of India	1925
State Bank of India (Calcutta)	1806
Reserve Bank of India	1935

Source: S.M. Edwardes, *The Gazetteer of Bombay City and Island*, vol. II, Bombay: Government Times Press,1910, p. 407.

The Bank of Allahabad was established in the year 1865. One of the oldest banks in India, it is still functional. The English Company successfully established the Bank of Bengal, Bank of Bombay, and Bank of Madras as units and named them

'Presidency Banks'. These banks were later merged in 1925 and became the Imperial Bank of India, which upon independence came to be known as the State Bank of India. Under the new Indian Coinage Act in 1906, a coin could be minted up to a denomination of one thousand rupees.[11] A new branch of the Royal Mint of London was opened at Bombay between 15 August 1918 and 31 December 1919 with the objective of coining the British sovereigns in India. After coining 12.95 lakh sovereigns, the branch was shut down in April 1919. It was later converted into the residence of the mint master, now known as the Mint House. In the year 1919, a gold refinery was set up in mint which employed the chlorine process for refining gold. It refined raw gold from South Africa and Indian mines. The silver refinery was started in 1929 with an installed annual capacity of 80 million ounces of silver.[12]

The Old Bank of Bombay and its Functioning in 1840

In the year 1842, the two-anna silver piece was introduced and gold coinage was regulated. Speculation began in the Bombay market from the years 1862–4. It was an important phase in the commerce of Bombay as it indicated great prosperity and large amounts of wealth pouring into the city, thus increasing the number of banking and financial associations leading to demoralized trading. By 1893, no gold coinage was seen except for ceremonial occasions. There was high demand for silver and the people took full advantage of the Coinage Acts until 1893. The re-coinage of coins in 1901–2 was once again started. The World Wars were challenging for Indian banking. In order to control the situation, bring monetary stability, and improve economic conditions, the government established the Reserve Bank of India on 1 April 1935. This was a landmark moment in the history of banking in India.[13]

Changes in the Coinage System

The Surat Mint finally came to be abolished in October 1815 by the English Government and the minting of currencies was shifted to Bombay. In the year 1824, the use of a new rupee, weighing 180 grains and containing 165 grains of silver and 15 grains of alloy, was proposed. The coinage in India was made uniform, first in 1835 and then in 1909. The English East India Company's rupee was ordered to take the place of the Mughal sicca rupee of Surat, although the Company's rupees varied largely from the sicca rupees. The latter contained 8 per cent more silver. In 1841, a two anna silver piece was introduced, and a proclamation was made to regulate the minting of gold coins, making it compulsory to bear on the obverse the portrait of Queen Victoria and on the reverse, a figure of a lion and a palm tree with the designation— 'The East India Company'. This proved that the English Company was the most influential body among the European powers. Another change in the Bombay Mint took place in 1844; this pertained to the minting of copper coins.[14] All of these changes made in Indian coinage led to debates, as a result of which the reconstruction came to be suggested in 1812, in 1827, and again in 1869. Even when decimal coinage was a rage, the rupee continued as the medium of exchange and constituted the legal money in which all the payments were made. Every rupee loan which the Government of India contracted and every currency note which it issued were all promises therefore to pay the owner in silver rupees.[15]

Bombay Mint in the 1850s

In 1835, the British government passed a law stating that only silver coins were to be issued as the legal tender in the territories of the East India Company. This uniform coinage was introduced for all the English possessions of James Princep who was then the Assay Master of the Calcutta Mint and much earlier of the Benares Mint. The silver rupee coin of 1835 had embossed the portrait of the English King William IV who was on the throne of the United Kingdom of Great Britain and Ireland. The rule of the East India Company came to an end in 1858. However, up to 1862, the coins continued to bear the designs and the title of the East India Company.[16] All rupees minted in the Bombay Mint were of pure silver bearing the portraits or busts of the ruling English sovereign. When silver rupees were short in supply, some gold rupees were also minted. The Bombay Mint was the only place in the country where gold could be refined. Therefore, bullion was imported to Bombay from other countries for minting, jewellery designing, and financial transaction.[17]

In 1827, the copper pie was introduced for circulation, and in March 1831, by proclamation, the old pice were made current until further orders at the established rate of 50 to the rupee and exchangeable for the supply in the General Treasury at the rate of 64 quarter annas for 50 of the old pice. In 1832, two important proclamations regarding the new coinage at the mint were issued by the Bombay government. The first one was related to the gold and silver currencies of the Bombay Presidency while the second was to do with the newly introduced copper coinage. The copper coins underwent changes both in denomination and weight besides adhering to the following pattern—the pie weighing 33 ½ grains to the one-twelfth of an anna. The quarter anna was to weigh 100 grains. The new copper coin was thus higher than that which it superseded and was also of a smaller denomination. The silver and gold coins, however, were allowed to remain unchanged, both in terms of its weight and standard.[18]

A petition was signed by the leading merchants of Bombay and submitted to the government, which in reply stated that it was not prepared to undertake the substitution of rupees that are in circulation with those from the new coinage. The Bombay government made the old rupee the bona fide coinage of the Bombay Mint and also exempted it from the charge of 2 per cent. Mint duty was also charged on re-coinage; such old rupees were receivable at the new mint by weight, in quantities not less than a thousand tolas and the usual bullion certificate was granted for an equal weight of current coins. Though this process, the owner of the old rupees had the option of exchanging these old notes for new coins at only the cost of the loss by wear and the interest accruing to the bullion certificates value.[19]

A change was made in the device on the copper coinage issued at the Bombay Mint in 1844. Hence, the quarter anna piece or pice was to have on the obverse the armorial bearing of the East India Company, by omitting 'East India Company' around the margin. The scales on the old coins were not to be retained in the new coins. Similar changes were made in the half anna and pie as well, substituting the words denoting their respective values for the scales. This new copper coinage was not to prejudice the currency of copper coins from the previously established devices. According to the Provision Act XIX and XXIV of 1861, an agreement was entered into with the Bank of Bombay on 28 February 1862, whereby the balance and business of H.M.S. General Treasury at the Presidency was transferred to the bank. The bank also took control of the issue and payment of government paper currency notes at the Presidency. This agreement came into operation on 1 March 1862 for a period of five years with or without modification as agreed upon by the government and the bank. The amount of government currency notes in circulation on 30 April 1862 was 15,000,000 rupees and a corresponding amount in silver coin or bullion (2,800,000 rupees and 12,200,000 rupees respectively) was in the game reserve with the Department of Issue at the same time. The Government of India sanctioned the sale of copper coin at a discount, and this measure helped the poorer classes, who were relived of the charge of one anna to two annas (6.5 to 12.5 per cent) made by the local shroffs on every rupee for which copper changes were given. The first coinage for India under the British Crown came into existence in the year 1862. These coins were embossed with the impression of Queen Victoria wearing an Imperial Crown adorned with gold, rubies, and embroidered robes, which depicted the wealth the Queen possessed.[20]

Until 1893, the operations of the Indian mints were regulated by the Coinage Acts noted in the margin, which provided for the free coinage of gold and silver for the public and the coinage of copper for government regiments. The gold coins struck in the mint under these acts were Mohurs, sovereigns and half-sovereigns of the nominal value of 15 rupees, 10 rupees and 5 rupees respectively. There was also a double Mohur of 30 rupees. However, no demand for gold coinage was observed; only during ceremonial occasions were gold coins struck. Silver was in high demand. The terms of the Coinage Acts state that up to 1893, any person supplying silver to the mint to the amount of 1,000 tolas and over was entitled to have it coined into rupees on payment of a seigniorage charge of 21 rupees per every 1,000 rupees of out-turn produced by his tender. The greatest out-turn during the free coinage period was during 1877–8, the year of great famine, when it reached a total of 110,439,039 rupees. Although this figure has seen a rise in the more recent years.[21]

The coinage of small silver and of copper coins was usually

undertaken at the Bombay Mint only when the coinage of rupees had not sufficed to keep the mint working full-time and the bulk of the subsidiary coinage was being carried out at the Calcutta Mint. For eighteen years, no copper coinage had been carried out in the Bombay mint. In June 1893, the Indian mints were closed for the free coinage of gold and silver on the recommendations of the Indian Currency Committee, and since then, no Bombay rupees has been coined except on government account or in connection with schemes for the conversion of currencies of certain local states. Shipments of silver weighing over 2,000,000 pounds, which had been consigned to India for coinage into rupees before the issue of the notification in June 1893, were taken over by the government from the importers at a valuation and converted into rupees on government account. The representations from Far-East traders had led to an agreement between the Government of India and the two of the local exchange banks for the coinage of British dollars in 1895. This was to happen at the Bombay Mint for the circulation in the Straits Settlements and Hong Kong, which was later demonetized in 1904 when the government of the colony issued a new coin called the Straits Settlements Dollar for circulation in their territories. This coin was struck in the Bombay Mint too.[22]

The rest of the silver coins of Mexican, British, and Hong Kong dollars ceased to be the legal tender with effect from 31 August 1904, after the Straits Settlements (Coinage) Order of 1903 authorized minting of the Straits Settlements dollar.[23] The coinage of the present rupee with the effigy of His Majesty King Edward VII commenced in January 1903. A new nickel coin of one anna in value was introduced and minted at the Bombay Mint in 1907.[24]

In 1919, a gold refinery was started in the Bombay Mint and employed the 'chlorine process' for gold refining. It refined raw gold which came from South Africa, Australia, and other Indian mines. The silver refinery was started later in 1929 due to the increasing demand for silver. It had an installed annual capacity of 80 million ounces of silver.[25]

Establishment of the Bank of Bombay in the Mid-Nineteenth Century

In the nineteenth century, banking in Bombay was carried by the Hindu Shroffs (moneylender), primarily until the establishment of the Bank of Bombay. These Shroffs, in many cases, possessed great wealth and capital and rendered considerable service to the government. Their business premise was for the most part the Bazaar Street, where bills and hundis were accepted and honoured from all parts of India. In 1835, the English government established a savings bank in the Bombay Castle called the Manor House, and in 1836, when commerce was progressing and expanding and the town had abundance of capital, the question of establishing a Bank of Bombay was first brought forward. The need for a bank was felt by the English government shortly. It withdrew the privilege of making deposits and transfers at the treasury; the difficulties experienced by the public were not taken seriously until 1840 when the Bank of Bombay, after many delays, was finally once again opened for business on 15 April 1840.[26]

The Bank Committee regretted the announcement of the postponement of the passing of the Charter Act by the Vice-President of the Council in India in consequence of a resolution to revise the list of shareholders and to frame a new one. The committee could no longer form any opinion on when the bank will be opened, the establishment being in the hands of the government and beyond the control of the committee. On 27 January 1840, by the order of the committee, William Walter Cargill was appointed as the Bank Secretary.[27] The Bombay town gradually developed into a thriving centre for merchant communities such as the Gujarati Banias, Jain Shroffs, Kutchi Bhatias, Parsis, Marwaris, Konkani Muslims, Baghdadi Jews, and European free traders or private merchants who traded on their own account or carried trade transactions for other interested traders. The system of 'hundi' became a powerful institution of trust between the creditor and debtor, acting as the instrument in building trading networks. Bansilal Abhirchand and Motishaw were the leading agents from the Marwar region in the Bombay trade and became well-known bankers later. Bombay became the most influential trading network in the last quarter of the eighteenth century and the first quarter of the nineteenth century until India's participation in the First World War.[28] There were twenty-one leading Hindu Shroffs from Bombay in 1845, namely Gunadass Crustnajee (1809), Sheram Dowlatram (1819), Chimodass Madodass (1824), Latchmandas Sewdass (1834), and others. They were the leading men in the field of inland exchange, and the sole conductors of it before the Old Bank of Bombay broke ground in 1840. The first Indians to be entrusted with a state mint were the Parsis, the Merjis in particular—the only family ever to engrave its initials on a national coin struck in the 1840s. The Aurangabad Mint bore the initials of Pestoni Merji and was widely known as 'Pestan Shai'.[29]

The Role of the Parsis in Building Bombay's Business in the Nineteenth Century

Parsis assumed an economic pre-eminence among the Indian communities in Bombay in the eighteenth and nineteenth centuries. They played a significant role in the development of the shipping industry in Bombay from the seventeenth century onwards. By the nineteenth century, the Parsi merchants functioned as agents, contractors, and suppliers for the British mercantile houses and also acted as their guaranteed brokers and ship builders. By the mid-nineteenth century, Parsis controlled an extensive commercial enterprise in Bombay and western India and dominated Bombay's trade. Many operations in local and overseas trade were carried by them, and they played a significant role from ranging and procurement to the distribution of goods on their own. Trade was conducted and connected through their own vessels. The Parsis and Bhandaris collaborated on the sale of European articles. They benefitted from the security offered by the British at Bombay and helped greatly in transforming the island of Bombay into the major entrepôt for western India. In the years 1830–60, Bombay's trade was connected to China through the initiative of the Parsis. They traded in the import of tea and export of cotton and opium to Canton, Amoy, and Fuzhou in China.[30]

The Parsis continued to prosper and hold an important status in the political and socio-economic life under British colonialism. By the mid-nineteenth century, their enterprise had diversified into the areas of banking, cotton textile manufacturing, and advanced technological industries and its connections with the international trade. The community played an important role in the setting up of the Bombay Mint and were given a special place in Bombay's mercantile operations. Pestonji Cursetji Shroff, an honourable Parsi trader, was given this privilege such as he got the opportunity to be the committee member of the Bank of Bombay and also the director of Eastern Financial Associations.[31]

Dadabhoy Pestonji-Wadia (1802–55) was the first Indian

who conspicuously invested in the banking enterprise in Bombay and held three-eighths of the Oriental Bank shares.[32] He was the member of the government-established Bank of Bombay in 1836 and was joined by other Parsi merchants, Jamshetji Jejeebhoy and Framji Cowasji Banaji, as the Directors. The Parsi families—Wadias, Davars, Banajis, and Readymoneys—were all associated with the early banking and financial history of Bombay in 1854.[33] Cowasji Nanabhoy Davar (1814–73) was the first successful entrepreneur of Bombay. Engaged in many enterprises, he was the broker to English companies. His own trading company traded with the firms in the Far East, participated in promoting four Bombay banks between 1846–63, and took initiative in the formation of the Steam Navigation Company. In 1854, he started the first steam-powered press and cotton textiles mill at Bombay. The same year, he floated a spinning company with a capital of 500,000 rupees contributed by fifty leading merchants. Davar had many shareholders on his side, all Parsis who supported him in these projects.[34]

A few banking firms set up as joint stocks were the only examples of collaboration between Indian and British businessmen. Dadabhoy Pestonji Wadia and Jejeebhoy Dadabhoy were among the promoters of Bank of Western India formed in 1842. The bank was renamed Oriental Bank later. The Parsis were also associated with the Bank of Bombay, which came to be known as the first modern bank in the city.[35]

A general remark put forward for the Old Bank of Bombay was that during the first seventeen years of its existence, it suffered very little loss. Some of them were head offices and some of them were branches. Dadabhoy Pestonji Wadia and Jejeebhoy Dadabhoy were considered undoubtedly wealthy as they rendered important services to the government. These leading men also assisted the bank and looked after its functioning during the Revolt of Sepoy Mutiny in 1857. They mostly belonged to the Bazaar Gate Street, 'where merchants mostly congregate'. These merchants gather and decide about the money and their investments in the bullion. The Bazaar Gate Street was managed by Atmaram Bhukun, who belonged to the Jain community among Banias, and his primary business was money lending.[36]

The Concept of the Indian Bazaar System at Village- and City-Levels

A term of Persian origin that gained currency in Indian and European languages, Bazaar 'refers to a market or marketplace, generally a permanent market or street shops'. It is also a place where peasants, towns people, land holders, rulers have historically converged in South Asia to conduct wholesale and retail trade and to gather information and news in the cities and towns of the region, where traders and merchants exchanged indigenous financial nexus and upheld the bill of exchange through the system of hundi. They traded with land produce and transacted in credit. *Beopar* means trade and *beopari* is the one who engages in trade. The traders and merchants (Mahajans) occupied the 'sphere of bazaar bankers and merchants working together at inland exchanges and operating through an old customary practice of lending and earning commission by the nexus of agencies (arhat) and hundi system'. The narrative constructed around the bazaar thus draws to an understanding that market occupies a different place in the Indian landscape. A few examples include the village bazaar of Chitpore (Calcutta, Charles D'Ogyly) and the Bohra Bazaar in the Fort area,

Bombay.[37] Amiya Kumar Bagchi stresses that 'the relationship between banking was predominated in India, and the system of public credit was first developed in the Italian city-states and later in England and Netherlands'. According to Om Prakash, Najaf Haider, and Shireen Moosvi, 'The credit system of Mughal India portrays a sophisticated system in which money deposited was used in the wider circulation and thus bill of exchange (hundis), prevailed and which also generated banking money when required.'[38]

In other words, traders engaged in relaying grain and other items collected in the villages by the 'trading farmers' to primary markets, the Haats, or to higher-level markets. They made their purchases at one market and sold at another. They were able to become the primary 'carriers' of overland trade because they owned cattle for use as transportation, either as pack animals or hitched to carts. Before the advent of the railways and an extensive network of good roads, their command of the primary means for transporting goods between the hinterland and the major entrepôts along the water highways secured them a vital intermediary role. Some also hired out their cattle, although only infrequently because *grihastha beoparis* tended not to involve themselves directly in the transportation of their goods to higher-order markets. 'In the land carriage,' as one local administrator noted perceptively, 'the carriers are also the principal traders, oftener purchasing at one market to sell at another than hiring carriage to settled merchants'.[39] As Bombay grew into a much larger trading centre, the Fort area became congested. Traders, shopkeepers, and agents gathered to conduct business. Therefore, we find many lofty structures in this area, now called Ballard Estate, and numerous bazaars sprang up due to the demand of trading from different commodities. Moti Bazaar Pear Street or Zaveri Bazaar, Bazaar Gate Street of Bombay, where Arabs and Baghdadi Jews traded in horses, precious metals, and perfumes, Null Bazar, Bhendi Bazaar, and Chor Bazaar were the names of bazaars which played an important role in the trade of Bombay.[40]

Bombay's Share Market and its Operation

In Bombay, the business of stock and shares was purely handled by Indians who had been dominant in this business. One of the leading brokers of the share market was Premchand Roychand, 'who gave to the stock and share brokers a standing and importance's not hitherto achieved'. The cotton mill industry helped the share market grow in the early 1870s which in turn increased the investments in the shares.[41] In 1877 the number of share brokers had increased to 318 from mere six brokers who were recognized by the banks in the 1840–50s. The number had steadily increased to sixty in 1860.[42]

The brokers originally had a meeting place at Cotton Green, where the Elphinstone Circle is now situated. They continued to meet and discuss trading business there until 1855. Cotton Green is presently a station on the Victoria Terminus Line. Since it was a centre where bundles of cotton were traded and merchants flocked to bid and buy cotton in wholesale, the place became a popular destination for the brokers. Later, they started meeting between the Old Fort walls and the Mercantile Bank. Finally, a stable place was found at Dalal Street and the brokers began assembling at this new venue, now called the Bombay Stock Exchange. After the brokers had organized themselves in 1875, they joined the leading mill-owners of Bombay and endeavoured to house the share bazaar in a suitable building. The frequent resort to excessive and unhealthy speculation and the use of wrongful means to achieve private gain led many brokers into destitution, forcing some order and cohesion in the 'chaotic' Dalal Street. A reported was published on 10 July 1875 in the *Times of India* stating that a meeting was held for the purpose of restrictions to deal with the differences which had arisen.[43] On 11 July 1875, the brokers set up a committee to draft rules for the Native Share and Stockbrokers Association which they had founded to protect 'the character status and interest of native share and stockbrokers. The aim of the Association was to promote honourable practice; to suppress malpractices; to settle disputes among the brokers; to decide all questions of usage and courtesy in conducting brokerage business.'[44] The Bombay Shareholders' Association submitted the following list in 1932 highlighting the number of directorships held by some prominent businessmen.[45]

Table 6.2: Names of Prominent Businessmen and their Directorships in the total number of Companies[46]

Names of the Businessmen	*Number of Companies for which Directorships were held:*
F.E. Dinshaw	65
Sir Purshotamdas Thakurdas	42
Sir Pheroze C. Sethna	34
H.P. Moody	14
Sir Fazulbhoy Currimbhoy Ebrahimbhoy	26
Sir Lalubhai Samaldas	26
N.B. Saklatwala	29

Source: James Maclean, *A Guide to Bombay*, 'Bombay Gazette', Bombay: Steam Press, 1889, p. 48.

The Origin of Banking in Bombay Island under the English East India Company

Sir George Birdwood, in his interesting 'Old Records of the India Office' from 1891, notes that in the year 1671 the East India Company banked with Alderman Edward Blackwell of London, and at one point of time, money amounting to 175,000 pounds lay in his hands. This was before the Bank of England was thought of and there were no banking companies, foreign or domestic, in Bombay until 1840.[47] The Bank of Bombay was started with a capital of Rs.5,250,000; its business being confined to receiving deposits, maintaining accounts of cash, and discounting bills, drafts, and other investments. Until the establishment of Government Paper Currency Office in 1860, it enjoyed the privilege of issuing bank notes. In October 1842, a company was formed in Bombay under the title of the Bank of Western India and with a capital of Rs.5,000,000 in order to facilitate exchange and legitimate the banking business. It later opened many branches in Calcutta, Colombo, Hong Kong, and Singapore. Another bank named the Oriental Bank was formed so that they could transfer the Government Bank from Bombay to London and double its capital. The Oriental Bank of London had a branch in Bombay under a Board of Directors and in 1833, the Agra and United Service Bank was established.[48]

In five years, three more banks were opened, of which two were branches—one of the North-Western Bank of India and the other, the London and Eastern Bank. The Chartered Mercantile Bank of India, London and China was local in origin and the capital of the three banks combined in 1855 was about Rs.15,000,000. In 1845, another banking company known as the Commercial Bank of India was formed, mainly on the suggestion of local merchants to invite more merchants to come to Bombay from the hinterland, invest their capital, and make more profits. On 15 June 1845, Cargill issued the following notice, 'The Bank of Western India will henceforth be carried on under a new deed of settlement under the name of the Oriental Bank.'[49]

The Oriental Bank was originally a co-partnership bank called the Bank of Western India. This bank was founded in Bombay in the year 1842 to conduct banking business from which Presidency Bank of Bombay was excluded by the terms of its charter from the East India Company. In 1845 the Bank of Western India moved its head office to London and became the Oriental Bank. later this bank was amalgamated in 1849 with the Bank of Ceylon, the Oriental Bank applied for a Royal Charter to operate anywhere east of the Cape of Good Hope.

Between 1855 and 1863, the branches of London and Eastern Bank and North-Western Bank of India shut their business in Bombay, but the Chartered Bank of India, Australia and China, incorporated by Royal Charter, opened its agency in Bombay; in 1860, a new bank, styled upon the Central Bank of Western India, was established with a capital of Rs.5,000,000. The banking directors were local, and they opened other branches in London, Calcutta, Madras, Hong Kong, Shanghai, Yokohama, Melbourne, Indore, Ahmedabad, Surat, and Sholapur.[50]

The American Civil War, Famines of Lancashire, and its Effects on the Business in Bombay

The American President Abraham Lincoln's abolition of slavery had led to the Civil War in the 1860s leading to the abrupt severing of trading links.[51] The year 1863–4 was important to India as it showed great prosperity, and therefore, large amount of wealth poured into the city of

Bombay owing to the cutting off of the American cotton supply to England. The supply of cotton to Lancashire was stopped and the English textile industry was obliged to look towards India for the supply of raw material. Bombay became an important export centre for cotton. Traders and merchants found this trade in cotton to be very lucrative and began trying their luck. There was soon a boom in the cotton trade and in 1861, the value of cotton export was recorded to be Rs.50,000,000. Three years later, the figure jumped to Rs.290,000,000; such a huge fluctuation had not been witnessed in the past. As a result, these merchants needed to safeguard their money and many new banks sprang up to give loans to people to deal in cotton trade. This wreaked havoc in the lives of Bombay merchants and the banks failed to cover up their debts. The situation worsened and caused panic in 1865 and eventually, the banks of Bombay faced the disgrace of liquidation proceedings in 1868.[52]

A consequence of the Lancashire cotton famine in 1825 was the termination of cotton staple production until 1861. This meant immense profit for the Indian cultivators of cotton, resulting in enormous imports of treasure, gold, and silver into Bombay. The sudden outpour of wealth thus produced an artificial boom leading to the growth of many companies in Bombay such as banks and financial associations, land reclamation schemes, cotton cleaning, pressing, and spinning companies, as well as hotels. The boom was accompanied with an outbreak of a reckless gambling spirit bringing ruin and disgrace to many old and reputed citizens and companies of Bombay. The magical wealth thus arrived and disappeared rather quickly which left many a businessmen in a state of despair.[53]

The rise and fall of the Bombay market created ripples which lasted for a short span of time. The crisis in the years

1861–5 was followed by the emergence of Bombay as the gateway city of western India and the commercial capital of the British rule. Due to its commanding role in trade, finance, and marketing of raw cotton from the hinterland in western and central India, Bombay markets drew together foreign capitalists and speculators with indigenous bankers, merchants, and middlemen. It enabled the consolidation of the position of Bombay merchants and bankers in global commercial and trading networks, thus propelling the city towards mass urbanization and industrialization by the late nineteenth century and making it the centre of one of the largest textile industries in Asia. This period also showed a sudden and rapid increase in the number of banking and financial associations. The wealth surge changed the trading ethics and the attitude of the trading communities, giving rise to the notion of false speculation that anyone can make a huge profit by investing their capital in Bombay Stock Exchange gained currency.[54]

Sir Bartle Frere, the Governor of Bombay (1862–72), held views similar to Mansfield regarding social distance from Indian which he called the 'colonial policy'. In December 1863 came the exhaustive lengthy report of European Pauperism submitted by the committee consisting of Revd. W.K. Fletcher, M. Scott, Charles Forjett, the Municipal Commissioner of Bombay, and Robert Haines. The construction of railways by two companies called the BBIC (Bombay Baroda and Central Indian Railway) and GIP (Great Indian Peninsula Railway Company) too contributed to the problems in the later years with the start of the Civil War in America. It rendered many working class Englishmen out of jobs. Though this phenomenon resulted in an economic boom and a share mania in Bombay due to heavy demand for Indian cotton, it also caused many Englishmen to come to India in search of employment.[55] The shares mania thus created an artificial boom for a short span of time and collapsed the general business in Bombay.

Another issue of debt which the businessmen in Bombay faced was that they had invested huge amounts of capital to tackle the growing population by reclaiming a section of the sea called the Back Bay. To spur the project, Premchand Roy Chand (1831–1906), new to the Bombay business, became the principal promoter of the Back Bay Company. His father Roy Chand Deep Chand, a Jain timber merchant in Surat, had come to Bombay in the early 1840s looking for better prospects. He started his career as a broker in bank shares and his career took a significant turn when he gained monopoly on brokering bank shares and amassed great wealth. So firmly did he establish himself in the Bombay business world that the reputable officials too considered him their close friend. Governor Frere Bartle appointed Premchand as the Director of the Bank of Bombay since his support was needed to beautify the city and to execute this project, funds were needed. A scheme was launched to improve the defence of the harbour in cooperation with the Bombay Chamber of Commerce in the year 1836. Many obsolete buildings were brought down and new construction of public buildings such as libraries, hospitals, and training institutes were established. Most of the private buildings that surround the magnificent Elphinstone Circle today were built to beautify Bombay with the profits earned by the merchants during the business boom. The Back Bay Company, however, was not very successful and ended in a disaster.[56] One of the causes for its downfall was that the Government of Bombay contributed towards 400 shares in the company which it later abandoned on 6 July 1864 for the public auction. After the Back Bay auction sale, the share market dwindled away, the confidence of the gullible public was lost, and it brought a wave of unimaginable speculations in the Bombay market to earn quick gains.[57]

The Bombay Market in the Period of Conjecture, 1862–4

There were eighteen local banks in Bombay besides five exchange banks, and none of these banks could survive by 1871 as the loss incurred was too high than the money invested. These banks had invested money worth 29 crores and in return received 7 crores, which forced these banks to shut down and only the exchange banks could survive. The Old Bank of Bombay was redeveloped in 1868. During the year 1880, the branch of the East India Land Credit and Finance Company of London closed their business in Bombay as they could not make any profit and the banking business faced acute stagnation owing to natural calamities such as plague and famine.[58]

The coinage of India then not only supplied equal currency to the demand of a large and increasing commerce but also catered to the material for the manufacture of silver ornaments which were worn by all Indian womens and who could afford to buy these ornaments. These large sums were removed from circulation, and therefore, occasionally lost altogether due to the general practices of hoarding. Lending due consideration to these different modes of employing and destroying coinage further led to the coinage of nearly sixty crore rupees, or sixty million sterling in the last twenty-two years, or the absorption of silver—a marked characteristic of the foreign commerce of India. It was evident that the imports of silver, required for minting coins, making payments, and meeting requirements of an increasing foreign trade, was being rapidly filled up.[59]

Colonel Sykes' paper records that in April 1842, India imported bullion in large quantities amounting to 15,184,000 pounds, or at an average rate of 1,898,000 pounds annually. In 1854, India imported precious metals for 18,993,865 pounds, at an average rate of 3,798,773 pounds annually. The total shipments of bullion to India and China were 144,817,541. Colonel Sykes' paper also throws light on the vast absorption of bullion by India as something mysterious and unaccountable, to which the saying of Pliny that India was 'the sink of precious metals, especially silver' is as applicable now as it was eighteen centuries ago. There were periods now and then when the white metal was scarce, but it was re-exported to England. The East India Company had to, during the first quarter of the nineteenth century, send its silver back more than once to replenish its coffers in Leaden Hall Street.[60]

The rupees minted from 1862–74 bore the same date—1862. In 1863, the Bombay Mint adopted a new pattern of adding dots or beads to its dyes to indicate the exact year of minting below the base of the coins or above the flower.[61] In 1864, there was an acute shortage of rupees due to the low imports of silver as the metal did not remain in the vaults of the banks and unknown quantity of silver went inland for purposes of hoarding and making ornaments and silver utensils. Currency notes had, for the first time, been put into circulation in 1862, but the people were less accustomed to their use. The Bank of Bombay notes though had been familiar for decades to the traders and merchants in the city. The Bank of Bombay in 1864, increased its rate of discount to as high as 23 per cent.

The situation of the metallic currency was so grave that the mercantile communities in their respective trading towns were alarmed at the silver famine which continued. It was globally believed that America had exhausted its surplus, that the French had no five-franc pieces to spare, and that the growth of the production of silver was difficult. Two prominent members of the Bombay mercantile community, namely Mr Michael Scott of Messrs, Ritchie, Stewart & Co., and Mr Alexander Brown of Messrs, Nicol & Co., observed that the monetary conditions in India were in the most unsatisfactory and unstable state. As its exclusive silver currency was no longer adequate for circulation among the increased populations, the white metal had become so popular that people wanted to hoard it in their vaults.[62]

Mr Walter Cassels, a far-sighted English merchant and a senior partner in the old eminent house of Messrs Peel, Cassels & Co., was alarmed and forced to address a letter to the Chamber of Commerce on 1 December 1864, complaining about the situation of the silver currency and urging the government to establish a gold standard, with a gold currency. His words were as follows, 'Notwithstanding such large importations, the demand for money has so far exceeded production'.[63]

The conditions of silver production in the world alarmed the countries importing the metal silver. This alarmed the Government of India to shut their mints for private coinage. It was under such monetary circumstances that the abnormal speculation at Bombay's capital market began. But in its annual report for 1863–4, the Chamber of Commerce recorded that during these years there was an increase in the number of financial companies and banks. The excessive speculation in all sorts of joint stock companies had plunged into the trading activities and faced a crisis in capital and credit. Twenty-five banks, thirty-nine financial institutions, seven land reclamation companies, and a few other miscellaneous agencies had to suffer this huge loss. To name a few banking companies, they were the Bombay Presidency Bank, Alliance Bank of Bombay, Bombay Trading and Banking Association, and Imperial Bank of Bombay.

Colonel Ballard was the most famous British Mint Master of Bombay Mint. He was appointed as the mint master (1863), at the time when the East India Company was taken over by the British Crown and therefore the Company's coinage had to be discontinued and withdrawn. The new coins were to bear the impression of the ruling monarch of the British throne. Therefore, the coinage of Bombay Mint was in high demand and this demand was fulfilled by Colonel Ballard. He became the Commissioner of Issue of the Currency Office for Bombay Circle later, from March 1862 to September 1870. It is in his memory that the reclaimed land from the sea is now known as the Ballard Estate. It is one of the oldest commercial centres of business in Bombay and houses many official buildings.[64]

The Bombay Mint till the year 1876, was under the administrative control of the Government of Bombay whereas the Calcutta Mint was under the control of the Government of India. A new policy was initiated in 1876, that the mint of Bombay come directly under the control of the Government of India. In 1877, Queen Victoria assumed the title of 'Empress of India' and therefore, the word 'Queen' was substituted by the word 'Empress' on the obverse of the coins. All the British colonial and Indian coins thereafter, until 1950, bore the dual inscription of both King and Emperor, i.e. King, by the Grace of God, and Emperor of India.[65] In 1879, Lieutenant Colonel White became the Mint Master at Bombay, followed by Colonel Riddle in 1890.

The old Bank of Bombay was reconstructed in 1868, and the Hong Kong and Shanghai Bank and the Agra Bank of London soon opened their branches in the city, in 1869. The Bank of Bengal was established in the year 1809 and opened its agency in Bombay in 1867. In the last quarter of the nineteenth century, the branch of the East India Land Credit and Finance Company of London shut their business in Bombay. The banking business performed well till the year 1890, but in the next fifteen years that followed, the business had to face acute stagnation due to the climatic calamities such as draught and plague.[66] This led to the termination of the land mortgage of Bank of India and London, the Agra Bank, and the Oriental Bank Corporation.

A Note on Jagannath Shankar Sheth, the Father of Private Banking in Bombay

Jagannath Shankar Sheth (1803–65), was well-known for his business as well as money lending activities in the early nineteenth-century Bombay. Shanker Sheth belonged to the artisan community of goldsmiths (Sonar), and he was the only Maratha among the prominent businessmen in Bombay during the colonial rule.[67] In pre-colonial times, private bankers such as Shankar Sheth, who had large number of resources at their disposal, helped the Company during its period of crisis—the time of war and campaigns—which required funds and financial assistance. The state treasury had to rely on these private individual bankers and the likes of Shankar Sheth lent money on interest to both private merchants as well to the European traders. Later, he became the Director of the Oriental Bank and the Chartered Mercantile Bank of India, London, and China.[68]

The Functioning of the Indigenous Money Market

The money market and banking system of India consisted of four main constituents—the Presidency Banks, the European

Exchange Banks, the Indian Stock Banks, and lastly, the Shroffs, Marwaris, Parsis, and other private bankers and money lenders who were involved in European money market as well as the local money market. The local money market included the Bank of Allahabad and the Alliance Bank of Shimla, which were the Indian joint stock banks under the European management, occupying perhaps an intermediate position. In the local money markets outside the main towns, European businessmen had their offices and foreign trade was entirely managed by Indians. In the period preceding 1899, the bazaar rate during the times of stringency was lower than the presidency bank rate and the connections between the European Money Market and the Local Money Market were incomplete.[69]

The relationship of the indigenous banking system with the joint stock banks long continued to shadow the Indian banking system. It was observed that the bazaar rates were generally higher than the prime rates charged by the presidency banks and their competitors. The Indian bankers faced much higher risks in the lending operations. It was also observed that during the low season, the bazaar rates often went below the rates charged by the joint stock banks leading to higher overhead expenses of the joint stock banks and long-cultivated relationship of the Indian bankers with their favoured customers. The indigenous bankers practised systematic discrimination in favour of members from their own community, who were generally considered their favoured clients. In periods of extreme monetary stringency, the indigenous bankers would ration out the less favoured clients. This shows how the indigenous bankers played their cards in a prudent manner.[70]

The indigenous money market ran its finances through Promissory Note Bills of Exchange using the system of hundis and other instruments of negotiation for trade conducted in wholesale over long distances. It is important to be noted that the biggest and the most reputable shroffs, the indigenous bankers in Bombay and Calcutta, regularly reported the daily bazaar rates to the official of monetary authorities of British India.

This information was annually published by the Controller of Currency and later, by the Reserve Bank of India since 1935.[71] Similar to the manner in which the Shanxi merchant bankers migrated all over China and built up an imperial credit network, so did the Marwari merchant bankers who migrated to every part of India and built the most extensive network of community credit which facilitated the inland exchange in the country. The two greatest Marwari banking firms of the nineteenth century belonged to Tarachand Ghanshyam and Bansilal Abirchand. They built their fortunes from trading in opium and cotton. In order to procure these goods, they moved far into the interiors of central India thus forming a trade network across the country. These goods were financed and later delivered in Bombay and Calcutta by the means of long-distance hundi transactions or bill of exchange. This denotes that the most significant dimension of the expansion of the capitalist world economy was creating a new type of bazaar economy that assisted, restricted, and reshaped the network of expansion.[72]

The banking communities included the Marwaris, Jains, and Nattukottai Chettis, who were the representatives of the highest development of indigenous banking in India. They had their offices and branches in important centres of Bombay, Calcutta, Delhi, and Rangoon. Of all the indigenous bankers, the Nattukottai Chettis were the most perfectly organized. E. Thurston observes in 1909, that the Nattukottai Chettis were as remarkable as the European merchants in organization, co-operation and business methods. A Nattukottai Chetti was believed to be a born banker. They had extensive business connections not only in India and Burma, but also in the Strait Settlements of Singapore, Ceylon, Saigon, Mauritius, and South Africa. Some of them even had business correspondents in London.[73]

Banking Communities of India and their Business Engagements

The principal caste engaged in the field of banking was the vaishya, which included the Jainas, Marwaris, and Chettis—the most important banking communities of India. The Jains were among the richest communities, well known for their generosity towards religious matters. The Marwaris, who were either Jainas or Vaishnavities, worshipped the deity of Vishnu, came from the Marwar state of Rajputana, and the residents of central India. The majority of Marwaris were settled while some travelled from one place to another in search of business and developed themselves as the 'Marwari' merchants and bankers. To conduct business, these Marwaris had migrated to the trading centres of Bombay and Calcutta.[74] The plague in Bombay in 1896 forced the Marwaris to move to Calcutta.[75] They traded in food grains, opium, silver, sugar, textiles, and indulged in money lending. Their business was organized around the joint-family system. Within the Marwari community, there were further groups such as Mahesaris, Bikaneris, Bagris, and Bhihanis, etc.[76] Author Medha M. Kudasiya in her book, *The Life and Times of G.D. Birla* has pointed out that the Marwaris has been a diasporic community and were connected with Marathas as bankers and military contractors, who only arrived in Bombay in large numbers between 1835 and the 1850s. The

Marwaris were not the only important business community but the Gujarati banias played an important role in the economy of western India while the Sindhis especially had a strong trading networks beyond north-western regions. The Chettiars from southern India played a significant role in the south Indian economy.[77]

The Chettis were another important business community belonging to the banking business. The name itself is used to denote a distinct caste. In Tamil, Chettis were merchants. They are sometimes called Chettiars or Nagarathas, and are well-known for trading and banking in south India. Among the Purvaththukude, the Chettis were small traders and money lenders by profession. Of all the Chettis, the Nattukottai Chettis were the most important bankers. They are the most charitable class in southern India and well known for liberally endowing towards temples and religious ceremonies.[78] The Jains and the Nattukottai Chettis are known for their wealth and riches. Other significant banking communities from the Punjab region were the Khatris and Aroras.

The Role of Presidency Banks and their Functioning

By the middle of the nineteenth century, London had become the world's banking capital and crucial links in the commercial chain could only be made due to access to colonial India. The first presidency bank was the Bank of Calcutta, opened on 2 June 1806 with a capital of Rs.5,000,000.[79] The presidency banks such as the Bank of Bengal was established as the Bank of Calcutta in 1806; the Government Bank was set up in 1806 and later reconstituted as the Bank of Madras in 1843; and the Bank of Bombay was set up in 1840s. These served as quasi-government bank for their respective presidencies. A plan was made later to merge the three Presidency banks into one central bank. The amalgamation of the three banks happened after the collapse of the Bank of Bombay in 1867. It was introduced in the Indian Legislative Council on 1 March 1920 and enacted in September 1920–1 when the Imperial Bank was formed.[80]

The presidency banks dominated other banks in India along with some exchange banks and several Indian joint stock banks. All of these banks operated in different segments of the economy. The exchange banks were mostly owned by Europeans and concentrated on financing foreign trade. Indian joint stock banks were generally undercapitalized and lacked the experience and capital.[81] The interest charged by the presidency banks was generally lower than the rate of the bazaar due to the tight condition of the market scenario. Another reason was when the cash keepers were dishonest and had little means of their own. The mechanism broke down because of the difficulty faced by the money agent in procuring funds on time.[82]

The presidency banks thus acted as the bankers to all other local banks. The status of the presidency bank as the 'bankers bank had noticeably grown during the recent years', and on many occasions have the Presidency rendered valuable assistance in quelling and incipient panic, or in coming to the relief of a local bank which through no fault of its own, was in temporary difficulties. The presidency bank was so important because during a time of crisis, other local banks could turn for help from this powerful bank and take its guidance in framing financial policy.[83] The presidency banks helped finance the internal trade of India by their purchases and re-discounting of internal Bill of Exchange, generally as *hundis*, to a large extent. These included the Shroffs, Mahajans, Chettis, money-lenders, and the others who either directly or by relations with these smaller bankers. On some occasions the amount of *hundi* held by the Banks of Bengal and Bank of Bombay had exceeded one-third of their total advances, and during the busy seasons, the proportion was rarely less than a three quarters. This shows the market trend and its impact on the presidency banks.[84]

The Transformation of the Old System into the New System of Saving Money

Several merchants and mill owners raised a part of their capital which they would keep or borrow from the Mahajans, who would give loan or interest on the money stored with them called the public deposits. This old system of money lending practice was pointed out by the Central Banking Enquiry Committee which stated, that 'was undoubtedly a reflex and transformation of the old system of money being kept in the safe custody of the Mahajans (money lender)'. In the middle of the nineteenth century, when industrial transition was on the way, transactions in shares were conducted with the help of a small group of brokers who gathered in the open space and functioned with the norms decided earlier by both parties without any fixed rules and regulation terms.[85]

The Hornby Vellard was one of the first engineering projects to be undertaken in Bombay. William Hornby, the Governor of Bombay, initiated the project in the early eighteenth century despite harsh opposition from the East India Company. The city, therefore, began to take shape with several civil engineering projects underway, marking the birth of the industrial revolution. The seven islands were finally merged into one single mass in 1845, and in 1853, the country's first railway connection was accomplished between Bombay and Thane. The city was under the rule of the Company's hands until the revolt in 1857. After the revolt of the Indian mutiny of 1857–8, the administration of British India was transferred from the English East India Company to the Royal British Crown from 1862 till India achieved her independence in 1947. Henceforth, the coins in circulation were minted under the direct authority of the British Crown. Later in 1876, Queen Victoria assumed the title of Empress of India, and from 1877, the obverse of the coins was changed to 'Victoria Empress'. The opening up of the Suez Canal in 1869 also meant that connections between Bombay and the rest of the world were open, resulting in Bombay becoming one of the major ports in India. The opening up of Suez Canal unlocked many gateways to many parts of the globe. Bombay's trade came to be connected to Europe through this route which made transportation cheap and easy. Just before gaining independence, the city witnessed an increase in trade through the Suez Canal.[86]

The second half of the nineteenth century was a period of regular famines and harvest failures due to bad weather conditions. There were two major famines in the 1870s, particularly the Madras famine of 1876–7 which was so severe that it cost many lives. Another reason for the prolonged depreciation was that the gold price and the exchange value in silver affected the rupee to decline continuously, leading to the closure of the Indian mints for free coinage in the 1893. The year 1893 was a also year of recession in Europe, America, and Australia, and the trade in the Far East was also affected by the Sino-Japanese war (1894–5), wars fought between China and Japan. Therefore, the Government of India had to take this step in order to tackle the grave situation brought about by natural calamities as well the bubonic plague in Bombay in 1896.[87]

Implementation of the Currency Commissions Reports in Bombay to Examine the Monetary Crisis

The Mansfield Commission by Lord Dufferin commenced in the year 1886. The Indian Currency Committee or Fowler Committee was a government committee appointed by the British-run Government of India on 29 April 1898 to examine the current situation in India. Until 1892, silver was the metal on which Indian currency and coinage had largely been based. In 1892, the Government of India announced its intent to 'close Indian mints to silver' and, in 1893, it brought this policy into force. There were other currency commissions to investigate and study the problems faced by the Currency Committee of India. The Currency Committee of 1898, during the exchange crisis arising from the fall of silver in relation to gold, raised the interest rates of the exchange banks and the presidency banks to much higher rates in the upcountry money markets. There emerged a huge difference between the bank rates and the bazaar rates. Since both of these followed their own laws of motion, this led to disparity and inequality of wealth which affected many businessmen. This state was to change with the merging of the presidency banks into the Imperial Bank of India in the year 1921 and with the establishment of the Reserve Bank of India.[88]

Therefore, the Fowler Commission by Elgin II in 1898; the Babington Smith Commission by Chelmsford in 1919; and the Hilton Young Commission by Linlithgow in 1926 came into force to keep a check on the activities of these banking houses. The Fowler Commission Report, carried by Mr J.H. Sleigh, Secretary and the Treasurer of the Bank of Bombay, and written in 1898, was an interesting report that docked in the details of the money market of Bombay and Calcutta. The bazaar rate was same in both these markets, however, while the exchange banks were starving to receive fixed deposits for short periods at 9, 10, and even 11 per cent per annum, the presidency bank was struggling to meet the demands for loans even at 12 and 13 per cent per annum. During these years, the presidency bank rates had not risen above 9 per cent. The conditions prevailing in the Indian money market in the year 1898 were in many respects very abnormal.[89] This shows that despite the money markets of both colonial port-cities—Bombay and Calcutta—the Presidency Bank of Bengal was established on 2 June 1806 and received its charter of incorporation from the East India Company in 1809. The first Bank of Bombay was established on 15 April 1840, which had its roots of origin in the initial Bank of Bombay which was established on 22 December 1720 and was called the Western Bank of Bombay under Charles Boone Governorship of Bombay. It was renamed the Bank of Madras on 1 July 1843. The founding of these banks in other presidencies put an end to the idea that the Bank of Bengal might become a bank for all of India.[90]

Till the year 1862, the banks had the right of note issue, and this was mandatory from 1839–62. In 1862, the management of note issue was taken over by the government, and in the same year, the right to note issue by the private bank was finally terminated. In 1876, the government had given away their right of appointing directors and their share of capital. Since that year onwards, the presidency banks lost their official status but remained different from other banks in being governed by a special Charter Act (The Presidency Banks Act of 1876).[91] The major cause for the fall in Indian rices lay in the government's attempts to hold a particular rate of exchange between the rupee and the sterling. To have a clear understanding, one must go back to the 'disastrous deflation' deliberately undertaken by America in 1920. This caused a similar deflation in many other countries which were anxious about preventing the depreciation of their currencies in terms of dollar. In this way, a general process of deflationary contraction was initiated in March 1920, after the short-lived post war boom, leading to a fall in prices all over the world. In India, following the recommendations of the Babington Smith Committee, the authorities had blundered into over-valuing the rupee at 2s. gold—a rate rendered untenable by the unexpected turn of circumstances. The sterling dollar cross-rate declined, thereby raising the rupee-sterling rate of 2s gold to 2s. 10¼d. on 11 February 1920. This extraordinary rate greatly encouraged the remittance of funds, partly genuine and partly speculative, to England. At the same time, the balance of trade became unfavourable; exports fell from Rs. 330 crores in 1919–20 to Rs. 258 crores in 1920–21, while imports, encouraged by the new rate of exchange, rose from Rs.208 crores to Rs.336 crores during this period.[92]

The Rise of Silver Metal Price during World War I

During the last quarter of the nineteenth century, World War I (1914–8) had already added more stringent conditions on the supply of silver metal to Bombay. The rising price of silver changed the old ratio, fixed in the early twentieth century, causing severe problems at the end of the first World War in 1918. The value of the rupee—a silver coin—had increased to 2s. The high rates of the rupee were fixed, and this increased the value of rupees which was not accepted by the Indian business communities. This happened following the recommendations of the Babington Smith Commission by Chelmsford in 1919, also known as the Indian Exchange and Currency Committee. They opposed this decision made by the Babington Smith Committee. Later, the Currency League was formed to pressurize the British government to withdraw. It was not accepted by Mahatma Gandhi that a lower rate of exchange would be in India's interest. The representatives of Indian business and the nationalists fought for the common Indian interest, and through their speeches, both Purshotamdas Thakurdas and Birla, paved their ways in making the British Government lower the rates to 1s 6d. The schism between Indian business and the British expatriates was noticed in the beginning of the 1920s. This resulted in further clashes between the Indian representatives and the British government.[93] In the words of Purshotamdas Thakurdas, since September 1931, the 'back door became [the] front door', as the rupee was completely delinked from gold and rooted in the sterling. It was said that the Indian currency was put in danger and did not receive its accurate value when exchanged.[94]

Purshotamdas Thakur was connected to the House of Tata, who sometimes also sided with the Birlas. He cooperated with the Tatas to form an anti-non-cooperation society in Bombay. He was also well known as the 'King Cotton' of Bombay and represented the Indian Merchants Chambers (IMC), which was established on 7 September 1907 in Bombay. The IMC was instituted to promote trade, commerce, and industry established by Indian entrepreneurs and played a significant role in consolidating Indian business interests and making the Indian economy self-reliant. Thakur also championed the cause of setting up nautical colleges and schools for the training of Indian seamen.[95] A new branch of the Royal Mint of London was opened in Bombay during the year 1918–19 with the objective of coining the British sovereigns in India. After coining 12.95 lakh sovereigns, the branch was shut in

April 1919. It was later converted into the residence of the Mint Master, now known as the Mint House. In 1919, a gold refinery was set up in the Bombay Mint. It employed the process of chlorination for the refining of gold. It refined raw gold which came from South Africa, Australia, and other Indian mines. The silver refinery later was started in 1929 due to the demand of silver which had an installed annual capacity of 80 million ounces of silver.[96]

Table 6.3: Types of Banks Present in Bombay City in the Year 1908

Mercantile Bank of London	1854	India, Ltd
Chartered Bank of London	1858	India
Australia, and China	1863	India, Ltd
National Bank of London	1863	India, Ltd
Bank of Bengal Calcutta	1867	Agency
Bank of Bombay	1868	Bombay
Hong Kong and Shanghai Banking Corporation	1869	
Yokohama Bank Limited…	1894	
Presidency Banks		
Bank of Bengal established as the Bank of Calcutta	1806	
Bank of Madras	1843	
Bank of Bombay	1840	

Source: S. M. Edwardes, *The Gazetteer of Bombay City and Island*, vol. II, Bombay: Government Times Press, 1910, p. 292.

The business was mostly transacted in Bombay in enhancing of exports of cotton, yarn and seeds and imports of piece-goods, bullion, machinery, etc. The presidency banks—the Bank of Bengal, established as the Bank of Calcutta in

1806; the Government Bank was set up in 1806 and later reconstituted as the Bank of Madras in 1843; and the Bank of Bombay, set up in 1840—served as the quasi-government bank for the respective presidencies. Later, a proposal was made to set up a central bank which would revolve around the other three presidency banks. The proposal to merge the presidency banks was revived after the collapse of the Bank of Bombay in 1867 as a consequence of the 'share mania', which had gripped the Bombay market in connection to the American Civil War. The war cut off the supply of American cotton to England causing an unprecedented boom in the Bombay market. In 1898, in the depositions before the Indian Currency Committee (also known as the Flower Committee), which drew attention to the mismanagement of banking facilities in India and the sudden rise in the rate of discount, Alfred de Rothschild designed a scheme for creating a bank with the same privileges as those at the Bank of England by dissolving the presidency banks.[97]

In 1901, after the death of Queen Victoria, King Edward VII ascended the throne and coins began to be issued in his name. In 1901–2, re-coinage of the 1840 rupees was undertaken under orders of the government. There were two kinds of 1840 rupees. In June 1901, orders were issued for the re-coinage of the first issue. Treasury officers were instructed to remit the description of coins to the mint along with their balances of coins withdrawn from circulation. In January 1902, orders were issued for the withdrawal and re-coinage of the second issue of 1840 coins. The minting of these coins began during the year 1906–7, and the first issues to the public were made from 1 August 1907. After the death of Edward VII in 1910, King George V (1911–36) occupied the throne and coins were now issued in his name. King Edward VIII succeeded King George V in January 1936, but before the coronation, he abdicated the throne in December 1936 in favour of the Duke of York. No coins were thus issued in his name.[98] The last English Monarch, the Duke of York came to the throne as George VI on 11 December 1936. He was coronated and crowned on 12 May 1937 and ruled from 1938–47. Indian coins were issued in his name. During the rule of King George VI, India attained freedom and the last Indian coinage, under British rule, had his effigy until 1950.[99] This plan of founding the Imperial Bank of India was taken up fifteen years later in 1913 by John Maynard Keynes, who revived these issues and proposed that an 'Imperial Bank of India' be set up as the State Bank of India. Its primary function would be to perform operations of central banking as well as commercial banking. The Chamberlain Commission was appointed in the year 1913 which studied the memorandum submitted by Keynes. However, it could not take a decision immediately and took several years for the Imperial Bank of India Bill to be passed. The bill facilitated the amalgamation of the three presidency banks which were introduced in the Indian Legislative Council on 1 March 1920. The Imperial Bank of India Bill was finally passed in September 1920.[100]

The First World War through the end of the Second World War, and two years thereafter until the independence of India, were challenging times for Indian banking. The initial years were turbulent, and it took its toll as many banks simply collapsed despite the Indian economy having gained indirect boost due to the war-related economic activities. Many banking firms saw a sharp decline just before the First World War in 1913 and would continue facing losses until 1917. The period before 1913, which had earlier seen a profitable business and boom, now saw the crash in the banking system due to the war. The total paid capital received by the banks was as low as 51 per cent of the total received by the joint stock banks. The banking crisis of 1913–17 is by far the most serious which India had suffered since the introduction of European banking into the country.[101] Destruction of Calcutta 'agency houses' during 1829–32 and the ruins of so many banks and financial companies during 1862–5 further brought about the disasters of 1913–17. The Indian banking system has perhaps not yet completely recovered from these impacts since speculation and mismanagement led to the decline of an overwhelming number of banks.[102] The First World War also added to the crisis of the government as it had issued gold sovereigns to the public which could be exchanged with currency notes. Another issue was that the severe shortage of precious metals and the rise in the prices of silver due to the ongoing war made the public hoard silver for personal profits. The war put the currency system of India to an acute test. The silver standard, for example, was maintained by the British government during the years of silver depreciation despite the repeated appeals from the Indian bureaucrats to move over to a gold standard in order to make a bimetallic standard internationally acceptable. While the tribute payments were fixed in sterling, the silver depreciation made the task more challenging for the managers of the British Indian finance companies.[103]

The Setting up the Reserve Bank of India in July 1926

The Reserve Bank of India was set up because of the order from the Royal Commission of Indian Currency, popularly known as the Hilton Young Commission. This commission was appointed in August 1925, 'to investigate and bring out a report on the Indian exchange, currency system and its functioning and if it required any modifications. The commission worked for the improvement of the Reserve Bank of India'. The bank aimed at managing a balance between price stability and thus improving the economic growth.[104] The Hilton Young Commission submitted its report in July 1926 to establish a central bank which would be called the 'Reserve Bank of India'. This bank was expected to control all other banking institutions. The Hilton Commission was the father of the Reserve Bank of India as it introduced the idea of opening a central bank to the Legislative Assembly on 25 January 1927. The bill was postponed twice after careful consideration but failed to be implemented, and later, it was reconsidered again due to constitutional reforms. In 1928, the Government of India published a new Gold Standard and Reserve Bank of India Bill, but that too failed.[105]

The Indian Central Banking Enquiry Committee revived the Bill of Opening the Bankers Bank, i.e. Reserve Bank of India in 1931. The committee appointed to investigate the report dated 14 March 1933, stated that the Reserve Bank Bill would be drafted on the recommendations of the London Committee introduced by the Finance Member, Sir George Schuster on 8 September 1933, and the Bill was received by the assent of the Viceroy and Governor-General, the Earl of Willingdon, on 6 March 1934. The Reserve Bank of India Act was adopted to constitute a Reserve Bank of India to regulate the issue of Bank notes, maintain reserves to secure monetary stability in the country, and open the currency and credit system in India. The Bill received the assent of the Governor-General on 5 March 1934. After many considerations, finally, the Reserve Bank of India was established on 1 January 1935, and its operation commenced on 1 April 1935 under the supervision of Sir Osborne Smith.[106]

The first Deputy Governors of the Reserve Bank were James Braid Taylor and Sikander Hyatt Khan, who had administrative knowledge and planning as they were earlier engaged in the government office. The Report on Currency and Finance was the first report published by the Reserve Bank of India. It covered the years 1935–6 and 1936–7, and replaced the Annual Report of the Office of Controller of the Currency, which was wound up in October 1937. The Reserve Bank of India initially issued bank notes bearing the portrait of King George VI and the signature of the Second Governor James Braid Taylor. The first Governor Osborne Smith could not issue bank notes due to the abdication of King Edward VIII resulting in delay and the need for a new design altogether.[107]

The Role of the First Governor of the Reserve Bank of India

In 1934, Sir Osborne Smith, a citizen of Australia, was appointed as the first Governor of the Reserve Bank of India. He was recommended by the Governor of the Bank of England, Lord Montagu Norman, to take up the post in December 1933. Finally, on 29 November 1934, the position was offered to Sir Osborne Arkell Smith. The appointment of Sir Osborne took place because the British trusted his capabilities and the Bank of England could rely on him and expect his unquestioned co-operation. His experience as a banker earned him a high repute. He was the Managing Governor of the Imperial Bank through the difficult years of depression where he introduced reforms which helped the bank perform well.[108]

During his tenure as the Governor of the Reserve Bank of India, Smith brought about one of the most significant developments in the arena of banking in the mid-twentieth century, which was also the period of rise and expansion of the exchange banks. In contrast to the official banks, namely the exchange banks and the presidency banks, which eschewed foreign exchange, the private banks that were established in the port cities put the Indian money market in direct contact with international finance. These banks had connections with international banks in Europe and America.

A Report on the Inauguration of the Reserve Bank of India's Office

The Reserve Bank of India at Bombay begins its business in the Bank Street in the Shaftesbury Avenue Theatre, where a plate is seen with the words 'Reserve Bank of India' embossed. The building holds a strong history of banking—it has housed many offices of the Imperial Bank of India. It has become more famous now as the head office of west India for the Reserve Bank. The Reserve Bank of India opened by taking over the Public Debt Office, the Public Accounts office, and the Currency Department.[109]

A Note on One Rupee Notes (Smallest Denomination in India)

The first note whose payment was guaranteed by the government was introduced in circulation for the first time through the Indian Paper Money Act of 1861. This act vested the power of issuing and circulating bank notes in the Government of India in March 1862. One of the most fascinating and important notes amongst all was the one-rupee note, issued for the first time as a promissory note on 30 November 1917 during the reign of King George V. These notes were issued as promissory notes in the Bombay Mint. These notes were printed due to the inability of the colonial authorities to produce silver coins which forced them to switch to paper currency. In July 1918, the German torpedoes sank a ship named *SS Shirala* carrying a consignment of one-rupee notes from England to India. These were a part of the second print—notes which were pre-signed and legal tender. It was also the first case where the notes which were pre-signed had sunk before they arrived to India from England.[110]

Another variation of the one-rupee note was introduced on 24 July 1940 in honour of King George V. It had a more elaborate design with a decorated border on the obverse. The note was first printed in England in 1935. It depicted a silver coin image of King George V on the left corner. The words, 'I promise to pay the bearer the sum of One Rupee on demand at any office of issue', were embossed upon it. Even though currency notes were issued by the Government of India in 1861, the one-rupee note was launched in 1917 because the silver used for the one-rupee coin was melted and used for making weapon components in the First World War. The printing of the one-rupee notes was also undertaken as a measure against the situation created by the United States for the Indian currency. The United States aggressively purchased silver from 1934 onwards and raised the price of silver, creating disruption for the Indian currency system due to export of silver currency. Another major cause was the outbreak of the Second World War in 1939, which cut the transport supply of silver from its source. Thus, these factors led to the introduction of rupee coins and reduced the fineness of the rupee coin from 11/12ths of fine silver to one half of fine silver. The introduction of rupee notes and coins thereby decisively moved India away from silver and ended the old-age system of silver currency. There arose a shortage in coins since the public tried to hoard these coins and therefore, the princely states in western India issued 'cash coupons' to meet the shortage. The Bombay and

Calcutta Tramways were notified to issue their own coupons in lieu of various denominations of small coins. These coins constituted a form of exigent money.[111] New denomination of the two-rupee coin was introduced for the first time in India on 19 February 1943. The printing of Indian one-rupee notes was first discontinued in 1926, then restarted in 1940 and continued until 1994, when it was stopped again as part of cost-cutting measures. Printing resumed for a second time in 2015. Until 1970, the Indian one-rupee note was also used as a currency in Persian and Gulf countries such as United Arab Emirates, Bahrain, Oman, etc. Thus, the journey of the one-rupee note in the history of Indian currency is rather enthralling.[112]

Special Features of the One Rupee Note—1st Issue

Issued on 30 November 1917.
Discontinued on 1 January 1926.
Printed in England.
Paper: White Hand-Made Moulded Paper.
3 signatories—M.M.S. Gubbay, A.C. McWatters, and H. Denning.
Watermark: Two varieties—star enclosed in a rectangle and rayed star.
The first pre-signed notes shipped from England.
The only issue of Indian paper money having a prefix 'O'.[113]

An Account of SS Breda Carrying RBI Cargo

On 23 December 1940, *SS Breda*—a Dutch cargo steamer carrying a consignment of bank note paper for the Reserve Bank of India—met with a fatal attack by German bombers who sunk the ship destroying valuable treasures it carried.

A similar incident took place on 14 April 1944 when the ship *Fort Stikine*, a British vessel built in Canada in 1942, exploded during its berth in the docks of Bombay, killing almost 1,300 people and injuring 3,000 others. The ship was carrying gold bullion on behalf of the Bank of England as a part of its cargo for Bombay.[114] This explosion of the ships which had valuable cargoes on board created a great loss for the owner as well as for the purpose with which it was brought to Bombay for business especially for the minting of currencies and payments. Both these incidents happened during the Second World War where the supply of bullion to the port of Bombay and other cities faced severe crisis and both these incidents created huge losses.

The Introduction of Decimal Coinage in India

India attained her freedom on 15 August 1947, and the effigy of the English monarch continued to appear on its coins until India became a republic. After 26 January 1950, different figurines appeared on the reverse of the coins. The English monarch effigies were replaced by the Ashoka Pillars. The King's portrait was replaced by the lion capital of Ashoka (the national emblem) whereas the reverse carried a large floral motif. The design of the note continued to be very similar to King George VI's one-rupee note. This significant change was made in the addition to the obverse and reverse template of the one-rupee coin of 1951. In the same year, the colour of the one-rupee coin was changed from green to violet. Another change made by the Indian government was that on one-rupee, half-rupee, and quarter-rupee coins, sheafs of corn were embossed; on two-anna and half-anna coins, there was a bull; and on one-paisa coins, there was a flying horse.[115]

India adopted the decimal system of coinage from 1 April

1957, under its first Prime Minister Pandit Jawaharlal Nehru. The lowest denomination introduced in this system was one paisa—a hundred paisa made a rupee. This paisa was called the 'naya paisa' to differentiate it from the old paisa. Later, 20 paisa coins made of aluminium-bronze was introduced from 1968 to 1971. This coin had a symbol of the lotus flower on its reverse. Thus, the fort figurines of the national animal, bird, flower, and fruits were used as effigies on the coins.[116]

In 1964, production of commemorative coins began and the first commemorative coin was minted in the memory of Pandit Jawaharlal Nehru. The Bombay Mint thus made a significant contribution to Indian coinage and gold refining and thus helped in controlling the quality of bullion.[117] The history of finance in India can be traced from the origin of Bombay Mint, which brought in bullion for minting currency, and thus the idea of banking institutions in Bombay which in turn gave rise to agency houses, created markets, and established the Reserve Bank of India to control the functioning of banks; this also led to the founding of the Bombay Stock Exchange for investing capitals and earning profits which contributed greatly to the business of Bombay.[118]

Notes

1. K.K. Chaudhari, *Maharashtra State Gazetteers, Greater Bombay District*, vol. II, Bombay: Gazetteers Department, Government of Maharashtra, 1987, p. 367.
2. The rupee was also used as the standard denomination of two Indian Ocean island states, Mauritius and Seychelles. A version of the rupee called rupiah is a currency of Indonesia. In the nineteenth century, the rupee used to be a silver coin, but in 1940, its silver content was reduced to 50 per cent and from 1947 onwards, the silver was no longer in use. This replacement of silver by alloy was called 'Fall of the Rupee' by

Oscar Wilde, when the value of silver halved between 1870 and 1895. The silver currency was very much prevalent in the Indian monetary system, and its fall was disastrous for the Indian economy.

3. Jonathan Williams, Joe Cribb, and Elizabeth Errington, *Money: A History*, London: British Museum Press, 1997, p. xxx.
4. Jurgen Oster Hammel, *The Transformation of the World: A Global History of the Nineteenth Century*, New Jersey: Princeton University, 2009, pp. 730–32.
5. H.F. Howard, 'The Imperial Bank of India', *The Economic Journal*, vol. 31, no. 122, London: Oxford University Press, 1921, pp. 147–71.
6. *Bombay Mint 150th Anniversary Celebrations*, Bombay: India Government Mint, 1 May 1982.
7. Ibid.
8. Ibid.
9. Ibid.
10. Ibid.
11. S.M. Edwardes, *The Gazetteer of Bombay City and Island*, vol. II, Bombay: Government Times Press, 1910, p. 407.
12. *Bombay Mint 150th Anniversary Celebrations.*
13. Ibid.
14. Ibid.
15. Ibid.
16. James Mackenzie, *Bombay Gazette*, Bombay: Steam Press, 1876, p. 45.
17. Edwardes, *The Gazetteer of Bombay City and Island*, p. 282.
18. G.V. Mulherkar, 'Coins of the East India Company at Bombay', in *The Bombay Explorer*, vol. I, Mumbai, July 1986, pp. 25–8.
19. Clive Dewey and C.A. Bayly, 'Rulers, Townsmen, and Bazaars: North Indian Society in the Age of British Expansion 1770–1870', in *Economic History Review*, ed. E.H. Hunt, vol. 38, Kendal: Titus Wilson and Son, 1985, p. 431.
20. Bazil Shaikh, Ranjeeta Dubey, and S.M. Khot, *Mint Road*

Milestones RBI At 75, Mumbai: Reserve Bank of India, 2010, p. 123.

21. K.K. Chaudhari, *Maharashtra State Gazetteers, Greater Bombay District*, vol. II, Bombay: Gazetteers Department, Government of Maharashtra, 1987, p. 367.
22. The rupee was also used as the standard denomination of two Indian Ocean island states, Mauritius and Seychelles. A version of the rupee called rupiah is a currency of Indonesia. In the nineteenth century, the rupee used to be a silver coin, but in 1940, its silver content was reduced to 50 per cent and from 1947 onwards, the silver was no longer in use. This replacement of silver by alloy was called 'Fall of the Rupee' by Oscar Wilde, when the value of silver halved between 1870 and 1895. The silver currency was very much prevalent in the Indian monetary system, and its fall was disastrous for the Indian economy.
23. Jonathan Williams, Joe Cribb, and Elizabeth Errington, *Money: A History*, London: British Museum Press, 1997, p. 43.
24. *Bombay Mint 150th Anniversary Celebrations.*
25. Ibid.
26. Doreen Soh, *From Cowries to Credit Cards: Stories of Singapore's Money*, Singapore: Federal Publications, 1990, p. 10.
27. Howard, 'The Imperial Bank of India', p. 168.
28. Ibid., p. 12.
29. James Maclean, *A Guide to Bombay*, Bombay: Steam Press, 1889, p. 41.
30. James Douglas, *Glimpses of Old Bombay and Western India*, London: Sampson Low, Marston & Co., 1900, p. 113.
31. This was the first Bombay Bank which dealt in European exchange and the Oriental Bank originated from this.
32. Doshabhai Framji Karaka, *History of the Parsis,* vol. II, London: Macmillan, 1884, pp. 38–40.
33. Ibid., p. 40.

34. Douglas, *Glimpses of Old Bombay and Western India*, p. 115.
35. Jesse S. Palsetia, 'Mad Dogs and Parses: the Bombay Riots of 1832', *Journal of the Royal Asiatic Society*, vol. II, no. 1, Third Series, April 2001, pp. 13–30.
36. Dharma Kumar and Tapan Ray Chaudhuri, *The Cambridge Economic History of India; 1757–1970*, vol. 2, Cambridge: Cambridge University Press, 1983, pp. 574–5.
37. D.E. Wacha, *A Financial Chapter in the History of Bombay City*, Bombay: Commercial Press, 1910, p. 38.
38. Rajat Kanta Ray, 'The Bazaar Changing Structural Characteristics of the Indigenous Section of Indian Economy before the Great Depression', *The Indian Economic and Social History Review*, no. 3, New Delhi: Sage Publication, 1988, pp. 263–318.
39. Amiya Kumar Bagchi, 'Money and Credit in Indian History: From Early Medieval Times', in *American Historical Review*, vol. 109, no. 1, February 2004.
40. Anand A. Yang, *Markets, Society, and the Colonial State in Gangetic Bihar*, Berkeley: University of California Press, 1999, p. 227.
41. Radhe Shyam Rungta, *The Rise of Business Corporations in India; 1851–1900*, London: Cambridge University Press, 1970, p. 208.
42. Wilfrid Atlay, *Report of the Bombay Stock Exchange Enquiry Committee*, Bombay: The Government Central Press, 1924, pp. 3–6.
43. Rungta, *The Rise of Business Corporations in India*, pp. 208–10.
44. Atlay, *Report of the Bombay Stock Exchange Enquiry Committee*, p. 4.
45. Amya Kumar Bagchi, *Private Investment in India 1900–1939*, London: Cambridge University Press, 1972, p. 208.
46. Maclean, *A Guide to Bombay*, p. 48.

47. Dwijendra Tripathi, *The Oxford History of Indian Business*, New Delhi: Oxford University Press, 2004, p. 80.
48. Ibid., p. 78.
49. Ibid., p. 119.
50. Williams, Monier, 'Monetary System of British India', in *Bombay Quarterly Review*, vol. VI, no. XII, October 1857, p. 258.
51. F.J. Faraday, 'A Financial Chapter in the History of Bombay City', *The Economic Journal*, vol. 21, no. 81, March 1911, pp. 69–71.
52. *Bombay Quarterly Review*, vol. VI, no. XII, pp. 258–9.
53. Ibid., p. 47.
54. Lakshmi Subramaniam, *Three Merchants of Bombay: Business Pioneers of the Nineteenth Century*, Delhi: Penguins Books, 2016, p. 149.
55. Rungta, *The Rise of Business Corporations in India*, p. 74.
56. The American Civil War came to an end in 1865.
57. S.L. Sinha, *Early European Banking in India*, London: MacMillan & Co., 1927, pp. 158–60.
58. Bombay has always been one of the principal ports and a centre for speculation, especially in silver and cotton.
59. D.E. Wacha, *A Financial Chapter in the History of Bombay City*, Bombay: A.J. Combridge & Co, 1910.
60. Aravind Ganachari, '"White Man's Embarrassment": European Vagrancy in the 19th Century Bombay', *Economic and Political Weekly*, vol. 37, no. 25, 22–8 June 2002, pp. 2477–86.
61. Tripathi, *The Oxford History of Indian Business*, pp. 102–3.
62. Ibid., pp. 259–61.
63. *Bombay Quarterly Review*, vol. VI, no. XII, October 1857, p. 256.
64. Ibid., p. 237.
65. Ibid., p. 260.
66. Maclean, *Guide to Bombay*, p. 125.
67. Bagchi, 'Money and Credit in Indian History', p. xxxii.

68. Sinha, *Early European Banking in India*, pp. 158–60.
69. Wacha, *A Financial Chapter in the History of Bombay City*, p. 70.
70. Ganachari, '"White Man's Embarrassment"', pp. 2477–86.
71. Rungta, *The Rise of Business Corporations in India*, p. 165.
72. Tripathi, *The Oxford History of Indian Business*, pp. 102–3.
73. Ibid., pp. 259–61.
74. *Bombay Quarterly Review*, vol. VI, no. XII, October 1857, p. 256.
75. Dwijendra Tripathi, Jyoti Jumani, p. 87.
76. Tripathi, *The Oxford History of Indian Business*, p. 237.
77. Medha M. Kudasiya, *The Life and Times of G. D. Birla*, New Delhi: Oxford University Press, 2003, pp. 4–5.
78. Ibid., p. 260.
79. Maclean, *Guide to Bombay*, p. 125.
80. Ibid., p. 126.
81. *Bombay Mint 150th Anniversary Celebration.*
82. Ibid.
83. Edwardes, *The Gazetteer of Bombay City and Island*, p. 291.
84. Rajat Kanta Ray, 'Asian Capital in the Age of European Domination: The Rise of the Bazaar, (1800–1914)', *Modern Asian Studies*, vol. 29, no. 3, July 1993, pp. 497–8.
85. Tripathi, *The Oxford History of Indian Business*, p. 78.
86. Asiya Siddiqi, *Trade and Finance in Colonial India 1750–1860*, Delhi: Oxford University Press, 1995, p. 47.
87. John Maynard Keynes, *Indian Currency and Finance*, London: MacMillan & Co., 1913, pp. 194–5.
88. *Indian Exchange and Currency (Babington Smith) Committee 1919: Vol 1, Report and Minority Report; Vol 2, Minutes of Evidence; Vol. 3, Appendices*, London: British Library-Asia and African Studies, 1920, pp. 657–9.
89. Ray, 'Asian Capital in the Age of European Domination', pp. 452–554.
90. Aditya Mukherjee, 'The Depression Years: Indian Capitalist's Critique of British Monetary and Fiscal Policy in India,

1929–39', in *Money and Credit in Indian History: From Early Medieval Times*, ed. Amiya Kumar Bagchi, New Delhi: Tulika Books, 2002, pp. 149–69.
91. Ibid., p. 500.
92. L.C. Jain, *The Indigenous Banking in India*, London: Macmillan & Co., 1929, p. 36.
93. Ibid., p. 169.
94. Ibid., p. 28.
95. Ibid., p. 30.
96. V.D. Divekar, 'Western India', in *The Cambridge Economic History of India, c.1757–1970*, ed. Dharma Kumar, vol. 2, Cambridge: Cambridge University Press, 1983, pp. 332–51.
97. Sinha, *Early European Banking*, p. 178.
98. Amiya Kumar Bagchi, *Money and Credit in Indian History: From Early Medieval Times*, New Delhi: Tulika Books, 2002, p. xxxiv.
99. Shaikh, Dubey and Khot, *Mint Road Milestones: RBI at 75*, pp. 34–5.
100. Jain, *The Indigenous Banking in India*, p. 146.
101. A.N. Porter and R.F. Holland, *Money, Finance, and Empire 1760–1960*, Great Britain: Frank Cass, 1985, p. 104.
102. Tripathi, *The Oxford History of Indian Business*, p. 262.
103. Keynes, *Indian Currency and Finance*, pp. 195–8.
104. Shaikh, Dubey and Khot, *Mint Road Milestones: RBI at 75*, 2010, p. 199.
105. Ibid., p. 200.
106. 'Reserve Bank Begins Business', 4 April 1935, https://rbi.org.in/scripts/brief_commence.aspx.
107. Ibid., pp. 262–3.
108. Jain, *The Indigenous Banking in India*, p. 150.
109. *Bombay Mint 150th Anniversary Celebrations.*
110. Ibid., p. 200.
111. Anand Chandavarkar, 'Central Bank and Government: An Untold Story from RBI's Early History', *Economic and Political Weekly*, vol. 35, no. 34, August 2000, pp. 3048–60.

112. Shaikh, Dubey and Khot, *Mint Road Milestones: RBI at 75*, pp. 34–6.
113. The Central Bank of India is one of the oldest banks in the country which even survived the crisis of 1913.
114. Jain, *The Indigenous Banking in India*, pp. 151–3.
115. Ibid., p. 165.
116. A.N. Porter and R.F. Holland, *Money, Finance, And Empire 1760–1960*, Great Britain: Frank Cass, 1985, p. 104.
117. Tripathi, *The Oxford History of Indian Business*, p. 262.
118. Chandavarkar, 'Central Bank and Government: An Untold Story from RBI's Early History', pp. 3048–60.

Conclusion

The book encapsulates a rich narrative on the bullion trade under Portuguese presence in western India in the seventeenth century. The island of Bombay was later transferred to the English monarch King Charles II of England in the year 1661 through a political alliance between the Portuguese and the English. The island of Bombay was developed under the Bombay Governor Gerald Aungier who laid the foundation of the most important financial institution—the Bombay Mint, the first English mint established by the English East India Company in 1676, and the Bank of Bombay was founded in 1720. It also examines the role of the Assay Masters and other functionaries associated with these institutions such as Gumastas and Saraf's. Efforts made by the Bombay government to replace the Portuguese currency with English money are also laid down.

During these years, Bombay emerged as the leading monetary and financial centre of British India. English coins minted in the Bombay Mint circulated in the Indian subcontinent and provided financial stability. The book also examines Bombay's international trading links with countries such as the Netherlands, Spain, and Hungary in Europe; Brazil, Mexico, and Peru in South America; and China and Japan in East Asia. It is from these countries that bullion was exported and imported into Bombay, to deliver to other hinterland port cities on the west coast of India.

The Bombay Island was under the Portuguese Estado da India from 1510–1660. The establishment of Portuguese power on the west coast of India is reviewed in the book. The Portuguese Viceroy Afonso de Albuquerque, to meet financial needs, established a mint in Goa in 1510 where Portuguese coins such as manoels, xerafins, pardaos, esperas and reis were minted.

Improvement in Portuguese transport technology brought new changes to the trading system. Portuguese trading ships, namely galleons, carracks, caravels, frigates, and naos, helped them compete for control of trade in the Indian Ocean. Introduction of the Cartaz system in Cochin in 1502 helped in the generation of revenues and the building of the Portuguese economy in western India in the sixteenth and seventeenth centuries. Prominent among them were the German and Italian merchants who were the financiers of Portuguese trade. The most important were the Fugger and Welser families, owing to their trading links and contributions. The book also examines the role of the European mercantile communities who played an important role in the development of Portuguese trade in western India.

In June 1661, the English monarch Charles II of England married the Portugal princess Catherine of Braganza. A part of her dowry was the territory of the port-region of Bombay. This was the alliance that made it possible for the Company to gain greater control over India. After considerable resistance from the Portuguese in India, the Bombay Island was finally handed over to the British on 18 February 1665. In need of additional finances to improve Britain's naval capability, Charles II of England turned to the English East India Company for a loan of 50,000 pounds. In return, the Company acquired the island of Bombay on an annual rent of 10 pounds per year from 1668.

Under the Governorship of Gerald Aungier (1669–77), important measures were undertaken to develop the Bombay Island. These included important institutions such as the Court of Judicature which was established in 1672, and the Bombay Mint in 1676. An Assay Master was appointed to regulate the functioning of the mint. However, malpractices and corruption continued to exist. The measures taken to deal with these situations are also examined in the work.

The book also closely examines policies introduced by the Bombay government to promote the bullion trade and fulfil their monetary concerns. These policies sought to replace Portuguese and other currencies in circulation with English currency. The Bombay government also sought to ensure that trade transactions were carried out in the English language and not Portuguese, which at the time was the *lingua franca* for mercantile transactions in the Indian Ocean. This would further ensure the British domination of markets in western India and assert the Company's authority over Bombay town and presidency.

To increase the revenue earnings and to develop the island required the participation of both Indian and European merchants engaged in the bullion trade. Prominent Indian merchants dealing in this trade included Virji Vohra, Bhimjee Parekh, Rustam Maneckji, Rama Kamati, Laldas Vithal Parekh, Jamshetjee Jejeebhoy, and Jaganath Shankar Seth. Prominent Armenian merchants were Khwaja Minaz and Khwaja Shamsuddin Giloni who traded in precious metals. Abdul Gaffur was one of the most influential merchants of western India based in Surat who had trading connections in Bombay and other port cities of west coast. Their contributions are also well detailed.

How the politics of the west coast of India in the late seventeenth and eighteenth centuries created disturbances in the trade of Bombay is also of crucial significance. Political conflicts which arose vis-à-vis the British and the Marathas, the Mughals, the Siddis, the Portuguese, the Dutch and the French are also assessed. The Maratha leader Kanhoji Angria from Kolaba and Khem Sawant of Sawantwadi were powerful rulers of the Konkan region, who confronted and challenged the prowess of the English East India Company in western India. They used skilful tactics to fight against the European vessels. Kanhoji Angria defended the Maratha sovereignty against the British, the Dutch, and the French powers contesting for control of the western coast of India. After Kanhoji's death, his son Sekhoji Angria's force was not powerful enough and he could continue his father's legacy only until 1733. The powers of the Angria declined due to the internal politics against the Peshwa. The Marathas came to the forefront of the political scenario and many arrangements were made with the English.

Through the creation of the Bombay Marine (1759–1829), law and order was sought to be imposed and greater protection and security could be ensured for merchants. Shipping paved way for trade. Development of the Bombay harbour played an important role in building Bombay's economy. Ship building in the mid-seventeenth century contributed greatly to the development of Bombay's naval power. Trading vessels were constructed by the Parsi merchant Lowji Nusserwanji Wadia with ten other Parsi carpenters who came from Surat to construct ships at the Bombay dock. It was well planned and built to carry goods for local and foreign trade. The growing strength of the Bombay Marine helped in increasing Bombay's trade and revenues as well. Eventually, the British realized the importance of the maritime industry in the island of Bombay for it was gifted with a strategic location and possessed natural harbours along the west coast of India, which they used to their advantage.

By the mid-eighteenth century, Bombay's bullion trade had grown substantially. The establishment of private agency houses in Bombay also promoted trade. Both Company officials and private traders participated and invested in bullion and other commodities. These agency houses created business and actively funded the merchants to invest their capital in trade. Private European agency houses included the Charles Forbes & Co., Bruce, Fawcett & Co., Shotton & Co., John Leckie, S. Beaufort, Alexander Adamson & Co., and four European firms of wine-merchants and shopkeepers—Baxter, Son & Co., John Mitchell & Co., Wooler & Co., and R. Mclean & Co. These firms traded on their own accounts and owned their own ships.

Government officials and private merchants, both British and Indian, contributed to the development of money supply in Bombay and western India. The contribution of individual Company servants and private traders such as Robert Cowan, William Wake, Francis Pym, Lawrence Sullivan, David Scott, Jonathan Duncan, and Henry Dundas is noteworthy. Some of them were Company's officials who established very profitable private trade on their own accounts. Private traders engaged in financing voyages, provided ships with cargoes, and were involved in buying and selling of foreign coins such as Spanish dollars, pillar dollars, Venetian crowns, and florins. The practice of the English Company employees trading on their own account was prohibited in the 1780s as the English government faced severe revenue losses.

Political significance was of great importance since financing wars which were fought, namely the Anglo-Maratha war and the Anglo-Mysore war, required large amounts of money supply. In 1780–1800, Bombay town faced an acute shortage of silver metal which led to the suspension of Bombay silver rupees. Between 1802 and 1818, the British asserted political control over western India. The third Anglo-Maratha war (1818–9) ended with all the territories of Gujarat, Karnataka, Konkan, and central India being a part of the enlarged Bombay Presidency. The defeat of the Marathas opened the way to the development of Bombay as an administrative centre and political capital.

Bombay's trading links with Europe, China, and Japan with regard to the import of bullion supply have also been discussed in the book. Commodities exported from the Bombay port were opium, cotton, silk and tea. From 1780–1810, the silver production fell sharply due to the political instability in Latin American independence movements as well as the American and French revolutions which obstructed silver supply to Bombay town and other ports of western India.

Bombay's China trade connection was primarily on the basis of opium exchanged for bullion, especially white metal-silver. The port town of Canton was a major centre for the supply of opium. The growing demand for opium in China from the late eighteenth century led to the importation of large amounts of gold and silver into western India. Parsi and Marwari firms played an important role in the trade of opium, cotton, silk and tea and thus established their own companies in Canton and other Chinese towns such as Amoy, Fuzhou, Ningbo, Souchou, and Nanjing. By the early nineteenth century, Bombay was a major centre of international trade with the Persian Gulf, the Malabar Coast, Coromandel, Bengal, and China. In the mid-nineteenth century, the first Opium War in 1839 and the treaty of Nanking in 1842 reduced Bombay's trading links with China substantially.

Silver supply was disrupted by revolutions in Latin America from 1810. The Latin American independence movement created social instability and pushed the Spanish out. By the

1820s, the global silver production had fallen more than 50 per cent from the late 1700s. From 1780–1810, the silver production fell sharply and was only regained in 1860–70. When political stability in Latin America was destabilized, it caused the production of silver to be affected in all corners of the globe. The white metal silver had 'conquered' the world's largest economy. Silver had always played a decisive role in India's economic development as well with its relations with the Western countries.

Subsequent development in the 1820s saw the end of the Company's monopoly over trade by 1833. In 1835, the British Indian government passed a law in which it stated that only silver coins issued by its mints would become the legal tender in its ruling territories. This brought a new change in India since it would have a uniform currency. The English East India Company's political control in the Indian subcontinent came to an end with the transfer of power to the British Crown. What King Charles II of England had handed over to the East India Company on 27 March 1668, namely the small islets of Bombay to the East India Company, was handed back to Queen Victoria. Thus, the leading commercial and financial capital, Bombay was transferred to the British Crown on 1 November 1858. This official announcement of Direct Crown Rule was read from the Royal Proclamation, from the steps of the Town Hall. This ended the East India Rule in India. However, until 1862, the coins still continued to bear the designs and title of the East India Company.

The Revolution of American Civil War in 1857 and the Lancashire cotton famine brought a new dynamic to Indian commerce since the American cotton supply was cut off to England. This shortage in cotton supply was met by the Indian cotton merchants, where the Bombay port played an important role. This created an upsurge and speculation in the Bombay market. Bombay handled 92 per cent of Indian raw-cotton exports in 1860, and since most of the cotton was paid in bullion, it led to the inflow of capital and created new opportunities for investments in construction projects to beautify the city. Western India saw many new banks being established during this period. However, later, these banks ended up in debt. To tackle this crisis, committees were set up to help merchants come out of the debt crises facing loss of property and wealth. The end of the American Civil War and the collapse of cotton prices resulted in panic and withdrawal of credit.

Bombay town owes a great deal to the prosperity earned during the share-mania that hit its businesses as well the merchants. It was a blessing in disguise as plenty of money flowed into Bombay and the increase in wealth helped many businessmen set up new enterprises and works of public utility. Under the Governorship of Sir Bartle Frere, the modernization of Bombay took root. He helped in improving and transforming the city of Bombay and making a township of merchants into a splendid and populous city. He 'believed that Bombay was one of the greatest cities of the east and she should be made the fairest too'.

The role of the bazaar was quite distinctive, as it acted as a site of interrogation, a stage for posing fundamental questions regarding Indian society under colonialism, and also for posing questions about narrative history. Certainly, the search for a colonial history through the venue of the bazaar highlights a past less familiar than the ones built around those other sites that have come to embody colonial Bombay. The narrative constructed around the bazaar thus draws us to a different reality because the market itself occupies a different place in the Indian landscape of business. Markets have long been a familiar and essential feature of the historical landscape, central places of exchange at which peasants, townspeople, landholders, and rulers have historically converged in South Asia to conduct wholesale and retail trade, to gather news and information, and to engage oneself in various social, cultural, religious, and political activities in the past and which is very active even in the present times.

The presence of the merchant communities of Bombay such as the Gujarati merchants, Jain Shroffs, Kutchi Bhatia merchants, Parsis, Marwaris, Konkani Muslim traders, and Armenian Jews played an important role in expanding the business of Bombay. Their contribution in the growth of banking business and other enterprises have shaped the city of Bombay into a financial centre and facilitated the creation of the Bombay market. Bombay thus became the most influential trading network in the last quarter of eighteenth century and the first quarter of the nineteenth century until India's participation in the First World War. The money market and banking system of India consisted of four main constituents—the Presidency Banks of Bombay, Bank of Bengal, Bank of Madras, and the European Exchange Banks. How it affected the business and its impact on the business of banking is well explained in the book. The Indian stock banks as well as the Shroffs, Marwaris, Parsis, and other private bankers and money lenders were involved in the European money market as well as the local money market. It gives us a clear understanding of how the money market impacted the banking business and merchant investments.

The supply of metals used for coinage declined in India during the early or late medieval period. This scarce supply of usual metals led to the decline of money which created substitutes in the form of other substances, likely to be introduced in the form of networks and credit systems. This proves that the media of exchange and credit networks had already existed from the ancient times.

The rise in the price of silver metal during World War I (1914–18) had already added a burden on the supply of silver in Bombay. The rising price of silver also changed the old ratio fixed in the early twentieth century, causing severe problems at the end of World War I in 1918. Another important cause for the rising prices of silver 1934 onwards was the US Government aggressively purchasing silver which raised the prices to the point of threatening to disrupt the Indian currency system because of the melting and export of silver rupees.

To examine the currency crisis which had gripped India during the period, especially Bombay after the World War I, commissions were set up. The Hilton Young Commission was introduced to examine the crisis of presidency banks and establish a central bank in Bombay. Hilton Young was popularly known as the father of the Reserve Bank of India as he played a dynamic role in building a central bank and forming committees to look into the affairs of banking in India. European agency houses and trading firms were established in order to run businesses in the city of Bombay. Various banking institutes also came into being. The committee looked forward to a bank which could govern other banks, control the monetary functioning and savings of businessmen, and use it for creating more wealth and investments in the business. To maintain monetary stability in India, on 20 December 1934, the British government issued a notification, and on 14 January 1935, the Reserve Bank of India came into existence.

World War II (1939–45) added to the crisis, and these war years had far reaching implications for India. In 1940 India made a transition from a silver currency to fiat currency. India took a decisive break from silver after almost a thousand years, freeing Indian currency from the constraints of silver and enormously reducing the transactions costs. Governor J.B. Taylor said, 'We ought to see whether we cannot take the opportunity of the war to liberate the Indian currency system as far as possible from the incubus of silver, a metal which does not seem to have any future before it'. This led to unprecedented inflation which was managed through the open market. It brought downfall to the banking business and reflected on the Indian economy. Many banking firms saw a sharp decline and had to be terminated due to the lack of business. The war years also disrupted the flow of bullion. Later, the Government of India took initiatives to play an active role in the economic life of the nation and an industrial policy resolution was adopted by the government in 1948 to adopt a mixed economy aiming to help the growth of finance and trade in India.

Bombay now serves the capital of a much larger territory. All the development of late seventeenth, eighteenth, nineteenth and twentieth centuries enabled Bombay to work effectively as the financial capital of India. Bombay Island's journey from a small-time trade centre dealing in dried fish, coconuts, and betel nuts through the transition of control from the Portuguese to the English, transforming it into a centre of bullion trade and a financial capital to the eventual development of the Reserve Bank of India on 1 April 1935 is quite significant. The period from 1661–1935 constitutes the critical phase in the development of Bombay town into a cosmopolitan port city and one of the leading commercial and financial capitals of India.

Mumbai (Bombay), owes its debt to many individuals both local and foreign who have worked together in bringing this transformation to Bombay's growth and development. It was not only the Portuguese, English, but also the Indian merchant communities who have contributed greatly in making Bombay a City of Hope and Commerce, for all those who strive to fulfil their dreams in this city.

APPENDICES

Appendix I

Letter of Accession of the Island of Bombay, by Sir Humprey Cooke on 3 March 1664.

Your honnors most humble and obedient
servant at Command,

ISLAND BOMBAIM 3d *March* 1664/5. HUMFREY COOKE.

HONOBLE,

The Inclosed, is Coppy of what I formerly wrott you over land; since when by his Majestys second Orders after much troubles and many delayes, I have received the possession of this Port and Island of Bombaim which was delivered me in his Majesty's name the 8th february past 1664/5. It is a very pleasant place and a good ayre, yeldeth greate quantity of Coconuts and rice; His Majesty's rents at present imports little more or lesse 700 *li.* per annum; as trade and commerce encreaseth so will his revenue, It is cituated very convenient for trade and commerce for all parts, as South seas, redd seas, Gulph of Persia, Coast of Malabar, Chormandell, Bay of Bengala, Pegu and other places; It is some eight miles in length, and five and a halfe broad, in it are five Churches, nine townes and villages, and uppwards of 20000 Soules as by the Churches information; the generall langwage is Portugueze; Banians, Mahometans, and gentills about the mayne and neighbouring Islands begins to flock hither to reside, so that in few yeares I question not but that it may bee as benneficiall unto the King his Majesty as Batavia is now to the Hollander. At the first, his Majesty must expect to bee out of monys for Fortifications, it beeing at present not alltogeather deffensible; Shipping will bee also very necessary to incourage merchants to trade for all parts, which will much advance our Kings revenues and custumes; I have given a very large relation of all unto his Majesty by these conveyances boath by sea and land which latter I send on purpose for inteligence unto him in regard the shipps bound for Europe from Suratt at this seasone will bee forced to make a winter voyage, so that in all probabillity the messe may arrive some monthes before them into England, when I doubt not but Mr. Secretary will communicate unto your Honour the needfull. Public Record Office. C.o. 77. Vol IX folio. 217

I have sent his Majesty a list of a generall muster, as also an account of all pay and disbursments since Sir Abraham Shipman, and myselfe entred the service, untyll the 3d of December 1664, which I hope will give satisfaction;

I have received your letter directed to Sir Abraham Shipman, dated the 8th March, and have taken notice of its contents; I rest ever

Your Honors most humble and obedient servant,

HUMFREY COOKE.

ISLAND OF BOMBAIM
the 3rd March, 1664/5.

[*Endorsed.*]

Bombaim,
H. Cooke from Bombaim,
3rd of March 64.

Source: Shafat Ahmad Khan, *The Anglo-Portuguese Negotiations Relating to Bombay, 1660–1677*, London: Oxford University Press, 1922, p. 471.

Appendix II
Table of Bullion

Table AI.1: Export of Gold and Silver to Asia by the English East India Company, 1660–1760

Period	*Silver*	*Gold*
1660–65	40,145	107,447
1666–70	22,910	167,366
1671–5	49,828	366,950
1676–80	179,252	515,662
1681–5	240,952	693,161
1686–90	30,567	87,918
1691–5	7,687	22,114
1696–1700	131,511	49,122
1701–5	166,885	–
1706–10	173,833	14,111
1711–5	167,503	14,579
1716–20	250,851	–
1721–5	289,349	–
1726–30	261,401	–
1731–5	260,102	–
1736–40	260,378	–
1741–5	257,882	–
1746–50	366,289	–
1751–5	398,041	–
1756–60	193,458	–

Source: K.N. Chaudhari, *The Trading World of Asia and the English East Company 1660–1760*, Cambridge: Cambridge University Press, 1978, p. 272.

Appendix III

Table AIII.1: Imports at Bombay from Places within the Presidency in the Early Nineteenth Century

Years	*Panwell and Concan*	*Guzerat*	*Surat*
1817–18	2,617,321	7,055,494	2,053,480
1818–19	2,360,363	7,276,187	2,137,803
1819–20	3,554,232	3,982,597	2,983,440
1820–21	4,621,806	3,310,266	1,965,164
1821–2	4,497,109	8,477,664	2,279,691
1822–3	4,641,928	6,015,491	2,494,195

Source: George Alexander Prinsep.

Table AIII.2: Description of Bullion Imported at Bombay and Surat in the Early Nineteenth Century

Years	*Value in Gold (Bombay Rupees)*	*Silver*	*Copper*
1817–18	561,338	11,535,160	425
1818–19	1,421,219	16,960,391	2,000
1819–20	495,079	6,600,664	—
1820–21	942,788	5,843,937	—
1821–2	525,108	1,399,229	650

Source: K.N. Chaudhari, *The Economic Development of India Under the East India Company 1814–1858*, Cambridge: Cambridge University Press, 1971, p. 129.

Appendix IV

The following is the relative list of the 'Bombay Current and Imaginary Coins' which existed in 1802:

2 reas = 1 urdee.

4 reas = 1 dooganey or single pice.

6 reas = 3 urdees = 1 dorea.

8 reas or 4 urdees = 1 fuddea or double pice.

31 fuddeas or pice = 1 anna.

12 pice or 4 annas = 1 quarter rupee.

25 pice or 8 annas = 1 half rupees.

50 pice or 16 annas = 1 rupee.

5 rupees or 80 annas = 1 paunchea.

15 rupees = 1 gold mohur.

Therefore, 2 reas, 1 anna, and 1 quarter-rupee were imaginary. In accounts, the coins were confined to the following reckoning:

100 reas to 1 rupee.

4 quarters = 1 rupee.

All accounts were kept in rupees, quarters, and reas.

Sources: James Mackenzie, *Maclean's Guide to Bombay*, Bombay: Bombay Gazette, Steam Press, 1876, p. 121.

Appendix V
Different Types of Currencies and Their Weighing Values

Currency and Weights (Approximate Conversion Rates)

1. Chinese: 1 tael = 1 liang = 0.0378 kg. of silver
2. Japanese: 1 kanime = 3.76 kg. of silver
3. Dutch: 1 florin (guilders) = 0.01 kg. of silver
4. Portuguese: cruzado, a unit of account generally taken to be equivalent to 1 Spanish dollar in Asia. 1 picul = 100 catties = 60.48 kg.
5. Spanish: 1 Spanish dollar (272 maravedis) = 0.025561 kg. of pure silver.
6. Portugal = 1 cruzado = 17 guilders.
7. 1 rupee = 400 reis
8. Mozambique: 200 reis = 1 cruzado
9. real = 6 cruzados
10. Maria Theresa Thaler = 6 cruzados
11. 1 Rupee = 2 cruzados.

Coins and Weights of Bombay: John Fryer's Records

3 lari = 1 xeraphin.
80 reis = 1 lari.
1 pice = 10 reis.
16 bujerookes = 1 piece of eight.

The reis are imaginary coins.

Calculation of Money Under the British Rule

1 pie = 1/3 pice = 1/12 anna
1 pie = ¼ anna = 1/64 rupee
1 anna = 1/16 rupee
1 mohur = 15 rupees

Unit of Measurement

1. Bahar: A unit of measurement used across China, the Malay world, the Indian subcontinent, and Arabia to denote the weight or mass of certain bulk goods.
2. Picul: A unit of weight commonly used in the early modern trade, the picul is equivalent to 1/3 of a bahar or 100 katis. 1 picul is equal to 60 kg. of silver.
3. Maund: A term used for varying units of weight in some Asian countries, especially India. 1 maund is equivalent to 37 kg.

Appendix VI

Table AVI.1: British private exports of silver to Asia, 1791–1806 (in £)

Year	*Bengal*	*Madras*	*Bombay*	*India Total*	*Canton*
1791–2	65,015	95,325	35,973	196,313	n/a
1792–3	59,703	13,121	0	72,824	n/a
1793–4	25,362	2,814	483	28,659	n/a
1794–5	36,102	505	1,563	38,170	n/a
1795–6	20,004	0	0	29,004	n/a
1796–7	29,466	0	0	29,466	n/a
1797–8	82,929	46,309	61,433	190,671	n/a
1798–9	226,776	82,742	199,508	509,026	n/a
1799–1800	69,872	4,268	4,841	78,981	19,863
1800–1	28,100	4,864	23,646	56,610	10,035
1801–2	137,492	101,232	15,190	253,914	26,890
1802–3	244,717	91,488	30,161	366,366	112,988
1803–4	217,170	88,472	60,595	366,237	50,633
1804–5	204,360	42,604	24,338	271,302	n/a
1805–6	72,336	65,593	48,840	186,769	n/a
Total	1,528,404	639,337	506,571	2,674,312	

Source: H.V. Bowen, 'Bullion for Trade, War and Debt-Relief: British Movements of Silver to, around, and from Asia, 1760–1833', *Modern Asian Studies*, vol. 44, no. 3, May 2010, 2009, p. 467.

Appendix VII

Table AVII.1: Gold coins Minted in Various Presidencies in the Early Nineteenth Century

Years ending 30 April		*Value of gold (in £)*	*Percentage of coinage by value*
1802–9	Bengal	93,220	0.88
1810–18		1,063,315	6.04
1819–20		90,077	1.46
1821–30		12,785	8.55
1808–9	Madras	171,515	16.04
1810–11		453,600	40.00
1812–17		608,323	30.33
1818–20		855,937	43.46
1802–10	Bombay	744,961	56.92
1811–14		1,041,266	52.73
1816, 1817, 1819, 1820		383,970	52.90
1823		36	1.46

Source: 'Bullion of Gold and Silver, Which was Imported to and Exported from Each Presidency of the English East India Company', *Parliamentary Papers*, vol. XLII, Great Britain, 1864, p. 309.

Appendix VIII
The Crash in Banking Business in India During the First World War

At least ninety-four banks in India failed between 1913 and 1918 as indicated in the following table:

Table AVIII.1: Failure of Banks, 1913–18

Years	*Numbers, of Banks which Failed*	*Authorised Capital (in Lakh)*	*Paid-up Capital (in Lakhs)*
1913	12	274	35
1914	42	710	109
1915	11	56	5
1916	13	231	4
1917	9	76	25
1918	7	209	1

Sources: 'Banking in India', *en.wikipedia.org.*

Appendix IX
The Humble Pie, the Smallest Minted Coin of Nineteenth-century India

'The Epitaph of the Pie'

Low and high
We all will sigh
When the poor little pie
Bids her last goodbye.

But her cost's is so high;
And what can she buy?
What trade she can ply?
She needs must eat the humble pie;

So let us not vie
To keep alive the pie
And without a plaintive cry
Peacefully let her die.

If you want the reason why
There need not be hue and cry,
Remember She'll in honour lie
With the silver rupee high!

This poetry was written by the Finance Secretary K.G. Ambegaonkar on 12 July, 1952, and the Finance Minister C.D. Deshmukh, when the minting of the smallest coin of the previous monetary system was discontinued after 1952. The ruling came from the Secretariat in Delhi to do so.

Source: Bombay Mint 150th Anniversary Celebrations, Bombay: India Government Mint, 1 May 1982.

Glossary

1. *Ashrafi*: The *ashrafi* is a term used for gold coin in Arabic and Persian. Another silver coin equivalent to the Portuguese *xerafin* was also called the ashrafi, which they had adopted and issued from Goa.
2. *Abbasi:* The term used for the Persian coins.
3. Anna: One-sixteenth of a rupee.
4. Angelina: English silver coins minted at the Bombay Mint.
5. Bania: Trader (a caste) or a trading community, originally from Gujarat.
6. Bazaar: A fixed place where people congregate to exchange goods.
7. *Bujuruks:* These coins were made of copper.
8. Caroline: English gold coins minted at the Bombay Mint.
9. Caravel: The sailing ship based on Arab and Mediterranean designs used during the fifteenth and sixteenth centuries. The caravel possessed two or three masts with lateen (triangular-shaped) sails. It is a highly maneuverable vessel favoured by the Portuguese and the Spanish in the early phase of European expansion. The caravels were chiefly used as trading vessels and were lightly armed. They have a round hull design and use both square and lateen sails. They were preferred by merchants and sailors for their speed, as well as easy handling in all wind conditions.

10. Carrack: A generic term of Arabic origin for a large and generally lightly-armed Portuguese trading ship. Used mainly in the sixteenth and early seventeenth centuries, the design characteristically featured a forecastle where the crew resided and an elevated poop deck. It was a term used for a large ocean-going vessel, sometimes synonymously used for galleon.
11. Cartaz: A safe conduct pass or license issued by the Portuguese. It granted the owners of the ship the license to navigate the high seas. The term originates from the Arabic word *Qirtas* meaning 'paper' or 'document'. The Portuguese first introduced the Cartaz in 1502 to protect their commercial interests on the west coast of India. It subsequently evolved as a means for the enforcement of monopoly over maritime trade. It was primarily claimed and asserted by the Portuguese and Spanish over the high seas, in the Atlantic, Pacific and Indian Oceans.
12. *Carreira da India*: A Portuguese system of shipping to and from India.
13. Cowry shells: A word of Indian origin (kauri), referring to small white seashells. Cowries were used as currency in parts of South-East Asia and Africa. The Maldives was the largest source of cowries.
14. Cruzados: A Portuguese silver coin. Cruzados worth 400 reis were worth about 10 per cent more than the Spanish-American real of eight. The silver content was just over 29 g. Four cruzados made a Portuguese escudo.
15. Copperoon: Copper coins were called Cooperoon by the English.
16. *Dhow/Dow*: In western India, an old-fashioned Arab vessel built with a long grab stem, rising as a long slope from the water, was called *dhow/dow.* It was like the keel, usually with one mast and lateen rig.

17. *Dugani/Doogany:* A small coin in circulation in Bombay, equal to a single pice of 4 reads.
18. *Ducat:* A currency of Italian origin, widely minted in western Europe in the early modern period. It was generally equivalent to about 3.5 g. of gold.
19. Escudo: An escudo was a gold coin with a face value equivalent to 4 cruzados or about 3.57 g. of gold. In terms of gold weight, this made it equivalent to the ducat.
20. *Estado da India*: This term refers to the Portuguese colonial possessions in the Indian Ocean which was administered from Goa. It consisted of forts and ports. The expression is often used interchangeably with terms such as 'Portuguese India' and 'Asia Portuguesa'.
21. EEIC: The English East India Company.
22. Flemish pound: The Flemish pound was equivalent to about 6 guilders in the late sixteenth and seventeenth centuries. This made it equivalent to about 2.4 reals of eight or 2.2 Portuguese cruzados. They were silver coins and made it equivalent to about 64 g. of coin-grade silver.
23. Frigate: The term refers to an open Portuguese naval craft that was often rowed during the sixteenth and seventeenth centuries and deployed in the East Indies. By the eighteenth century the term referred to a naval sailing vessel featuring three masts and armed with up to 50 cannons. Frigates were usually deployed as vessels of war on account of their speed and excellent handling abilities.
24. Fuddea/Fedea: A small denomination coin current in sixteenth-and seventeenth-century Bombay.
25. Galleon: A type of ocean-going sailing vessel from the sixteenth to eighteenth centuries that was deployed either as a vessel of burden or in naval wars. Galleons feature an elongated hull and multiple decks, especially

if designed to house artillery, and three to five masts. Galleons supplanted the carracks as commercial ships, not least because they could sail faster and were easier to handle under various wind and sea conditions. The term galleon was often used as a synonym for carrack during the early seventeenth century.

26. Gallevat or Gallivan: It was used as a war-boat with oars in small draughts of water in the west coast of India till the eighteenth century. A Ghurab never went into action unless accompanied by gallivants. They were large row boats built like grabs but smaller in dimension; this was light in built and meant for faster speed. Some gallivants had wooden decks to carry 6 to 8 two- or four-pounder guns. They carried 40 to 50 oars and could be rowed four miles an hour.
27. Gumastas: An authorized agent who carries out business transactions and assists in businesses such as obtaining licenses, business permits, and other legal matters. The Gumastas act as a middleman between the owner and government authorities.
28. *Hons:* The hons are mentioned either by names, places or mints. They were very popular in the Deccan. The Muslim rulers of the Deccan also issued gold coins known as the Padshahi, Muhammad Shahi, and Ibrahimi Nisani hons. Smaller denominations of the hons were Pratap, Dharans, Falams, and Chakrams—all minted in gold in medieval Maharashtra.
29. *Hundi*: This hundi system was a traditional way of practicing informal banking system in India. It is a system of credit and Bills of Exchange, involving the transfer of funds between parties without any official paperwork.
30. Hong Merchants: A new type of client-merchants who came to light in the Canton port of China in the

early eighteenth century. Co-Hong was the corporate organization of the Hong Merchants.

31. Hoppo: In charge of maritime customs, who were appointed to control maritime trade and collect custom revenues at the port.
32. *Kacherris*: A fixed place of administrative office or a government department.
33. *Kaffir*: A term of Arabic origin used to designate a person who is not a Muslim. The Spanish and the Portuguese adopted this expression during the early modern period and often employed it as a pejorative. It generically referred to persons of colour, especially Africans, South Indians, and the people of the Indies.
34. Khoja/Khwaja: Derived from the Persian language in the seventeenth century, the term was sometimes used as an equivalent or counterpart to the Portuguese Senhor or Dutch Heer. Khoja was used as a title to signify rich merchants.
35. Lateen sail: A triangular-shaped sail.
36. Larin: A gold coin used in the Persian Gulf, west coast of India, and the Maldives.
37. Lari: Lari was a silver coin of Persian origin which was made of doubled silver wire. This thick wire used for making a lari was made of fine-quality silver without any alloy. It assumed the name 'lari' from the place Lar, at the north of Persian Gulf. It was brought by the Persian merchants to the Konkan and was accepted by the people and the Sultans of Bijapur.
38. *Vereenigde Oost-Indische Compagnie*: The Dutch East India Company.
39. Pardao: The name pardao generally refers to silver and gold coins. The gold pardao in India was equivalent to one gold pagoda. The value of the pagoda, depending on

location, fluctuated between 75 and 120 suivers (3.75 and 6 Dutch guilders). The Portuguese minted silver pardaos in Goa with a face value of five tangas at 60 reis each or 300 reis in total. For this reason, the silver pardao was often interchangeable with the Spanish-American real of eight. The VOC minted its own version of the silver pardao for conducting trade along the Malabar Coast.

40. *Pie*: one-twelfth of an anna, e.g., 11-10-6 is 11 rupees, 10 annas and 6 pies.
41. *Purcchas*: Official documents or business records.
42. Respondentia: Credit money which the merchants had invested with the aim of earning profit. It was a kind of maritime insurance.
43. Real*:* A currency unit in Spain and the Spanish Americas. The best-known coins in the world are the ones struck in Mexico and Bolivia with a face-value of eight (reals-of-eight / pieces of eight) as well as in face value of four reals.
44. Real-of-Eight: Spanish-American coin of eight reals face-value minted in present-day Mexico and Bolivia. This coin ranked among the first globally traded and recognized 'currencies' and were widely accepted not only in the Americas but also in East and South-East Asia. Period documents refer to the real of eight by a host of other names, including 'piece of eight' and later as the 'Spanish dollar'. The silver content of the real-of-eight remained stable at about 27.07 g.
45. Real-of-Four: Spanish coin of four reals in face-value, a half of a real-of-eight.
46. Reas/Rees: A small denomination coin, reas is equivalent to one-twenty-fifth of an anna and four-hundredth part of a rupee. Accounts were kept at Bombay in rupees, quarters, and reas till as late as 1834.

47. Rupee: The rupee was initially a heavy silver coin weighing generally 180 g. It was the most popular and widely circulated silver currency in the eighteenth century, equivalent to one-sixteenth of an anna. The rupee was the Indian currency equal to about 2s. up to 1872, and 16d. in 1900; now it equals 13.3d. approximately.
48. Rupiah*:* The Rupiah was a silver piece introduced by the Afghan ruler Sher Shah Suri, the Emperor of Delhi in 1542 AD.
49. Sahukar: The term sahukar is used in Marathi documents in the early period as a merchant capitalist, but later, it denotes a money-lender, banker, trader, or entrepreneur. The Peshwas have been the principal borrowers from the saucers of Pune.
50. Sarrafs: An Arabic word 'Sayrafi' meaning money-testing, they conducted business transactions in the market.
51. Shahbandhar: A term of Persian origin meaning 'King of the Port'; in the Indian subcontinent and around the western Indian Ocean, it was used to refer to the port-master or harbour-master.
52. Shroff: In the Bombay Presidency, it is a term for an indigenous banker who also acts as a money lender and a dealer in gold and silver bullion.
53. Sicca: This term comes from the word Sicca, a new rupee coin introduced in 1773 by the East India Company after they took over Bengal, Bihar, and Orissa. It remained in use until 1935.
54. Sycee: It was made of indigenous Chinese silver which contained an average of 12 grains of gold per pound of silver, whereas Mexican silver contained about 4 grains.
55. Tael: A unit of weight measurement commonly used across East Asia and South-East Asia. Tael is equivalent to one-sixteenth of Kati (about 37.3 g.).

56. Taka: An important silver coin of the seventeenth century which was in circulation in West Bengal.
57. Tinnies: English coins made of tin.
58. VOC: *Vereenigade Oostindische Compagnie* (VOC) or the United Netherlands Chartered East India Company was established in 1602. The Company was formed by merging six regional trading companies (so-called fore-companies or pioneer companies), and it was given a wide range of powers by a Charter from the Dutch State General. These included the right to enter treaties and alliances, wage wars, and raise taxes to build forts, appoint governors, and pronounce justice. After 1619, its administrative centre in Asia became Batavia in the northern coast of Java.
59. Xerafin: A silver coin formerly used in Goa and other Portuguese ports. Its value varied in Portuguese currency from 300 to 360 reas. The word has an Arabic origin from the word Ashrafi denoting gold dinar, but it was occasionally used for gold coins.

Bibliography

Primary Sources

Old / Rare Published Books

Anderson, Philip, *The English in Western India; History of the Factory at Surat, of Bombay and the Subordinate Factories on the Western Coast*, London: Smith & Taylor, 1856.

Albion, R.G., *Forests and Sea Power*, Cambridge: Harvard University Press, 1926.

Burnell, John, *Bombay in the Days of Queen Anne*, London: Hakluyt Society, 1933.

Bruce's Annals, vol. II, Court Letter to Surat and Bombay, 22 February 1671.

Birdwood, George, *Report on the Old Records of the Indian Office*, London: W.H. Allen, 1891.

Douglas, James, *Round about Bombay*, Bombay: The Bombay Gazette, Steam Press, 1886.

———, *Bombay and Western India*, vol. II, London: Sampson Low, Marston and Company, 1893.

Drewitt, F. Dawtrey, *Bombay in the Days of George IV: Memoirs of Sir Edward West*, London: Longmans, Green & Co., 1907.

Fonseca, Da Nicolas Jose, *An Historical and Archaeological Sketch of the City of Goa*, Bombay: Thacker & Co., 1878.

Forrest, George W., *Selections from the Letters, Despatches, and Other State Papers Preserved in the Bombay Secretariat*, vols. I and II, Maratha Series, Bombay: Bombay Government Press, 1892.

Foster William, *The English Factories in India*, vol. IV, Oxford: Clarendon Press, 1923.

——— and George Birdwood, *The First Letter Book of the East India Company 1600–1619*, London: Bernard Quaritch, 1893.

Furber, Holden, *John Company at Work*, Cambridge: Harvard University Press, 1948.

Gense, J.H. and R.D. Banaji, *The Gaikwads of Baroda*, vol. II, Bombay: D.B. Taraporewala Sons & Co, 1939.

Laval de Pyrard, Francois, *The Voyage of Francois Pyrard of Laval to the East Indies, the Maldives, the Moluccas, and Brazil*, ed. and tr. Albert Gray and H.C.P. Bell, vol. II, London: Hakluyt Society, 1890.

Mookerjee, Radha Kumud, *Indian Shipping and Maritime Activity from the Earliest Times*, Bombay: Longmans Green & Co., 1912.

Malabari, B.M., *Bombay in the Making (1661–1726)*, London: T. Fisher Unwin, 1910.

Pollard, A.F., *The British Empire*, London: The League of the Empire, George Philip & Sons Ltd., 1909.

Panikkar, K.M., *Malabar and the Dutch*, Bombay: D.B. Taraporewala Sons & Co., 1932.

———, *Malabar and the Portuguese*, Bombay: D.B. Taraporewala Sons & Co., 1929.

Roe, Thomas, *The Embassy of Sir Thomas Roe to India, 1615–19*, repr., London: Oxford University Press, 1926.

Roberts, E.P., *History of British India under the Company and the Crown*, Oxford: Clarendon Press, 1938.

R.H., Major, *Travels of Niccolo Conti in India in the Fifteenth Century*, London: Hakluyt Society, 1857.

Rousselet, Luis, *Travels in Central India, and its Native Princes*, London: Bickers & Sons, 1882.

Sherer, J.W., 'Papers Relating to Coinage at Indian Mint', *Home Miscellaneous*, vol. 437, no. 33, 1824.

Sewell, Robert, *A Forgotten Empire*, London: Swan Sonenshein & Co., 1900.

Sarkar, Jadunath, *Economics of British India*, Calcutta: Kunta Line Press, 1913.

Shafaat, Ahmad Khan, *Anglo-Portuguese Negotiations Relating to Bombay: 1660–1677*, London: Oxford University Press, 1922.

Thompson, Edward and G.T. Garratt, *Rise and Fulfillment of British Rule in India*, London: Macmillan, 1935.

Thurston, Edgar, *Coins Catalogue N.Z*, Madras: Government Central Press, 1878.

Wilbur, Eyer Marguerite, *The East India Company and the British Empire in the Far East*, Stanford: Stanford University Press, 1945.

Gazetteers

Campbell James, *Gazetteer of Bombay Presidency*, vol. III, pt. I, Thana: Government Central Press, 1882.

———, *A Statistical Account of the Town and Island of Bombay, Trade and Fortification*, vol. II, Bombay: Government Central Press, 1894.

———, *Gazetteer of the Bombay Presidency—Gujarat, Surat and Broach*, vol. III, Bombay: Government Central Press, 1899.

Chaudhari, K.K., *Maharashtra State Gazetteers*, vols. II and III, Bombay: Gazetteers Department of Maharashtra, 1986.

Edwardes, S.M., *The Gazetteer of Bombay City and Island*, vol. I–III, repr., Bombay: The Government Times Press, 1909.

Forrest W., George, *Selections from the Letters, Despatches, and Other State Papers Preserved in the Bombay Secretariat*, Maratha Series, vols. I and II, Bombay: Bombay Government Press, 1887.

Gazetteer of the Bombay Presidency, Gujarat Surat and Broach, vol. II, Bombay: Government Central Press, 1877.

Gazetteer of the Bombay Presidency, vol. XIII, pt. II, Bombay: Government Central Press, 1882.

Imperial Gazetteer of India, Bombay Presidency, vol. I, Calcutta: Superintendent of Government Printing Press, 1909.

Thana District Gazetteer, Maharashtra State Gazetteer, vol. III, Bombay: Government of Maharashtra, 1986.

The Imperial Gazetteer of India, Atlas, vol. XXVI, Oxford: Clarendon Press, 1909.

Archival Records

Maharashtra State Archives, Collection of Papers, Records of the Bombay Government, Received from The India Office, vol. I, 1661–4.

Maharashtra State Archives, Collection of Papers, Records of the Bombay Government, Received from The India Office, vol. III, 1668–9.

Maharashtra State Archives, Collection of Papers, Records of the Bombay Government, Received from The India Office, vol. V, 1671–3.

Maharashtra State Archives, Collection of Papers, Records of the Bombay Government, Received from The India Office, vol. VI, 1673–5.

Maharashtra State Archives, Financial Department Diary, 7/A, 1813.

Maharashtra State Archives, Financial Department Diary, 7/B, 1813.

Maharashtra State Archives, Financial Department Diary, 7/C, 1813.

Maharashtra State Archives, Financial Department Diary, 12/A, 1814.

Maharashtra State Archives, Public Department Diary, 2/A, 1724.

Reports of Committee of Correspondence, 1722–4, India Office Library.

Reports of Committee of Correspondence, July 1724.

Maharashtra State Archives, Public Department Diary, 11/B, 1727–34.

Maharashtra State Archives, Public Department Diary, 10/A, 1737.

Maharashtra State Archives, Public Department Diary, 11/A, 1738.

Maharashtra State Archives, Public Department Diary, 11/ B, 1738.

Maharashtra State Archives, Public Department Diary, 10/B, 1739.

Maharashtra State Archives, Public Department Diary, 14/ I, 1741.

Maharashtra State Archives, Public Department Diary, 14/II, 1741.

Maharashtra State Archives, Public Department Diary, 14/III, 1741.

Maharashtra State Archives, Public Department Diary, 15/A, 1741–2.

Maharashtra State Archives, Public Department Diary, 15/B, 21 April 1742.

Maharashtra State Archives, Public Department Diary, 16/A, 18 March 1743.

Maharashtra State Archives, Public Department Diary, 18/I, 1745.

Maharashtra State Archives, Public Department Diary, 24/I, 1751.

Maharashtra State Archives, Public Department Diary, 26/II, 1753.

Maharashtra State Archives, Secret & Political Department Diary, 30/1756.

Maharashtra State Archives, Public Department Diary, 41/1763.

Maharashtra State Archives, Public Department Diary, 45/I, 1765.

Maharashtra State Archives, Public Department Diary, 45/II, 1765.

Maharashtra State Archives, Public Department Diary, no. 5, 55/ III, 1770.

Maharashtra State Archives, Public Department Diary, 59/III, 1771.

Maharashtra State Archives, Secret and Political Department Diary, 39/1789.

Maharashtra State Archives, Secret and Political Department Diary, 165/1805.

Maharashtra State Archives, Revenue Department, vol. 39/797, 1837.

Parliamentary Papers of Great Britain, vol. XLII, no. 309, 1864.

Secondary Sources

Books

Albuquerque, Teresa, *Bombay: A History*, New Delhi: Promilla, 1992.

Almadi, D.R., *The Beginnings of Banking on Bombay Island*, Bombay: Maharashtra Archives Bulletin no.12, Government of Maharashtra, 1979.

Atlay, Wilfrid, *Report of the Bombay Stock Exchange Enquiry Committee*, Bombay: Government Central Press, 1924.

Arasaratnam, S., *Merchants, Companies and Commerce on the Coromandel Coast, 1650–1740*, New Delhi: Oxford University Press, 1986.

Bagchi, Amiya Kumar, *Private Investment in India 1900–1939*, London: Cambridge University Press, 1972.

———, ed., *Money, Credit in Indian History; From Early Medieval Times*, New Delhi: Tulika Books, 2002.

Diffie, Bailey W. and George D. Winius, *Foundations of the Portuguese Empire (1415–1580)*, vol. I, New York: Minnesota Press, 1977.

Tavernier, Jean-Baptiste, *Travels in India*, Delhi: Low Price Publications, 2007.

Barber, William J., *British Economic Thought, and India (1600–1858)*, London: Oxford University Press, 1975.

Barros De, Joseph, *Portuguese Coin and Currency in Goa*, Panjim: Oriental Numismatic Society of Great Britain, 1990.

Bombay Mint, 150th Anniversary Celebrations, Bombay: India Government Mint, 1 May 1982.

Borschberg, Peter, *The Singapore and Melaka Straits*, Singapore: National University of Singapore Press, 2010.

Bouchon, Genevieve, *'To Portuguese Expansion', Regent of the Sea: Cannanore's Response, 1507–1528*, New Delhi: Oxford University Press, 1988.

Bowen, V.H., *The Business of Empire: The East India Company and Imperial Britain, 1756–1833*, New York: Cambridge University Press, 2006.

Boxer, C.R., *Portuguese Conquest and Commerce in Southern Asia (1500–1750)*, London: Variorum Reprints, 1985.

——, *The Portuguese Seaborne Empire, 1415–1825*, London: Hutchinson, 1969.

——, *The Tragic History of the Sea (1589–1622)*, Cambridge: Hakluyt Society, 1959.

——, *Portuguese India in the Mid-Seventeenth Century*, New Delhi: Oxford University Press, 1980.

Burnell, John, *Bombay in the Days of Queen Anne*, London: Hakluyt Society, 1933.

Chaudhuri, K.N., *Trade and Civilization in the Indian Ocean*, New Delhi: Munshiram Manoharlal, 1985.

——, *Trade and Civilization in the Indian Ocean: An Economic History from the Rise of Islam to 1750*, Cambridge: Cambridge University Press, 1986.

Chaudhury, Sushil and Morineau Michael, *Merchants, Companies and Trade*, Cambridge: Cambridge University Press, 1999.

Choksey, R.D., *Economic Life in Bombay Gujarat (1800–1939)*, London: Asia Publishing House, 1969.

Clapham, J., *The Bank of England: A History*, vol. II, Cambridge: Cambridge University Press, 1966.

Correa, Gaspar, *Lendas da India Por Gaspar Correa*, vol. III, London: United Kingdom, 1862.

S.J., Correia Alfonso J., *Indo-Portuguese History Sources and Problems*, Bombay: Oxford University Press, 1981.

Cottrell, Arthur, *Western Power in Asia: Its Slow Rise and Swift Fall 1445–1999*, Singapore: John Wiley, 2010.

Danvers, F.C., *The Portuguese in India: Being a History of the Rise and Decline of their Eastern Empire*, vol. II, London: Frankcass, 1966.

Darryl, Alden and Warren Dean, *The People and Politics of Portuguese India during the Sixteenth and Early Seventeenth Centuries*, Gainesville: University Press of Florida, 1977.

David, M.D., *Bombay: The City of Dreams*, Bombay: Himalayan Publishing House, 1998.

———, *History of Bombay*, Bombay: University of Bombay Press, 1973.

De Souza, Teotonio R., *Medieval Goa: A Socio-Economic History*, New Delhi: Concept Publishing Company, 1979.

Disney, Anthony, and Emily Booth, *Vasco da Gama and the Linking of Europe and Asia*, New Delhi: Oxford University Press, 2000.

Disney, A.R., *A History of Portugal and the Portuguese Empire*, vol. II, Cambridge: Cambridge University Press, 2009.

———, *Twilight of the Pepper Empire: Portuguese Trade in Southwest India in the Early Seventeenth Century*, London: Harvard University Press, 1978.

Dossal, Mariam, *Imperial Designs and Indian Realities: The Planning of Bombay City, 1845–1875*, Bombay: Oxford University Press, 1991.

———, *Theatre of Conflict and City of Hope: Mumbai, 1600 to Present Times*, New Delhi: Oxford University Press, 2010.

Elmore, H.M., *'British Mariner's Directory and Guide to the Trade and Navigation of the Indian and China Sea': With an Account of the Trade, Mercantile Habits, Manners, and Customs of the Natives*, UK: Cambridge University Press, 2012.

Fairbank, John King and Merle Goldman, *China: A New History*, Cambridge: Harvard University Press, 2006.

Furber, Holden, *Bombay Presidency in the Mid-Eighteenth Century*, Bombay: Oxford University Press, 1965.

Gentzler, J. Mason, ed., *Changing China: Readings in the History of China from the Opium War to the Present*, New York: Praeger, 1977.

Gokhale, Govind Balkrishna, *Surat in the Seventeenth Century*, Bombay: Popular Prakashan, 1979.

Gupchup, Vijaya, *Bombay: Social Change 1813–1857*, Bombay: Popular Book Depot, 1993.

Gupta, Ashin Das, *India and the Indian Ocean in the Eighteenth Century*, New Delhi: Oxford University Press, 1994.

———, *Indian Merchant and the Decline of Surat, c.1700–1750*, Germany: Wiesbaden, 1979.

Holden, Furber, *Bombay's Presidency in the Mid-Eighteenth Century*, Bombay: Asia Publishing House, 1965.

Hutchinson, Lester, *European Free Booters in Mughal India*, Bombay: Asia Publishing House, 1964.

Jain, L.C., *The Indigenous Banking in India*, London: Macmillan, 1929.

Kahate, G.R., *The Bombay Mint*, Bombay: India Government Mint, 1986.

Karaka, Doshabhai Framji, *History of the Parsis*, London: Macmillan, 1884.

Keynes, John Maynard, *Indian Currency and Finance*, London: MacMillan, 1913.

Kudasiya, M. Medha, *The Life and Times of G.D. Birla*, New Delhi: Oxford University Press, 2003.

Kosambi, Meera, *Bombay in Transition: The Growth and Social Ecology of a Colonial City, 1880–1980*, Stockholm: Almqvist and Witsell International, 1986.

Kulkarni, A.R., *The Marathas, 1600–1848*, New Delhi: Books and Books Publication, 1996.

Lovell, Jullia, *The Opium War*, London: Picador, 2011.

Maclean, James, *A Guide to Bombay*, Bombay: Bombay Gazette Stream Press, 1877.

Pearson, M.N., *Coastal Western India: Studies from the Portuguese Records*, New Delhi: Concept Publishing House, 1981.

Malabari, B.M. Phiroze, *Bombay in the Making (1661–1726)*, London: T. Fisher Unwin, 1910.

Malekandathi, Pius, *Portuguese Cochin and the Maritime Trade of India (1500–1663)*, New Delhi: Manohar Publications, 2001.

Maloni, Ruby, *European Merchant, Capital and the Indian Economy*, New Delhi: Manohar Publications, 1992.

——, *Surat: Port of the Mughal Empire*, Mumbai: Himalaya Publishing House, 2003.

Masani, R.P., *Britain in India*, London: Oxford University Press, 1960.

Mathew, K.M., *History of the Portuguese Navigation in India, 1497–1600*, Delhi: Mittal Publication, 1988.

——, *Indo-Portuguese Trade and the Fugger's of Germany*, New Delhi: Manohar Publication, 1997.

——, *Mariners, Merchants, and Indian Oceans: Studies in Maritime History*, New Delhi: Manohar Publications, 1995.

——, *Portuguese Trade with India during the Sixteenth Century*, New Delhi: Manohar Publications, 1983.

McGuire, John, Bertola Patrick and Reeves Peter, ed., *Evolution of World Economy, Precious Metals and India*, New Delhi: Oxford University Press, 2001.

McPherson, Kenneth, *The Indian Ocean: A History of People and Sea*, Delhi: Oxford University Press, 1993.

Mhamai, S.K., *Fourth Centenary Volume of the Goa Archives (1595–1995)*, Goa: Directorate of Archives and Archaeology, 2001.

Moody, J.R.P., *Jamshedji Jejeebhoy: The First Parsee Baronet*, Bombay, 1959.

Morehouse, Geoffrey, *India Britannica*, London: Harvill Press, 1983.

Nightingale, Pamela, *Trade and Empire in Western India: 1784–1806*, London: Cambridge University Press, 1970.

Oster Hammel, Jurgen, *The Transformation of the World: A Global History of the Nineteenth Century*, New Jersey: Princeton University, 2009.

Panikkar, K.M., *A History of Kerala (1498–1801)*, Annamalai: Annamalai University Press, 1960.

——, *Asia and Western Dominances: A Survey of the Vasco-Da-Gama Epoch of the Asian History, 1498–1945*, London: Allen & Unwin, 1959.

Parry, J.H., *The European Reconnaissance*, New York: Walker and Company, 1968.

Pinto, Celsa, *Trade and Finance in Portuguese India*, New Delhi: Concept Publishing Company, 1951.

Prakash, Om, *Portuguese in India*, vol. I, New Delhi: Anmol Publications, 2002.

Pursell, Victor, *South and East Asia since 1800*, Cambridge: Cambridge University Press, 1965.

Ranganathan, Murali, *Govind Narayan's Mumbai: An Urban Biography from 1863*, London: Anthem Press, 2008.

Rao, P.R., *Portuguese Rule in Goa, 1510–1961*, Delhi: Asia Publishing House, 1963.

Ray, Aniruddha, *Studies in History of the Deccan, Medieval and Modern*, Delhi: Pragati Publication, 2002.

Rego, A. da Silva, *Portuguese Colonization in the Sixteenth Century: A Study of the Royal Ordinances (Regimentos)*, Johannesburg: Witwatersrand University Press, 1959.

Renford, K. Raymond, *The Non-Official British in India to 1920,* Delhi: Oxford University Press, 1987.

Roderick, Ptak and Dietmar Rothermund, *Emporia Commodities and Entrepreneurs in Asian Maritime Trade (1400–1750)*, Germany: Franz Steiner Verlag, 1991.

Rodrigues, Dulcinea Correa, *Bombay Fort in the Eighteenth Century*, Bombay: Himalaya Publishing House, 1994.

Roy, Tirthankar, *The East India Company*, New Delhi: Penguin Group, 2012.

Rossabi, Morris, *A History of China*, USA: Wiley Blackwell Publishing, 2014.

Rungta, Radhe Shyam, *The Rise of Business Corporations in India; 1851–1900*, London: Cambridge University Press, 1970.

Russel Wood, A.J.R., *A World on the Move, The Portuguese in Asia, Africa, and America: 1415–1808*, New York: St. Martin's Press, 1993.

——, *The Portuguese Empire, 1415–1808*, Baltimore: John Hopkins University Press, 1992.

Scammell, G.V., 'Indigenous Assistance in the Establishment of the Portuguese Power in Asia in the Sixteenth Century', *Modern Asian Studies*, vol. 14, no. 1, Cambridge University Press, 1980, pp. 1–11.

Shastri, B.S., *Goa-Kanara Portuguese Relations, 1498–1763*, New Delhi: Concept Publishing Company, 2000.

———, *Studies in Indo-Portuguese History*, New Delhi: Prakashan Publishing, 1981.

Shaik, Bazil, *The Conjuror's Trick: An Interpretive History of Paper Money in India*, Mumbai: Marg Publications, 2020.

———, Ranteeta Dubey and S.M. Khot, *Mint Road Milestones: RBI AT 75*, Mumbai: Marg Publications, 2010.

Shete, H. Baburao, *Bombay: A Photorama*, Bombay: Bombay Municipal Corporation of Greater Bombay, 1981.

Sinha, S.L.N., *History of the Reserve Bank of India (1935–51)*, vol. I, Bombay: Reserve Bank of India, 1970.

———, *Early European Banking in India*, London: Macmillan, 1927.

Singh, B.S., *European Agency House in Bengal*, Kolkata: Firma Mukhopadhyay, 1966.

Soh, Doreen, *From Cowries to Credit Cards: Stories of Singapore's Money*, Singapore: Federal Publications, 1990.

Steensgaard, Neil, *The Asian Trade Revolution of the Seventeenth Century*, Chicago: Scandinavian Institute of Asian Studies, 1974.

Subramanian, Lakshmi, *Three Merchants of Bombay: Business Pioneers of the Nineteenth Century*, Delhi: Penguin Books, 2016.

Subramaniam, Sanjay, *Money and the Market in India: 1100–1700*, Delhi: Oxford University Press, 1998.

———, *The Career and Legend of Vasco da Gama*, New Delhi: Cambridge University Press, 1977.

———, *Improvising Empire: Portuguese Trade and Settlement in the Bay of Bengal, 1500–1700*, Delhi: Oxford University Press, 1990.

——, *The Political Economy of Commerce: Southern India (1500–1650)*, Cambridge: Cambridge University Press, 2002.

Supple, B.E., *Commercial Crisis and Change in England: 1600–1642*, Cambridge: Cambridge University Press, 1964.

Tchitcherov, Alexander I., *India: Changing Economic Structure in the Sixteenth-Eighteenth Centuries*, New Delhi: Manohar Publishers, 1998.

Tindal, Gillian, *City of Gold: The Biography of Bombay*, London: Maurice Temple Smith, 1982.

Tripathi, Dwijendra, *The Oxford History of Indian Business*, New Delhi: Oxford University Press, 2004.

Tripathi, Dwijendra and Jyoti Jumani, *The Concise Oxford History of Indian Business*, New Delhi: Oxford University Press, 2007.

Villars, Pierre, *A History of Gold and Money (1450–1920)*, London: Oxford University Press, 1976.

Wacha, D.E., *A Financial Chapter in the History of Bombay City*, Bombay: Commercial Press, 1910.

Wadia, A.R., *The Bombay Dockyard and the Wadia Master Builder*, Bombay: R.A. Wadia, 1957.

Whiteway, R.S., *Rise of the Portuguese Power in India, 1497–1550*, Patna: Janaki Prakashan, 1979.

Wild, Anthony, *The East India Company Trade and Conquest from 1600*, London: HarperCollins, 1999.

Williams, Jonathan, Joe Cribb and Elizabeth Errington, *Money: A History*, London: British Museum Press, 1997.

Yang, A. Anand, *Markets, Society, and the Colonial Sate in Gangetic Bihar*, Berkeley: University of California Press, 1999.

Articles

Avati, M.P., 'Bombay Buccaneers', *The Bombay Explorer*, vol. 3, 1987.

Afonso, John Correia, 'Indo-Portuguese Ivories of the Hera's Collection', *Indica*, vol. 3, no. 2, 1994.

Arunachalam, B., 'The Bombay Marine', in *Mumbai by the Sea*, ed. B. Arunachalam, Mumbai: Maritime History Society, 2004.

Bagchi, Amiya Kumar, 'Money and Credit in Indian History: From Early Medieval Times', *American Historical Review*, vol. 109, no. 1, February 2004.

Brenner, Robert, 'The Social Basis of English Commercial Expansion, 1550–1650', in *Merchant Networks in the Early Modern World*, ed. Sanjay Subrahmanyam, vol. 8, London: Routledge, 1996.

Bouchon, Genevieve, 'Sixteenth Century Malabar and the Indian Ocean', in *India and the Indian Ocean 1500–1800*, ed. Ashin Gupta and M.N. Pearson, London: Oxford University Press, 1987.

Bowen, H.V., 'Investment and Empire in the Later Eighteenth Century: East India Stockholding, 1756–1791', in *Economic History Review*, vol. 42, no. 2, 1989.

Moloughney, Brian and Xia Weizhong, 'Silver and the Fall of the Ming', in *Metal and Monies in an Emerging Global Economy*, ed. Dennis O Flynn and Arturo Giraldez, vol. 14, Variorum: Ashgate Publishing Company, 1997.

Chakrabarti, Shubhra, 'Intra Sigent Shroffs and the English India Company's Currency Reforms in Bengal 1757–1800', *The Indian Economic and Social History Review*, vol. 34, no. 1, 1997.

Chandra, Satish, 'Exploration in History, Commerce and Politics', *The Indian Ocean Review*, vol. 1, no. 4, 1988.

Chaudhuri, K.N., 'World Silver Flows and Monetary Factors as a Force of International Economic Integration, 1658–1758', in *Metals and Monies in an Emerging Global Economy*, ed. Dennis O. Flynn and Arturo Giraldez, vol. 14, Variorum: Ashgate Publishing Company, 1997.

Da Cunha, J. Gerson, 'The Origin of Bombay', *The Journal of the Bombay Royal Asiatic Society*, 1900.

David, M.D., 'Historic Bassein', *Indica*, ed. S.J. Afonso Correa, vol. 24, 1978.

Dewey, Clive and A.C. Bayly, 'Rulers, Townsmen, and Bazaars: North Indian Society in the Age of British Expansion, 1770–1870', *Economic History Review*, ed. E.H. Hunt, vol. 38, 1985.

Dossal, Mariam, 'Continuity and Change: The Portuguese Presence in British Bombay, *c.*1661–1860', in *Vasco da Gama and the Linking of Europe and Asia*, ed. Anthony Disney and Emily Booth, New Delhi: Oxford University Press, 2000.

———, 'The Call of the Sea: Maritime Mumbai, *c.*1660–2000', in *Ports, Towns Cities*, ed. Lakshmi Subramanian, Mumbai: Marg Publication, 2008.

Duncan, T. Bentley, 'Navigation between Portugal and Asia in the Sixteenth and Seventeenth Centuries', in *An Expanding World: European Commercial Expansion in Early Modern Asia*, ed. Om Prakash, vol. 10, Vermont: Ashgate Publishing, 1997.

Elbi, M.M., 'The Portuguese Caravel and European Ship Building: Phases of Development and Diversity', *Revista da Universidade de Coimbra*, vol. 33, no. 25, 1985.

Faraday, J.F., 'A Financial Chapter in the History of Bombay City', *The Economic Journal*, vol. 21, no. 81, 1911.

Fernandez-Armestro, Felipe, 'Indian Ocean in World History', in *Vasco da Gama and the Linking of Europe and Asia*, ed. Anthony Disney and Emily Booth, Delhi: Oxford University Press, 2000.

Flynn, O Dennis and Arturo Giraldez, 'Born with a Silver Spoon: The Origin of World Trade in 1571', in *An Expanding World Series*, ed. A.J.R. Russell-Wood, vol. 14, Variorum: Ashgate Publishing Company, 1997.

Furber, Holden, 'Asia and the West as Partners before Empire and After', *The Journal of the Asian Studies*, vol. XXVIII, no. 4, 1969.

Mulherkar, G.V., 'Coins of the East India Company at Bombay', *The Bombay Explorer*, vol. 1, 1986.

Ganachari, Aravind, 'White Man's Embracement's European Vagrancy in the 19th Century Bombay', *Economic and Political Weekly*, vol. 37, no. 25, 22–8 June 2002.

Ganguli, B.N., 'Dadabhoy Naoroji and the Mechanism of "External Drain', *The Indian Economic and Social History Review*, vol. II, no. 2, 1965.

Glamann, Kristof, 'The Dutch East India Company's Trade in Japanese Copper, 1645–1736', *Scandinavian Economic History Review*, 1953.

Gupta, Ashin Das, 'The Broker at Mughal Surat, *c.*1740', *Revista de Cultura Review*, no. 13–4, January 1991.

Gupta, V.B., 'Imports of Treasure and Surat in the Seventeenth Century', in *Metal and Monies in an Emerging Global Economy*, ed. Dennis O. Flynn, and Arturo Giraldez, vol. 14, Variorum: Ashgate Publishing Company, 1997.

———, 'Imports of Treasure and Surat's Trade in the Seventeenth Century', in *Metals and Monies in an Emerging Global Economy*, ed. Dennis O. Flynn and Arturo Giraldez, vol. 14, Variorum: Ashgate Publishing Company, 1997.

Haider, Najaf, 'Precious Metal Flows and Currency and Circular in the Mughal Empire', *Journal of the Economic and Social History of the Orient*, vol. 39, no. 3, 1996.

Howard, H.F., 'The Imperial Bank of India', *The Economic Journal*, vol. 31, no. 122, 1921.

Kulkarni, A.R., 'Money and Banking under the Marathas: Seventeenth Century to AD 1848', in *Money and Credit in Indian History from Early Medieval Times*, ed. Amiya Kumar Bagchi, New Delhi: Tulika Books, 2002.

Kumar, Dharma and Tapan Ray Chaudhuri, *The Cambridge Economic History of India; 1757–1970*, vol. 2, Cambridge: Cambridge University Press, 1983, pp. 574–5.

Knappert, Jan, 'The Indian Ocean before 1500', *Indian Ocean Newsletter*, vol. VI, no. 2, 1985.

Lentin, Sifra, 'Imperial Japan's Trade with Bombay', Bombay: Gateway House, 20 March 2019.

Maloni, Ruby, 'Surat to Bombay: Changing Definitions of a Port City', in *Surat: Port of the Mughal Empire*, ed. Ruby Maloni, Mumbai: Himalaya Publishing House, 2003.

Marshall, P.J., 'Private Trade in the Indian Ocean Before 1800', in *An Expanding World: European Commercial Expansion in Early Modern Asia*, ed. Om Prakash, vol. 10, Vermont: Ashgate Publishing, 1997.

Mathew, K.S., 'The Portuguese Chronicles of the Sixteenth Century and the Socio-Economic History of India', *12th Conference of the International Association of Historian of Asia*, Hong Kong, 24–8 June 1991.

——, 'Trade and Economy of Coastal Gujarat in the Sixteenth Century', *The Journal of the Oriental Institute*, vol. 34, no. 3–4, 1985.

—— and Safar Khwaja, 'The Merchant Governor of Surat and the Indo-Portuguese Trade in the Early Sixteenth Century', *Proceedings of the Indian History Congress*, vol. 43, Kurukshetra, 1982.

——, 'The Economy of Bassein in the Sixteenth Century', in *Indica*, ed. John Afonso Correa, vol. 24, Bombay: Anand Press, 1978.

McPherson, Kenneth, 'East Africa and the Indian Ocean', *The Indian Ocean Review*, vol. 1, no. 2, 1988.

McPherson, Kenneth, 'Power, Status and Belief', *The Indian Ocean Review*, vol. 1. no. 2, 1988.

Mookerji, Radha Kumud, 'Indian Shipping and Maritime Activity from the Earlier Times', *The Journal of Asian Studies*, vol. XX, November 1960.

Moraes, George, 'Pre-Portuguese Culture of Goa', *Proceedings of the International Goan Convention*, 28 March 2011.

Morris, David, 'The Central Administration of the East India Company, 1773–1834', *The Journal of Asian Studies*, vol. XX, no. 1, 1960.

—— and Stein Burton, 'The Economic History of India: A Bibliographic Essay', *The Journal of Economic History*, vol. XXI, 1966.

Mukherjee, Aditya, 'The Depression Years: Indian Capitalist's Critique of British Monetary and Financial Policy in India,

1929–39', in *Money and Credit in Indian History from Early Medieval Times*, ed. Amiya Kumar Bagchi, New Delhi: Tulika Books, 2002.

Nightingale, Pamela, *Trade and Empire in the Western India: 1784–1806*, Cambridge South Asian Studies, no. 9, Cambridge University Press, 1970.

——, 'The Survival of the Presidency 1784–1792', in *Trade and Empire in Western India: 1784–1806*, Cambridge: Cambridge University Press, 2007.

Palsetia, Jesse S., 'Mad Dogs and Parses: the Bombay Riots of 1832', *Journal of the Royal Asiatic Society*, vol. II, no. 1, Third Series, London: Cambridge University Press, April 2001.

Pearson, M.N., 'Asia and World Precious Metal Flows in the Early Modern Period', in *Evolution of World Economy, Precious Metals and India*, ed. John McGuire, Bertola Patrick, and Peter Reeves, New Delhi: Oxford University Press, 2001.

——, 'Early Relations between the Portuguese and Gujarat', *Indica*, vol. 35, Mumbai, September 1998.

Prakash, Om, 'The Indian Maritime Merchant, 1500–1800', *Journal of the Economic and Social History of the Orient*, vol. 47, no. 3, 2004.

——, 'The Portuguese in the Far-East, 1540–1640', in *Vasco da Gama and the Linking of Europe and Asia*, ed. Anthony Disney and Emily Booth, New Delhi: Oxford University Press, 2000.

——, 'European Commercial Expansion in Early Modern Asia', in *An Expanding World: The European Impact on World History 1450–1800*, ed. A.J.R. Russell-Wood, vol. 10, Variorum: Ashgate Publishing Company, 1997.

——, 'The Trading World of Asia and the English East India Company, 1600–1760', *The Indian Economic and Social History Review*, vol. XVII, no. 3, July–September 1980.

Ray, Rajat Kanta, 'The Bazaar Changing Structural Characteristics of the Indigenous Section of Indian Economy before the Great Depression', *The Indian Economic and Social History Review*, 1988.

——, 'Indigenous Banking and Commission Agency in India's Colonial Economy', in *Money and Credit in Indian History: From Early Medieval Times*, ed. Amiya Kumar Bagchi, New Delhi: Tulika Books, 2002, pp. 118–30.

Richards, John F., 'The Opium Industry in British India', *The Indian Economic and Social History Review*, vol. 39, no. 3–4, 2002.

Roy Le, Christian John, 'Portuguese India and its Historical Records', *Hispanic American Historical Review*, no. XXV, 1945.

Ryuto, Shimada, 'The Golden Age of Japanese Copper: The Intra-Asian Copper Trade of the Dutch East India Company', in *Intra-Asian Trade and the World Market*, ed. A.J.H. Latham and Heita Kawakatsu, London: Routledge, 2006.

Schlosberg, Henry, 'European Cartography of the West Coast of India', *Indica*, vol. 27, 1990.

Shaik, Bazil, 'Fortune, Probity and Prudence (A Brief Narrative of Banking in Bombay)', *The Bombay Explorer*, no. 47, Mumbai, 2006.

Siddiqi, Asiya, 'Money and Prices in the Earlier Stage of Empire: India and Britain 1760–1840', *The Indian Economic and Social History Review*, vol. XVIII, no. 3–4, 1981.

—— 'The Business World of Jamshedji Jeejeebhoy', in *Trade and Finance in Colonial India 1750–1860*, Delhi, Oxford University Press, 1995.

Silberling, N.J., 'Financial and Monetary Policy of Great Britain during Napoleonic Wars', *Quarterly Journal of Economics*, vol. XXXVIII, 1924.

Subramaniam, Lakshmi, 'Bombay and the West Coast in the 1740s', *Indian Economic and Social History Review*, vol. 18–19, New Delhi: Vikas Publishing House, 1981.

Sugihara, Kaoru, 'Japan as an Engine of the Asian International Economy, *c.*1880–1936', *Japan Forum*, vol. 2, 1990.

Maynard, Thomas, 'Anglo-Portuguese Relation: 1650–1810', in *Trade Inquisition and the English Nation in Portugal, 1650–1810*, ed. L.M.E. Shaw, London: Carcanet, 1989.

Tracy, James D., 'The Rise of the Merchant Empires: Long Distance Trade in the Early Modern World, 1350–1750', in *Library of Congress Cataloguing in Publication Data*, New York: Cambridge University Press, 1990.

Wadia, Rushed, 'Trade and the Raj', in *Across Oceans of Flowing Silks from Canton to Bombay: 18th and 20th Centuries, and No Parsi is an Island*, ed. Ranjit Hoskote, Nancy Adajania, and J. Godrej Pheroza, Mumbai: Marg Publications, 2013.

Watson, Bruce, 'Fortifications and the "Idea" of Force in Early English East India Company Relations with India', in *An Expanding World*, ed. M.N. Pearson, vol. 24, Variorum: Ash gate Publishing Company, 1997.

White, David L., 'Parsis in the Commercial World of Western India, 1700–1750', *The Indian Economic and Social History Review*, vol. XXIV, no. 2, 1987.

Williams, Monier, 'Monetary System of British India', in *Bombay Quarterly Review*, vol. VI, no. 12, October 1857.

Wretts-Smith, Mildred, The Business of the East India Company-1680–1681', *The Indian Economic and Social Review*, vol. I, no. 2, 1963.

Index

www.ingramcontent.com/pod-product-compliance
Lightning Source LLC
Chambersburg PA
CBHW051358240926
51852CB00004B/90/J
9789366277110